Philosophy

VOLUME 3

Karl Jaspers

Philosophy

VOLUME 3

Translated by E. B. Ashton

The University of Chicago Press

Chicago and London

Originally published in 1932 as Philosophie
© *1932, 1948, 1956 by Springer-Verlag, Berlin-Göttingen-Heidelberg*

International Standard Book Number: 0-226-39494-8
Library of Congress Catalog Card Number: 69-19922

THE UNIVERSITY OF CHICAGO PRESS, CHICAGO 60637
THE UNIVERSITY OF CHICAGO PRESS, LTD., LONDON

Contents

VOLUME 3

General Contents

Volume 3

Book Three

METAPHYSICS

Transcendence

What it means to "be" is the unending question of philosophizing.

As *defined being* it is knowable. The categories show the basic modes of its definition. Their establishment in logic makes us explicitly conscious of the modes of being: being in the sense of "being known and conceived" becomes objective in its ramifications and in its diversity. But this does not exhaust being proper.

As *empirical reality*, being includes something I must take for granted, something covered, but not penetrated, by my thought. In world orientation I have taken hold of this reality which defies surveyal as a whole but permits knowledge and relative cognition of its several sides, and of any single thing's particular being. Being in the sense of "being in the realm of cognition" always carries at its bounds whatever is outside the realm of cognition. But this mundane being—cognition plus the cognitively recognized unknown—does not exhaust being either.

From mundane being, breaking through it, I come to myself as possible *Existenz*. There my being lies in freedom and communication and is aimed at other free being. It is an interior being that has yet to decide whether and what it is, a being that cannot get out of itself and cannot observe itself. But even this being is not one with which all things would be exhaustible. It is not only together with other free beings; it refers in itself to a being that is not Existenz but its *transcendence*.

Thus, when I want to know what being is, it appears to me *disjoint*, the more so the more relentlessly I keep asking, and the less I let myself

be deceived by some construction of being. I do not have *the* being anywhere; I always have only *a* being. *The* being comes down to the empty
definition of an undefinably ambiguous communicative function—the
statement I make in the copula "is"—but there is no tenable way for it
to become a *concept* comprising the common features of all being. It
does not become the whole of a gist expressed in all the modes of being,
much less a *specific being* with the distinction of emerging as the source
of all things. Whenever I try to grasp being *qua* being, I fail.

To my mind, the entire question of being *qua* being is not quite
intelligible. To my cogent, conscious insight it can be demonstrated that
the modes of being are disjoint; but this will remain a matter of indifference because cognition en route to objective being unquestioningly
presupposes the unity of that being anyway, even though it is not subject to cognition. To bring the disjointness of being as such to mind is a
free act. Not till I choose between adoption and rejection do I face the
disjointness of being as the situation that concerns me and, in boundary
situations, challenges me to raise the true question about being.

It is thus not as vital existence, nor as consciousness at large, that I
experience the disjointnesss of being. Possible Existenz alone will be
struck by this disjointness and will *search* for being as if it were lost and
recoverable. What characterizes possible Existenz, as distinct from
existence, is that in this search for being it is truly itself. This is what as
possible Existenz I cannot get away from: I do not have the ground of
being in existence; nor in the varied definitions of some particular being
as an object of knowledge and cognition; nor in my isolated self; nor
even in communication. Nowhere do I have what it is to "be." I come
up against limits everywhere, moved by the search for being that is tied
to my freedom because it is my freedom. When I do not search for being,
it is as if I myself ceased to be. I seem to find it in the concrete historicity
of my active existence, yet whenever I want to grasp it in philosophizing, I must see it slip out of my hands.

When I face this being as transcendence, I am seeking the ultimate
ground in a singular fashion. The ground seems to open up, but it no
sooner comes into view than it dissolves again; if I mean to grasp it, I
take hold of nothing. If I try to advance to the source of being, I drop
into the unfathomable. I never get to know, substantially, what is. Yet
this abyss, a void for the intellect, can fill up for Existenz. I am transcending where this depth has opened and the search as such has
become a finding in temporal existence; for a man's possible Existenz
may turn his transcending of temporal existence into a *unity of presence
and search*—a presence which is nothing but the search that has not
been detached from what he is seeking. I can seek only by anticipating

what I am to find. Transcendence must be present where I seek it. In transcending I have no objective knowledge of being, as in world orientation, nor do I come to be aware of it as of myself in the elucidation of Existenz. I know about it, rather, in an inner action which lets me stay with this intrinsic being even as I fail. Without finding it as an objective support, Existenz can look to this being for the strength to uplift itself in existence, to rise to itself and to transcendence in one.

The modes of this search for being by possible Existenz are ways to transcendence. Their elucidation is philosophical metaphysics.

Discontent with All Being that Is Not Transcendence

Factual cognition lets me understand its limits. I can understand that cognition and its contents are not outright being, that they are only the kind of being which in my consciousness aims at a being as objectively extant. This being was the mundane one, the being of the world.

Philosophical world orientation has shown us that the world does not rest in itself. The world proved to be inconclusive; its cognition as a self-sustained, self-contained, self-sufficient whole became impossible.

A sense of these limits was the start of the breakthrough to possible Existenz and the start of philosophizing. In my thinking I came to be struck by an antithesis which, though I do not understand it cognitively, I do grasp as possible Existenz: by the antithesis of extant being and the being which I am in my freedom. In this antithesis the extant side was always objective, clear, and generally valid, but the side of freedom remained nonobjective and indefinite. Without claiming general validity, freedom aimed at unconditional validity. In existential elucidation a specific manner of thinking made freedom communicable in awakening appeals. What led to this elucidation was discontent with merely general, merely mundane existence. But no definitive satisfaction could be obtained in existential elucidation either.

Yet Existenz can grasp itself in its own freedom only if at the same time, and in the same act, it will perceive something other than itself. Strict unconditionality makes me aware, not only that my existence is not selfmade and is the helpless prey of certain doom, but that I do not have myself alone to thank for my freedom either. In some way or other, the realization of unconditionality will occur only in relation to its transcendence.

There are three possibilities. Either transcendence will be expressly *denied*—but as Existenz finds transcendence incessantly thrust upon it as a concomitant possibility, this denial must be actively reiterated and thus maintained as negative conduct toward transcendence. Or an Existenz will *oppose* transcendence so as to realize itself in a struggle with it. Or an Existenz will seek its way in the world *with* transcendence. For any possible Existenz, whether without, against, or with transcendence, transcendence remains the ceaseless question. These three possibilities are elements in the motion of our existential sense of transcendence in temporal existence.

To me as Existenz absolute independence is indeed my true unconditionality in temporal existence, but it also drives me to despair. I am aware that as flatly self-based I would have to sink into the void. For my self-realization I depend on a fulfillment that comes to me. I am not myself if I happen to default; I relate to myself as if selfhood were bestowed upon me. The test of the possibility of my Existenz is the knowledge that it rests upon transcendence. I close the door to my becoming Existenz if I take it for being proper.

This is why in breaking through mundane existence I do seize my freedom with the passionate sense of a decision about being itself. And yet I cannot take freedom for the ultimate, for only in time is it the way to the realization of an Existenz that is still merely possible. Freedom is not being-in-itself. In transcendence freedom ceases because decision has an end; in trancendence there is neither freedom nor unfreedom. Being free—the most profound appeal to us as long as it is still up to us what we are—is not the same as being transcendent. Confined to itself, even freedom withers. It seeks its fulfillment in transcendence, which as such opens only to freedom, and whatever this fulfillment is will turn into a possibility for freedom: into the possibility of perfection or of reconciliation, of redemption or of pain at transcendent being. In every case the *end of possible self-sufficiency* is freedom's ultimate satisfaction in temporal existence.

The view of transcendence gives to Existenz its proper sense of being finite. That human cognition is finite can be made clear by contrast, by construing other possibilities of cognition; and the finiteness of existence lies in the fact that it always has something outside it, and that all its forms simply originate and pass away. The finiteness of cognition and of existence might be conceived as overcome by construing an infinite expansion.

Existenz, on the other hand, can grasp itself neither as finite in contrast to a conceivable perfection of endlessness nor as finite in contrast to anything else that is finite. But when a leap beyond all thoughts of finiteness and infinity has made it sure of itself, Existenz knows that it is inseparable from other Existenz and not detached from the authority to which it relates, however infinite the difference.

If I were to call this relation finiteness, this finiteness of Existenz could not be cogitatively construed and dialectically voided like those other, earlier finitenesses. It would be finiteness pure and simple. It would not be intelligent but comprehended in the act of a freedom that aims at itself and thus confronts its transcendence. The intelligible finitenesses would be relativized and on their part would acquire existential relevance only if the consciousness of a transcendently related Existenz should reach back to animate them.

What relates to transcendence is not understood in accord with its infinite character if I call it finite, and if I call it infinite I miss its essential discontent. Existenz cannot say of itself that it is finite, or infinite, or both. It is the infinite and therefore insurmountable discontent that is as one with the search for transcendence. Existenz is either in relation to transcendence or not at all. In this relation lies its discontent or else, with temporal existence voided, its chance of satisfaction.

Reality of Metaphysical Thinking and Reality of Transcendence

1. Objectification of Transcendence

Transcendence is not defined in categories; it does not exist as empirical reality; nor does it lie in the presence of my freedom as such. It is thus not in any of the modes of being that lend themselves to objectively articulated thought, or to cognition as existence which I have to take for granted, or to elucidation in an appeal to my potential. But if something appears to itself in existence, whatever is can be for it only in the form of consciousness, and in consequence, with Existenz tied to existence, the being of transcendence too assumes for Existenz the form of objective being.

Metaphysical objectivity has a specific character prior to all temporary concretions. It is the function of a *language* that makes transcendence intelligible in the consciousness of Existenz. The language of this objectivity enables an Existenz to bring to mind what it cannot know as consciousness at large. It is not a general language, not a language of all Existenz as a community of rational beings; it is always a historic language. It will link some and be inaccessible to others. Diluted into a generality, it is entirely different only in the ways of its creation and original adoption.

In existence the transcendent language is like *another world* of objects. Our word for the objects of this world is *ciphers*. While in world orientation each object is itself, identical for everyone and thus explorable with general validity, the objective language of this second world is audible to possible Existenz alone. Yet everything objective is a possible cipher if it is adopted in transcending, brought to mind in a way that will make transcendence appear in it.

The metaphysical objects are outwardly visible for consciousness at large as well, in the vast abundance of historically given myths, metaphysics, and religious dogmatics. Theirs is a multifarious world, splintered into many languages, hence without entirety and at first like the unintelligible noise of a Babylonian confusion. In this world one realm of metaphysical objects seems heterogeneous to the next, and yet not absolutely disparate. For it is possible to address one another, as though in a language which I do not understand as yet but can come closer to understanding, without having made it my own. Metaphysical objectifications of transcendence are ascertainments that adjoin in the possibility of historic communication, but without definable borderlines. While in metaphysical objectivity there is thus no substantial identity for an observer who wants a scientific definition of one generally valid metaphysics, there is in that objectivity the possibility of historic community by way of a language whose understanding forms a bond between men.

2. Stages of Reality at Large

The question here is in what sense metaphysical objectivity as a language is real.

All reality lies for us in the correlation of something objective with a subject actively aimed at the objectivity. Empirical reality, for instance, is critically grasped as a known object in the activity of investigation. For a scientific consciousness at large, empirical reality is compelling. But transcendence is not a compelling reality; on the other hand, if we are possible Existenz in existence, we notice throughout the realities something which in empirical definition is no longer the thing we have experienced. It is a *reality as the limit of empirical reality*—something we can grasp only as empirical reality but cannot explore because it exceeds that reality.

One such reality, not noticed by any consciousness at large except negatively, was Existenz. When another human being is known and understood as an object and calculably steerable by creating situations, there still remains something incalculable—something only negatively comprehensible, by the endlessness of the factors in question, but positively manifested to my active self-being as the absolute uniqueness of the Existenz I communicate with. The incalculability is mutually real as the depth of being between Existenz and Existenz, but to my thoughts it is ambiguous. The endless frictions, deceptions, discomfitures, and possibilities in my relations with others, those difficulties in which I come to experience myself, are either consequences of pure nature as downright otherness, the hard mutual impediments of unexistential existence, or they are the darkness of a possible Existenz that has yet to open itself to elucidation by offering to communicate existentially. This reality of Existenz is a limit of empirical reality, and yet it is most tangibly, most presently real—a reality from which I would shut myself off if I were to take empirical reality for the only one there is. Then I would experience those disturbances which keep crossing me up in a world that seems so clearly calculable. I would experience them in myself as unconscious, irrational motivations, and in others as actions and purposes I could not expect. My very desire to take nothing but objective clarity for truth and reality keeps me entangled in indissoluble darkness.

Only as possible Existenz can I sense the real being of transcendence at the bounds of the empirical reality which I know in consciousness at large, and at the bounds of the existential reality that is revealed to me in communication.

Frequently, for example, the very thing that matters to us in a situation is an accident. Then, if we say it is all a combination of necessary, lawful, causal links anyway, there will indeed be nothing else for generally valid knowledge— and yet, in the concrete situation we keep feeling the sting of the incalculable as the crucial reality. We may ask how the incalculable can be real if it defies cognition; but to assert an all-encompassing machinery of causal links, to say that some things just cannot be calculated yet although in principle all things are calculable, is an untrue anticipation. Only in the boundary situation of historic determinacy can possible Existenz feel in incalculable chance the strictly real limit of empirical reality.

Every distinct concept of reality delimits it against something unreal. As possible Existenz I ask for *absolute reality*—not scientifically, not by determining reality, but by recollecting myself from all particularity. Absolute reality is to me transcendent; but in the immanence of empirical existence and Existenz I can experience limits where I feel its presence.

Transcendence is the reality an Existenz will ask for, but to ask for it in generally valid terms is impossible. It is impossible because transcendence strikes me as a *reality without possibility,* as the absolute reality beyond which there is nothing. Before transcendence I stand mute. In my cognition of an empirical reality, I understand its possibility from the conditions of its realization; my cognition helps me as I seek to change the concrete reality to suit my purpose. In my grasp of self-being I am aware of a possibility whose reality depends on my free choice; this possibility gives me no object for a goal, nor any plan for my way, but it is the substantial space from which the appeal for realization goes to my self-being. For transcendent reality, on the other hand, there is no retranslation into possibility. This is why it is not empirical: it lacks any conceivable possibility from which it might have turned real—not in the sense of a defect, but because this division of possibility and reality is the defect of empirical reality, which always has an otherness outside of it. And it is why transcendent reality is not Existenz: it lacks the possibility of decision—again not in the sense of a defect but the other way round, because the possibility of decision expresses the defects of Existenz in temporal existence.

It is where I come up against *reality that will not turn into possibility* that I encounter transcendence.

If transcendent reality does not occur as empirical, and if it is not Existenz either, we might infer that it lies in a *beyond*. Metaphysics would be the knowledge of an ulterior world located elsewhere, without access from the real world. In transcending I would be taking the road to this other world, on which fortunate, favored individuals may at times feel able to report.

This duplication of the world proves deceptive. What is transposed into the other world, in fantastic enlargements, reductions, and combinations, is nothing but things and events found in this world as well. Images and tales from that world, sprung from the imagination of the narrator or the construing intellect, become objects of fear and solace by being treated like other empirical realities. The beyond as just another reality is an untenable illusion.

How, then, can we approach the reality of transcendence? For an individual acting on his initiative—all by himself, so to speak—it is impossible to find out what it is. But an unfathomable tradition will tell him in the language of metaphysical objectivity what his ties to the tradition let him experience as his own present reality.

3. Metaphysics between a Knowledge of Tradition and the Existential Presence of Transcendence

In historical world orientation, the language handed down in myths, metaphysics, and theology can be outwardly known as the variety of metaphysical objects. But this knowledge of metaphysics as an empirical reality of human existence is not metaphysics itself. A man can have it even if he views it as the history of human errors.

Since it is only in a situation of flatly historic concreteness, rather, that transcendent reality can be truly present, metaphysics is the thinking that refers to this indubitable reality, the thinking that brings it to mind in a medium of hearing generalities.

Philosophical metaphysics, therefore, stands between the metaphysical tradition—as a possibility to understand and to adopt its language—and the existentially real presence of the transcendence in which, in the sphere of possible thought, I believe.

The metaphyiscal tradition is the premise, not of the outward knowledge of world orientation alone, but of the inner adoption that lets me hear the content of the cipher language as a striking transcendent reality. After all, a knowledge of the empirical reality of metaphysics in history makes no real sense unless it springs from a personal, present metaphysics which the searcher understands on traditional grounds. Without that source, the history of metaphysics would be a collection of curios, capable of satisfying only a mind that considers itself liberated from these disturbances of a rationalized existence. The metaphysics that has come down to us becomes a possibility for every present one.

Transcendent reality, on the other hand, has no way of entering into the metaphysical thought. The thought which originally lends a voice to the existential collision with transcendence will be expressed, of course, in historically concrete terms; it will demonstrate on the strength of truth, and when it proclaims truth it will admit no possibility of its being otherwise. *As a thought*, however, detached from the origin of its reality, it will soon be an *existential possibility*. Metaphysics is philosophical thought regarding transcendence; its entire substance lies in the origins of the transcendent experience, and its seriousness lies in making that experience possible. Metaphysics as a traditional possibility is not an absurd retranslation of transcendent reality into a logical and psychological possibility. It is a possibility for Existenz, a means of its self-elucidation in contact with absolute reality.

The *adoption* of tradition, the act that makes a man's own existential proximity to transcendence possible, lies in that in-between area of philosophical metaphysics in which the visualization of truth is not yet the reality of its presence. In this philosophizing (as distinct from the mere outward knowledge of doctrines) we deal with past metaphysics in communication with the alien Existenz that brought it forth, and we respect the distance which separates us from the reality of that Existenz. We regard our philosophizing as the readiness of an Existenz that has yet to show whether visualization will assure it of the reality of transcendence rather than of the possibility.

The reality of metaphysical philosophizing stands between the absolutely present reality of transcendence and the empirical reality of historically given metaphysics. It is the thinking which does not preach, does not stand before a real transcendence, does not explore what others have believed—the thinking which shows, rather, that everything that exists can become a cipher in the general medium of possible Existenz.

The difficulty is that metaphysics—though originally facing the absolute reality of a transcendence conceived as not adequately communicable—cannot do *without* generality but grows vacuous when it is *purely* general.

4. Materialization and Denial of Transcendence

The reality of transcendence appears immanently only in the language of objectivity, but it does not exist as an empirical object. Hence the possibility of either *materializing* transcendence, by a confusion of the realities, or *denying* transcendence and making an absolute of empirical reality.

Materialization makes transcendence deceptively present in the form of tangible particular reality. Instead of seeing it *in* empirical reality, we see it *as* empirical reality. We lose transcendence when superstition makes us absolutize what exists in the world, exists materially and yet unreally in the sense we mean it. Whatever we do under this delusion of supersensuality is magic. We cling to the finite and treat it like transcendence, and yet we do not control it even as finite.

Positivism, on the other hand, lets us admit nothing but empirical reality. A positivist will reject metaphysics as fantasizing, though he can by no means control or destroy the human reality of this fantasizing. He will examine the historical reality of metaphysics in human existence, since man is naturally prone to metaphysical needs, which in turn have lent form to their contents and thus influenced his existence. Whether the faith in these contents was illusory or not, the positivist can, in any case, determine what was believed and what factual effects this belief has had; he can take an inventory and organize his material. He can then describe the factual ways of dealing with metaphysical contents in cults, rites, festivals, and in past thinking. Finally he can understand the consequences which these ways of dealing have had for the practical conduct of life, in rational and irrational attitudes toward the empirical world.

Superstition materializes things, and positivistic unbelief dissolves them into illusions. To both of them the metaphysical objectivity looks opaque rather than transparent. They do not hear the language of transcendence; superstition transforms it into mundane existence and treats it like empirical reality, while unbelief transforms it into fantasies whose supposed cognition shows them to be null and void, measured by the reality of world orientation.

A materialized transcendence and an existing beyond are illusions created by the tribulations of existence: by means of a knowledge, without having to break through to the freedom of Existenz, the superstitious would like to get around the cares, the perils, the sense of absolute destruction involved in existence.

Positivists, on the other hand, cannot even properly ask about transcendence, since they do not leave the standpoint of consciousness at large. From this standpoint the transcendent language is not even recognizable as an existing language. Pure immanence without transcendence remains nothing but deaf and dumb existence.

Since transcendent reality is neither empirical existence as a materialized transcendence nor another world in the beyond, its experience depends on the *rupture of immanence*, on the break in which Existenz at the historic moment encounters being. Transcendence is located neither in this world nor in another. Its location is a boundary—but a boundary on which I face transcendence if I truly am.

Superstition and positivism are enemies on the same plane, but on this plane positivism is the winner. There are no objective miracles. There are no ghosts, no visions, no feats of magic. What exists as a fact in reality is subject to rules and laws and can be methodically established. Those other phenomena, reported time and again in good faith and due to fraud or hysteria, are indeed not logically impossible, but the specific certainty with which we understand them to be impossible rests on the entirety of knowledge. The real impossibility results from the fact that such phenomena conflict with the premises on which empirical cognition can take place at all. This does not make the flat impossibility cogent, however. Rather, its certainty is an existentially based one, a certainty which is precisely not logical, although elucidated in logical ways. To reckon with really impossible phenomena as realities, even to consider their possibility seriously and positively, will set a man abysmally apart from another who is filled with the certainty that they are impossible, for this certainty is both a premise of thoughtful positivistic mundane knowledge and the correlate of a genuine relation to transcendence. Like a mostly veiled symptom, these matters of superstition make us feel the factual lack of communication between men who in matters of existence seem to show so much mutual understanding and solidarity.

5. *The Question of Illusion or Reality*

The historical facts about the beliefs of mankind give rise to a nagging, inescapable question. Have men been led astray for thousands of years by phantasms that are examined adequately if we look upon them as on psychopathological phenomena? Was it an error that fashioned all those human personalities and unique creations, and are the strange stirrings in even the contemporary psyche mere remnants of this error, whose definitive eradication is now due? Are they just the irrelevant emotional clouds on an otherwise enlightened existence, or is there in us a lostness that makes us long to get back to the experience of true being?

In primitive states of mind these questions about metaphysical things do not arise as yet. In those states, what we distinguish as reality and dream, as body and soul, as distinct categories, has not yet been separated. The effective rubbing of two sticks to make fire and the causally ineffective pouring of water to make rain seem to be acts of the same sort. All is still physical and mental at once; nature is not yet inanimate, the mind not yet immaterial. In the immediate entirety of existence there is as yet no differentiation of the modes of being, and thus no definite knowledge. To ask real questions about reality, man must have thought, investigated, and oriented himself by distinctions. He must have excluded possible delusions and acquired the inescapable reality concepts of empirical knowledge: real is what can be measured, what our senses can perceive in space and time according to rules, what can be controlled or calculated, at least, by appropriate measures.

Only in this critically developed consciousness will the question of illusion or reality arise. But there—given philosophical lucidity—the alternative *does not apply to metaphysical objectivity*. Materialized, this objectivity is an illusion for knowledge, but it is reality for the Existenz that hears in it the language of transcendence. As possible Existenz alone will ask about transcendence, possible Existenz alone will understand the answer.

Impermanence of Metaphysical Objectivity

Objective for our consciousness is extant being. This is given in its own presence. The object is close to us because it exists either physically, tangibly, or as a necessary conception. As such an empirical or cogently valid object, it is this alone and does not mean anything else.

Yet at the same time, because it is something other than ourselves, the object stands at a distance. Even in scientific thinking this distance compels a boundary question: as it is, the object is for our consciousness at large; but what is it in itself? We now conceive it as a *phenomenon*, and in the thoughts of Existenz—already looking beyond itself on other grounds, toward transcendent being—this phenomenality of all objects is understood as the sublimation of mere existence. To me as consciousness at large the downright otherness of transcendence was no more than the still vacuous boundary concept of being-in-itself; to come to myself in this consciousness I only need to know and to have the mere object. As Existenz, however, I am not myself until I grasp transcendence. Conceiving the diversity of empirical and valid objects does not yet make me myself. As Existenz I do not stop at a general sense of the phenomenality of all things; instead, objects turn for me into a peculiar form of transcendent language.

When objects come to be phenomena of transcendence, they will show distinguishing features. An object that is such a phenomenon must be *evanescent* for our consciousness, since it is not extant being but the language of transcendent being for the being of freedom. Existenz throughout comes to itself in the disappearance of things that merely exist, and so it does in the direction of transcendence: solely in objects which as such do not endure for our consciousness. Thus there are three methodically comprehensible modes of the impermanence of metaphysical objects.

First: as an object, whether conceptual or visual, the metaphysical objectivity is not the object itself, but a *symbol.*

Second: for the intellect a clear conception of the metaphysical object will lead to its *logical collapse;* the conception proves to be a circle, or a tautology, or a self-contradiction.

Third: due to the metaphysical intention, it is absolute reality which a free Existenz grasps in finite, empirical reality. The absolute makes the empirical reality seem as though it were not truly real, while in the sense of empirical reality the absolute one is unreal. Being and nonbeing reverse their relationship *in constant alternation.*

1. Symbolic Thinking

We talk of meaning in the sense of signs and images, of parables, comparisons, allegories, metaphors. The basic difference between mundane and metaphysical meaning is whether, in the relation of the image to that which it represents, the represented thing itself could also be grasped as an object or whether the image is simply an image for something not accessible in any other way. In other words, whether that for which the image stands might be said or shown directly, or whether it exists for us only insofar as it is in the image. In the latter case alone do we speak of symbols in the exact sense of a metaphysical meaning that must be existentially grasped in the image and cannot be conceived as just an object. The parable that stays within the world is a translation or image of something which in itself is equally objective, of something thinkable or visual; but the metaphysical symbol is the objectification of something nonobjective in itself. The nonobjectivity as such is not given; the objectivity of the symbol is not meant as the object it is. We cannot interpret the symbol, except by other symbols. To understand a symbol does therefore not mean to know its meaning rationally, to be able to translate the symbol; what it means is that an Existenz experiences in the symbolic intention this incomparable reference to something transcendent, and that it has this experience at the boundary where the object disappears.

The object which is a symbol cannot be held fast as an existing reality of transcendence; it can only be heard as its language. Existence and symbolic being are like two aspects in the one world that shows itself either to consciousness at large or to possible Existenz. If I see the world as cognizable with general validity, as empirically given without signifying anything as yet, it is existence. If I grasp it as a parable of true being, it is a symbol. Existence permits generally valid cognition and exploration as a being in relations; symbolic being is the historically concrete language that permits an Existenz to look into the depths of being. It is itself alone, unrelated to anything else. Only by immersing myself in it can I comprehend it or lose it.

Immersion in symbols is not the mystical immersion, the entrance into the nonobjectiveness of transcendence by way of an objectless and thus incommunicable union. Rather, as I hear the symbolic language, the phenomenon of transcendence is articulated for my Existenz in the medium of bright consciousness, *with the subject-object dichotomy maintained*. The I, instead of dissolving in the face of its transcendence, gains in depth as a finite self-being. Like the elucidation of consciousness in world orientation, elucidation in the symbol proceeds here by way of objectivity. In world orientation the objectivity is extant, infinitely subdivided existence; in symbolic deepening it is the language as a transient passage. Phenomenal lucidity and the communicative depth of possible Existenz find their expression in the richly developed, subdivided, and always vanishing world of symbols.

2. *Logical Collapse*

What can be shown or proven is a finite insight into something particular. In the sense of this being, Existenz and transcendence do not exist. When they are conceived, the thought assumes logical forms that destroy it as an insight. The relevance of the thought must be tested by other than logical criteria—namely, by its power to elucidate Existenz by appealing to freedom, or to conjure transcendence by blithely collapsing as an object itself. When argument as an expression of transcending is disguised as proof, the proof is not what was really meant, and it will fail. The worth of such nonprobative proving shows as communicability of the unknowable factors on which transcending depends.

If to philosophize is to ponder transcendence, what will show at the crucial point is a *circle* that wipes out the thought as a demonstrable insight but demonstrates its philosophical character by its expressive vigor and scope. The circle may be reduced to a *tautology* when it is fundamentally grasped and the substance abbreviated into statements which are objectively meaningless but which will affect a possible Existenz.

Opposed to circle and tautology is the *self-contradiction* that wipes out not just the proof but the proposition itself; it is the real destruction of the objectivity of metaphysical thoughts. No profound expression of transcendence can help making itself vanish in such a contradiction, since as an object it cannot last without losing transcendence.

3. *Alternation of Being and Nonbeing*

The phenomenon of transcendence stands on the borderline of two worlds that interact like being and nonbeing. The forms of their objectivity reflect this situation. To me as consciousness at large, the empirical object is real and all other objects are unreal; to me as Existenz, the empirical becomes unreal before the true reality of transcendence. The relationship is reversible depending on the mode of the appercipient self-being; the essence of the object is changed when I am Existenz and when I slide back into mere existence.

This is why no experience—which we have in consciousness at large —can by empirical and logical compulsion create an objective certainty that there is transcendence. And conversely, the truer our grasp of transcendent being, the more decisively will its objective supports be destroyed.

Yet there is no separating the two worlds. A purely empirical existence is indeed like a decline from being to mere knowledge, but for us transcendence is not detached from the temporal reality in which it appears. A finite, empirical reality may become absolutely real without, as finite, being absolute; the finite as such can vanish without spoiling transcendence.

In our sense of symbols lies an extraordinary *sense of reality* that differs essentially from our knowledge of empirically present existence. Objectively, of course, an observer cannot distinguish a sensory dependence on existence from participation in the supersensory realities in it; for moments, a grasp of transcendence in immanent phenomena may look as if transcendence were materialized. In cases of conflict, however, and at turning points of the process of temporal existence it will appear what has been true. In the agonies of disappearing empirical reality, the lift to transcendence is the surest manifestation of its not being materialized.

Historicity of Metaphysics

1. Disappearance as the Essence of Historicity

The common feature of the three modes of formal metaphysical objectivity was that they will not let the particular object last. They will always void it again; they are not forms of continuity but forms of disappearance. The question is why this must be so.

At the limits of world orientation we have seen possible Existenz transcend to itself as relating to its transcendence—a transcendence which becomes phenomenal for an existential consciousness in the form of metaphysical objectivity. Possible Existenz transcends because there can be no immanent satisfaction of existence in itself, while the satisfaction of possible Existenz in existence is more than immanent. Yet the pursuit of this satisfaction does not aim at a future being, which as the ultimate goal of temporal existence would be its essence; nor does it aim at being in a beyond, which would be nothing but another world detached from ours. The satisfaction lies in the being which appears presently to itself: for us, transcendence is real only as *presence in time*.

In transcendence as a reality in historic form, the sense of being is always self-sufficient, not to be repeated and not to be copied. If the appearance of Existenz is historic rather than general, and if it is only becoming, not yet being—not like the passive becoming of existence, however, but by freely realizing itself in the extant medium—the transcendence that appears to it must also become historic. It is a certainty, not a knowledge, that is derived from the historic phenomenon. That transcendence will change its appearance along with Existenz is no argument against its truth and reality; indeed, its appearance must necessarily have the aspect of change if it is to be a language heard by Existenz in temporal existence.

This historic change would be impossible if transcendent truth could be fixed in extant objectivity. It is part of the historicity of Existenz in temporal existence that all metaphysical objectivity must disappear. Because the metaphysical object can achieve permanence only at the cost of untruth, Existenz must, in searching for transcendent truth, experience the same historic changes which it undergoes itself.

For the Existenz that appears to itself in existence, the form of the phenomenon of transcendence, of every true moment of quiet self-sufficiency, remains in the unrest of historically self-created motion.

2. *The Unvanished Substance*

What has disappeared remains as substance. The objectivity alone has been submerged to resurrect its content in a new form. Whatever Existenz experiences as its transcendence will be brought to present lucidity by what it hears from its past. No more than I invent and make my own language do I invent and make the metaphysical symbolism, the language in which transcendence is experienced.

The original transcendent experience occurs in absolute historic concreteness. If I call this "hearing" transcendence itself, in its primary language, then metaphysical objectivity—in thoughts, images, symbols —is a *second language* which makes it possible for the first, original one to be communicated.

As a child I awaken to consciousness with the language of transcendence: I hear that language from the past before I experience it myself and inquire about it. Later, having come to full consciousness, I deliberately expand the past for myself into a universal one, beyond the unconscious tradition I have received. History lies before me as an inexhaustible source of possible appeals to me. I enter into communication with things forgotten and buried, with strange worlds, and with the transcendence that has been experienced there.

I have two ways of approaching this past.

For my orientation in the world I come to know the history of religions and philosophies, of myths, revelations, and dogmas, of theologies and metaphysics. These are the *capita mortua* of what was once a phenomenon of being proper for free Existenz. I trace their transformations in the course of time, the new, desultory departures, the diversity of independent worlds. I seek a logical, typological, psychological, and sociological cognition of links and dependencies. But I am thus dealing with a material which in this way I do not really understand.

Knowing the documents and monuments, the narratives and the restored visuality of acts and types of conduct that have happened once, and of the thinking performed in them—knowing those is only a premise of the second approach. It is because I myself am struck by transcendence that I now seek to get close to the past, to understand it as I am awakened by it, whether in attraction or in repulsion. If the first way taught me only about objectivities that are extinct, the second will let me experience my own present historicity that will transform the otherness and adapt it to me, or else let it remain an accompanying possibility.

3. The Three Meanings of Generality in Metaphysical Thinking

To become audible for me from the past and in the factual present, the transcendent language must in some sense be a general one. Without generality, the experience of an absolutely dark sense of being would leave me helpless for lack of self-communication. But the meaning of generality in metaphysics is heterogeneous. I must make distinctions if I want to avoid the endless self-deceptions that occur in transcending, and the effects they have in practice.

When we explore the history of metaphysics, we seek an *objective* universal. We can search for the "primeval religious forms" that arise originally and yet identically everywhere; and psychologically, looking at the general human unconscious, we can find the universal images which under the right conditions may occur to anyone at any time—in imgination, dreams, and insanity as well as in the mythical ideas of nations. But precisely this universal, whose abstraction fosters and befits our cognition of the extant objectivities, proves meaningless for transcending. It is metaphysically void, a merely formal network or material fabric. I do not aquire an understanding of languages by studying the sounds, the word formations, the grammatical constructions that occur throughout; I do not understand man if I look only at his generally human features, at the basic human situations, and at the supposedly natural human consciousness; and neither are those general things the contents of metaphysics.

The history of metaphysics, therefore, is not, as in science, the field for acquainting myself with the general side of its existence. It is the field for penetrating, on grounds of my own potential, the historic Existenz which is always one and always singular. The historically determined, and in the above-mentioned sense not at all general, element is here the truth, but not as a case of a universal possibility. It is truth as the one-time revelation of an Existenz that is now addressing me, questioning me, and making demands on me. It is a truth of which new forms of truth are transformations or transpositions.

Yet in another sense this penetration on the basis of my own potential is still a search for the substance as *relatively general*. What my transcending refers to is unutterable, but objectivity is the utterable *reflection* of transcendence. As transcendence comes to be objectified in a phenomenon, the objectivity as such brings a general side into my original, unelucidated existential attitude toward transcendence.

Since no communication is possible without the form of a universal, that general side becomes a language, but this does not make it the content of the language. As in existential elucidation the conception of a universal is true only when an individual fulfills it, so the truth of metaphysical objectivity lies in the real transcendent relation it serves to accomplish. The universal needs the complement of newly present Existenz, just as it was originally borne by Existenz. If a stated metaphysics has assumed a general form, I can understand it only if I look through it at the source of the statement. What has been stated only in objective terms is meaningless as a metaphysical idea. It takes an approach to its roots and an adoptive transposition to reveal its truth to each historic Existenz. No mere intellect will succeed in this "looking through," nor is it capable of direct communication.

The point is that this relatively general side of the historic phenomena of transcendence lies in their communicability between the men they link. Though it has its fulfillment only in each individual, the "second language" does seem to express a transcendent being that is identical for many. The expression itself has originated either with individuals at times we can determine, or indeterminably in the tradition of a community from times immemorial.

We cannot, therefore, grasp the metaphysical substance in this general side as extant and timeless in itself, as breaking through now and then and becoming visible in time. We cannot know it as the one general transcendence, not even if we were to bring all particular truth from the history of metaphysics together into a whole.

And yet, in every true attitude toward transcendence lies a sense of being *independent of me*. My historicity does not produce it; it produces me, my self, *as* I become aware of it. As ineffability precedes all effability in the objective realm, so does the reality of transcendence precede its language.

For I as Existenz grasp my transcendence, but *not as mine alone.* Transcendence is more than it is for me. Although it will open to Existenz alone, Existenz cannot treat it as its private intrinsic being.

Thus transcendence as the universal and the One does not become objectively conceivable, let alone knowable, and yet it must be. The paradox of transcendence lies in the fact that we can *grasp it only historically* but cannot adequately *conceive it as being historic* itself.

It is not itself either in generality for a consciousness at large, like objects, or in historicity, like Existenz. For Existenz the reality of transcendence is the *sole universal,* that of which there is no particular case any more; it is the *inconceivable unity of the general and the particular* that has nothing distinguishable without or within. Where it is conceived in distinctions or seen as an image, transcendence is already a historic phenomenon and not universal.

The universal was thus, first, the objective form under which the particular is *subsumed* as a case. Secondly, it was the objectivity *fulfilled* by the present Existenz that grasps transcendence in it. And thirdly, it was the ineffable and unimaginable singularity that is *encountered* as the only reality.

The first universal, as the form of the existence and objectiveness of metaphysics in man, is knowable, but as I know it I tend to think of it at the same time as the existence of a radical delusion.

The second universal is what I face in an ascertaining faith: the sphere of communication in my understanding of myself and among those who hold beliefs in common.

The third universal is the transcendent being that is flatly inaccessible by way of general conception and yet, for all its inconceivability, is conceived in transcending: as the paradoxical unity of universal and particular, as that which it is in itself and thus cannot be for me.

The consequence of these three meanings of generality in metaphysics is a threefold mode of its claim to validity.

The generality of *existing* metaphysics does *not make it metaphysically valid*. It is vain to argue that the individual must conform to something because all experience shows it is intrinsically human. The very question whether there are forms of metaphysical need lies on a plane on which no decisions pro or con are possible.

The general transcendent *language* is *transferable* in its historic form, but *not universally valid*. That language is nothing but the relatively general objectivity that serves to communicate unconditional faith as the sense of being of a particular Existenz.

The general inaccessible *uniqueness* of transcendence is its *reality*. To encounter it in the historic phenomenon is the truth of metaphysics, although this unique universal itself never becomes an object. An ontologically conceived generality of transcendent being, valid for everyone, is impossible.

Existence as the Form of the Historic Appearance of Transcendence

1. Community and Struggle in the Transcendent Relation

The historic appearance of transcendence in an objectified symbol establishes a singular kind of community. Not only is my historicity communicative, but in an expanded historicity Existenz will follow the substance of the tradition from which it grew. The historicity of the metaphysical substance means that if an Existenz adheres to its own traditional revelation of transcendence, if it adheres to it in the particular form it has encountered and in the particular language it has heard, it is doing so not on the ground that the revelation is one form of truth among others, that it is "also true," but because to Existenz this truth is truth pure and simple, the truth whereby its self-being will stand or fall.

To an existing Existenz transcendent truth is not a timeless extant one, to be comprehended like rational insights. This is why it must have this historic form. Yet as long as that truth keeps a free existential community in motion, an Existenz that does not confuse the meanings of the universal will keep an open mind for other truth. The unconditionality with which it adheres to its own truth while recognizing that it is historic —this very unconditionality would make it shun any exclusiveness and any claim to universality, and would prevent it from granting the character of timelessly valid rational truths to its own forms of historic truths. And if asked whether the transcendently related being of the self might rest upon an accident of history, such an Existenz would answer Yes. Historicity brings forth a sense of *not being all*, a posture of not regarding oneself as the *sole* type of being there ought to be.

Historical reality shows us a different picture. Symbols become community-founding powers that are taken for the one and only truth, excluding or destroying any other. The darkness of transcendence blends into the obscurity of vital passions. This is the way of those who resist lucidity, who want to live in passionate intoxication, with blind self-existence untouchable. Valid now is that which is unquestioned. Made to look tremendously right by the fact that they are fighting for transcendence, men may yield to the savagery of instinctive violence. The symbol may found a community without communication.

This fanaticism can arise when the heterogeneous meanings of the universal are confused and taken for one and the same. Really transcendent truth is consciously understood as historic and thus not universal, as unconditional and thus not generally valid.

Struggles will inevitably result from the historicity of phenomenal transcendence, however, when a community's *existence* collides with the existence of another, due to the mundane situation of both. It is as though transcendence were unwilling to surrender its ever-particular historic appearance without a struggle. That men of this particular type, with this particular historic substance of being, ought to live on earth will seem to such men like an absolute commandment from a hidden source. Their battle is not merely one for self-preservation, waged by blind existence; it aims at the future of human life, which shall be so that men will know this specific historicity of a transcending consciousness and will adopt it as their past. And this goal can be attained not only in victory but in truthful failure.

In existence there is no sublimating this most profound clash of substances with existential roots. The tale of the three rings[1] does not reflect our situation. What we know in the various aspects of religion is not one truth in different form; it is the sole universal of transcendence, rather, which in mundane existence makes irreconcilable truth fight in the form of currently historic universals. This struggle has kindled greater passions than have the vital interests of existence. In the faith in trancendence everything seems at stake—not just the believer's being, but being itself.

2. The Three Spheres of Shaping Metaphysical Objectivity

Mythology, theology, and philosophy are attempts at an explicit and objective expression and representation of transcendent being. Mythology tries by an overflowing, ever-changing wealth of tales, figures, and interpretations, by the unfoldment of a knowledge of transcendence that pervades mundane knowledge and accompanies it. Theology tries on the ground of historically fixed revelation, claiming a rationally based, systematically perfected knowledge of truth. Philosophical metaphysics tries by pondering transcendence in existence, by thoughts that reach the ultimate origins and limits of existence, turn somersaults, and require present fulfillment by a historic Existenz. In philosophical metaphysics we adopt mythical reality from everywhere and seek to understand what is alien to us in mythology and revelation.

The proximity and interpenetration of the three formative spheres serve only to exacerbate their mutual rejection. But even as enemies they remain tied to each other. The unhistoric, ever-recurring typicality of their formations will not let the struggle between them rest—yet no clear fronts can evolve, with the struggle hidden in the individual soul as an irreversible motion.

Philosophy rejects the mythos that gave it birth. It pits rational, reasoned insight against the telling of tales that impress it as dreams and delusions. But some day, grown independent, philosophy looks back and tries to comprehend the myths as truth. Then they are either

---

1. A parable on religion from Lessing's *Nathan the Wise*, based on a story from Boccaccio's *Decameron*. The owner of a ring that will endear its wearer to God and men has two perfect copies made and on his deathbed gives each of his three sons a ring with the assurance that it is the original. The sons, each claiming on the strength of the father's word to possess the true talisman, appeal to a judge, who finds that as no ring has endeared the wearer to his brothers, all three seem false; not till the parties and their progeny have striven for a thousand years to *earn* the love of God and men may "a wiser judge" be able to resolve the issue. —TRANSLATOR.

viewed as *disguises* of philosophical insight for those still unable to grasp it in the form of thought—and also for the philosophizing individual himself, at moments when his certainty of being overcomes him in this visual form rather than by thought—or what is seen in the mythos is the actual *expression of a truth* to which no thought gives us access. In philosophical thinking we can only notice that there are things which seem inaccessible to us although their pure conception in the myths presupposes a way of thinking in their direction. Where a rational grasp of the mythical core is claimed for it, philosophical truth becomes peculiarly empty, or else it may prove to be mere uninvolved thinking *about* things. Struck by this experience, philosophy returns to being when it becomes true as thinking *in* the myth, just as it is true as thinking *in* life, *in* world orientation.

Philosophy also rejects theology because of theology's dependence on revelation, but the two come together again where revelation impresses philosophy as a historic form of phenomenal transcendence. Theology, then, is a truth that means something to philosophy even though its universality has been lost. Noticing that attempts to solidify and close our philosophizing in merely generally valid rationality make our philosophizing fatuous, we take conscious hold of its current historic substance even in the theological tradition. We transform this tradition, but we do not deny it.

Theology, on the other hand, rejects the myths as pagan but appropriates a mass of them, integrating and thus transforming them into parts of its entirety. It rejects philosophy as an autocratic form of absolute truth but appropriates it, whether as a preliminary stage of its own truth or as a means of expressing contents of its revelation.

In the temporal existence of the soul this struggle between the formative spheres of transcendent truth will continue because it is the medium in which the motion of transcendent objectivity occurs, and because this motion cannot come to the firm halt of definitive objectification wherever Existenz retains its freedom. The struggle ceases, leaving the unfree repose of the grave, where men lapse into the paganism of theosophical materializations—now grown superstitious—or into a purely rationalistic philosophy that pretends by knowledge to make sure of true being. Only in this absence of any struggle, in this dead immobility of one of the three forms, can philosophers come to regard the myths as poetic, random, entertaining reveries, and theology as a delusive aberration of fanatical priests that has now been overcome. In the judgment of theologians, on the other hand, the myths may then be heathenish devil's work, and philosophy a self-deification of man in his subjectivity and relativity.

3. The Transcendent Language in the Stages of Metaphysical Consciousness

The historicity of metaphysics, we have seen, means first its diversity—which from outside, however, can only be viewed and explored as a dead accumulation—and secondly, it means that Existenz will always see *its past relating to itself*.

The second mode of historicity is the tie of possible Existenz to the tradition of the three formative spheres of objective symbols. This tie includes an interaction between the traditional metaphysical substance and *its free adoption*. As the symbols go through history, they congeal into general validities; to regain their original voice they need to be animated by each individual in the personal historicity of his fate. It is true that to be preserved from oblivion they must be passed on according to definite rules and obeyed by the new generations, but it is also true that only emancipation from this required obedience will bring the individual so to himself that he can dispense with intermediaries in grasping his transcendence. There can be no existential commitment unless I break free of tradition, unless I translate its substance into present being for myself, unless I dare to risk being without the fixed form of tradition. But the objectivity of tradition is a premise of freedom, for freedom as such cannot be propagated as a tradition; it can only be acquired by the individual. Handed down, it is not freedom any more; enjoyed without a struggle, it is lost. The tradition of freedom is simply an indirect appeal from individuals who dared it to the later individuals who hear their voices. It is the secret community of those who are themselves, a community that will be ostracized and, as far as possible, silenced by all the servants of the objective tradition—by churches and parties and rationalistic philosophical schools, and by contemporary public opinion as the matter of course in which all understand one another.

The history of our metaphysical consciousness has grown by stages and leaps of our knowledge. As we understand it, we see it preceded by stages of consciousness. In these we visualize what historicity has been, and we comprehend that because we bear it in ourselves. In our knowledge of the stages, we draft the way to present historicity, which is at the same time the way to train ourselves for adoption. This draft, however, cannot claim to be a valid objective knowledge of the one universal course of consciousness. It can do no more than illuminate the history of the true sense of being of one who experiences his history in his time.

While cogent thought lies on one plane and a comprehension of its possible insights by everyone—athwart the different stages of consciousness, so to speak—requires only intellectual training, metaphysical contents are split not only into heterogeneous possibilities opposed to each other but into possibilities that belong together and succeed one another in stages. Their truth depends upon the stage of consciousness at which we hear it in this language. What lies at a later stage we cannot understand as yet; what lies at an earlier one we cannot adequately fulfill any more. The realization of metaphysical thinking is tied to a current stage of consciousness, while purely external thought seems universally transferable.

But to know the stages is *never a result*. It *remains an idea*. The most magnificent draft was made by Hegel in his *Phenomenology,* and countless other schemata of the stages have been drafted since. For moments they may look as though comprehending a general, lawful, necessary sequence; dialectical evidence, psychological and logical, and its partial confirmation by historical science suggest a deeper insight than these schemata really give. For the stages as a whole are historic and unforeseeable, without a visible beginning or a visible goal, and without a process we can understand as necessary. They are neither a linear sequence nor a universal.

Historic adoption of metaphysical objectivity means therefore to *comprehend it as a truth advancing by stages toward myself*. Yet this comprehension—which in the medium of historical orientation is itself metaphysical—remains true only if I see through its own schemata, if I do not stabilize in a universal image what is real only in my Existenz.

The truth that metaphysical objectivity lies on no single plane is of crucial importance. Upon this insight depends my possible communication with an alien substance, as well as my ability to understand my own substance without confusion.

A further consequence is an attitude in which I know the possibility of *making false demands* upon the other. There is, of course, no limit to the readiness of possible Existenz to question things and look for words to express total openmindedness, and yet I hesitate where thoughts would penetrate transcendence. Thoughts cannot convey a knowledge of God, only a consciousness of the way transcendence enters our soul *in our situation*. To say what has been my experience; not to shroud abysses and antinomies; to see transcendence itself in the light of questionability—all this is called for because my sense of freedom demands veracity as the expression of the unknown ground of my being. It seems to be the deity's own will that every way of seeking after truth be dared at the risk of error. We need not fear unveiling what it would conceal; what we have to fear is falsehood. Yet this daring all, and saying all, is limited to my own stage of consciousness. Not every man is ready to conceive each thought and to think it truly, to be struck by each fact and to sense the cipher in it. In dealing with children it is a teacher's business to decide responsibly what they can be told at a time; yet a risk remains, and in adults the stages of consciousness are even less knowable. It may be a matter of humanity and thus of truthfulness to hold my tongue without letting the other feel it, for in the end, what every individual will ask himself is up to him. All thoughts can no more be asked of all men than any thought can be forbidden to any. In a book the author is addressing his own stage of consciousness and need not limit himself; but in a concrete situation it adds to my hesitancy that I know about the stages without knowing them in the particular, and without objective knowledge of my own stage. There is a time for all things. The great leaps and crises change the whole of man, as if organs of sight were evolving, and others decaying. Men who really belong together may be kept apart by a discrepancy in their stages of consciousness. One may have had a radical basic experience in the existence which the other has not shared, and as a result each metaphysical symbol will have shifted in his language. The symbol strengthens me by its lucidity and clarifies my thought, but its objective unequivocality is so inappreciable that I see it through my current self-being with a sense of looking in it at the substance of being itself.

Metaphysical Methods

The standpoint to which we have come has three consequences in metaphysical practice. It means that from this standpoint certain methods are *to be rejected,* that a positive attitude toward past metaphysics will be shown in *adoption,* and that *present methods* will be limited to definable ways and will simultaneously become the key to adoption.

1. Rejected Methods

Prophetic metaphysics can proclaim its tenets on grounds of original certainty. Its exponents believe they have taken the step to a knowledge of intrinsic being. But what can thus truly be done at the outset of human philosophizing cannot succeed in the light of reflection, of mundane knowledge and an assurance of freedom—not, that is, except at the price of a blindness that may suggest community without communication but cannot allow one self to speak to another self. Hence the distrust we feel of prophetic metaphysics: what may historically, at the existential moment, overcome an individual as absolute certainty of transcendence in objective language—this is what such metaphysics would impose by force as generally valid truth. Even before they are done, while developing their thought structures, the prophets lose their own ground. Incapable of irony at those structures of theirs, they expatiate in them on the original substance, which possession already makes fade. In other historic situations, prophetic metaphysics was a creative gestation and expression of the transcendent experience; but today, without the original substance, it can be no more than an untruthful repetition of the outward form of preaching in the service of superstitious spiritual rapine.

No less impossible for us is a *scientific* investigation of transcendent being. As in world orientation the sciences have their topic in the objects of knowledge and cognition, metaphysics is here supposed to become a valid knowledge of transcendence. In analogy to theories of natural science with its methods of empiricism and conclusiveness, it is proposed to make transcendence cognoscible for consciousness at large by a *world hypothesis*. At the limit of all given things transcendence is conceived as a being that *underlies* them. A hypothesis of this underlying is drawn up from the facts of world orientation and the experiences of satisfaction and discontent in existence, taking the fullest possible account of all that occurs. Taken literally, the manner of speaking used in true philosophy, with its distinction of appearance from being, does suggest such a relationship; but this unavoidable manner of speaking must not be solidified into a mundane relation in the sense of the definite categories "appearance"and "being." It is not a means of expressing metaphysical thought unless, transcending the definiteness of the terms, I conceive in them the being that is positively manifest to a vigorous Existenz but not to be conquered as knowledge. As a world hypothesis, being would not be transcendent; as underlying, it would only be more or less probable and devoid of all real certainty. It would be objective, no longer in need of freedom as the organ of its ascertainment. Unless the hypothesis happens to attain some significance to empirical research —thus demonstrating at the same time its essential heterogeneity to all transcendence—it is void because it involves neither cognition nor a transcendent manifestation. In the world hypothesis, we treat transcendence as a supposedly existing being, which cognitive skill would let us ferret out. We seek to prove by the standards of noncontradictoriness what only a free self-being can ask about and seize upon. The necessary concomitant of such doings is a lack of understanding for all the existential metaphysics of thousands of years. The historically given metaphyical texts will be outwardly received, marked true or false by our own rationalistic standards, corrected, modified, and taken into our own edifice. These endeavors are pleasing to the exponents of a supposedly scientific approach—whom a fulfilled metaphysics displeases because it is not to be had by means of pure theory, without the condition that a man be free and act at his own peril. Also insinuating itself here may be a mythical element of genuine parentage. At all events, whatever is not either scientific world orientation or real metaphysics is unsubstantial in every sense.

2. Present Adoption

In adoptive metaphysics, searching freely for transcendence, we proceed differently. It cannot occur to us to devise a new transcendence; instead, we must try to unearth the buried language it has acquired over thousands of years. But the way to adopt this language is identical to that in which our present is adopted as a real presence. Metaphysics is metaphysical history adopted from each present day, and likewise is it the present made manifest by metaphysical history. It is fulfillment from tradition by the self-becoming Existenz of the individual who hears the language of the world, the immensely rich and profound world which is entered by all being that comes to matter to him.

The criterion of truthfulness in adoptive metaphysics is the scope of the empirical realities and existential possibilities perceived, the scope of the historic tradition that we make our own. While prophetic metaphysics usually confines itself to a few lines, an adoptive one is open to every possibility—and that precisely in awareness of its limitations. While prophetic metaphysics ignores the world to concentrate on mere world schemata, and ignores all other Existenz to pursue its own violent, uncommunicative course, an adoptive one is always newly engendered from mundane knowledge and existential communication.

3. Present Methods

Transcendence is what envelops us day in, day out, if we respond. Philosophy cannot give metaphysics, but it can awaken it and make it lucid.

If an attempt to express metaphysical contents methodically and systematically takes us away from their origin in present historicity and into a *relatively general sphere,* our thoughts will be kept meaningful only by their links with the original historicity and by the impulses that come from it. From this source alone can such thinking derive the decisive capacity for measure and criticism.

Philosophy as this metaphysical thinking without a really present source is *playing a game.* We unfold possibilities for Existenz; we make them available; but because they are no more than possible, we do not go beyond the question either. The present impact in this sort of play remains noncommittal and must not be confused with the decisive reality of Existenz. Metaphysical play is serious if it rests upon the search for Existenz, and if its contents are existential possibilities. It grows out of the seriousness of existential unconditionality that comes to appear in existence. The seriousness of mere existence, the purposive tackling of empirical things, has to do only with the causal, the legal, the tangible; it is objectively compelling, but its ground is ephemeral and at times will vanish altogether. The liberating existential seriousness is play in objective thinking, but its ground is unconditional, and absolute when it disappears. And it is this seriousness which in turn suspends all objectivity in the material seriousness of existence and in the thoughts of philosophizing.

The game has to do with possibilities. Transcendence is, of course, the being that cannot be turned into a possibility; but when the object of the game is the ground that lies beyond all possibilities, the manner of its conception is a possibility again. Possibility as the medium of mundane knowledge is the insight that what I am thinking of might also be different. Possibility in existential elucidation is an appeal to the freedom of the self. But possibility in philosophical metaphysics is the game of trying, recollecting, anticipating in objective form what can be present only in a historically concrete sense of being: the transcendent reality that has no possibility.

This sort of play would just be random toying if it did not involve commitment by its relation to possible Existenz. What makes it truthful is that once upon a time there was a moment when it really was present language, or that such a moment might come. And that a declared transcendent language unobtrusively presents itself as play, as a mere possibility, makes for the authenticity of the individual, freely self-becoming Existenz. A genuine Existenz may playfully anticipate what hitherto was manifested only as a possible language, but it can perceive its being only in reality, at the historic moment.

A systematics of metaphysical play results from three modes of transcending.

1. Beyond the being that is defined in categories, my thought transcends from the definite to the undefinable. In categorial thinking I tend to view definability in categories as the mark of all being, and an absolutizing of some or all of the categories would lead me to a definition of transcendence—in other words, to an ontology. But this *formal transcending* leaves the way to transcendence open. It is an originally philosophical experience, empty still, but present in thinking as such. Thought and metaphysical ascertainment coincide in it.

2. Instead of sufficing unto itself, the being of Existenz comes to feel transcendence as one with its self-being. This is why we could not

eliminate transcendence from existential elucidation, why metaphysical objectivities would keep occurring in order to develop possibilities of Existenz. Existenz as such is bound to ask for, and about, transcendent being. In metaphysics we explicitly make a topic of the *existential relations to transcendence*. We conceive, not transcendence itself, but its way of entering into the self-being of possible Existenz.

3. Beyond the empirical reality we know in world orientation, and beyond the reality of freedom which appeals to us in the elucidation of Existenz, our thoughts transcend in the endeavor to *read* all being as a *cipher script of transcendence* that may be decipherable for Existenz. The perusal of the cipher script is either a thoughtful comprehension of the kind of reading we do in art and letters, or it is the creation of a philosophical language for the thoughts that would unriddle being as a cipher. This is the significance of philosophical metaphysics. In the world images of such metaphysics we do not really mean those images. They are the form we use to make statements about transcendence.

The *search* for transcendence lies in the existential relations to it; its *presence* lies in cipher writing; the *space* for both is held open by formal transcending. But existential elucidation alone will lend weight to the formal thought experiences we have in philosophizing, as well as our reading of the cipher script. Without roots in Existenz they would veer into all kinds of random endlessness.

Formal
Transcending

2

In world orientation, being seemed to us the most self-evident of things. Not until we asked what it meant to be, then, did it strike us as not quite a matter of course.

The first result was that being is not the same in everything that exists and can be conceived. *Lists of categories* serve to classify what is, according to the modes of being. Each category characterizes a mode or species of being—for example, reality, validity, substance, quality, quantity, matter, form, life, consciousness, and so forth. The statement that something is does not mean the same thing everywhere.

The second result was that being, once splintered by our inquiry, cannot be restored as *one* being. If we try to ask about being as such, about the being typified and represented by all modes of being, we do not get an answer any more. Being has now been dissolved, and its disjointness is the lasting result of immanent thinking.

Since it was always only a particular mode of being which our thoughts and thinkabilities covered, no cognition in the world can answer our question about being. The only way that will let us seek an answer is still that of a transcending elucidation of being, without new objective cognition.

This is why, having left immanence as the diversity of being, we now attempt in transcending to ascertain true being as the one and only one. This being does not come under any category. From all being in categories—which for lack of a common immanent category of being is always specific—the way of failing thought leads to transcendence as the one being. I may call this "above-being" if I want to express that every category of being is inadequate to it and will drag it down to the immanence of a particular. And I may call it "nonbeing" if I want to express that this being lies in no category that means a being.

In formal transcending we aim at being itself. The question about it, a question that is raised at every stage of philosophizing, has here an end but does not receive an answer. A rational adequacy between question and answer is here flatly impossible. All that remains possible instead, in philosophizing, is the existential adequacy of thoughts that are presently fulfilling but objectively still empty.

Principles of Formal Transcending

1. From the Thinkable to the Unthinkable

The general forms of thinkability are the categories. Thinking as such means that I must inevitably think in categories even of the absolute, of being-in-itself. But the moment I do so, I have it in mind as a definite object in the world, distinct from other objects. I am no longer thinking of that which I meant.

After this experience I may try not to think of the absolute at all. But I cannot manage that either. Once having thought of what being is not, I cannot help thinking of being; in conceiving the nonabsolute, I indirectly touch upon the being of the absolute. Everywhere in thought, so to speak, there is a place where something will be directly posited as absolute, because I cannot exist and think without the appearance of an absolute, whether in the involuntary absolutization of a particular or in the conscious unconditionality of my own free self-being. In the endless flux of things that are, I cannot escape from my pursuit of being, nor from seizing it either in true or in deceptive forms.

I can, therefore, neither conceive this absolute being nor give up trying to conceive it. This being is transcendence, because I cannot grasp it but must transcend to it in thoughts that are completed when I cannot think them.

Unable, in my thinking, to hold fast to a thought of transcendence, I must, in the same thinking, void the things I have thought. This is what happens in transcending from the thinkable to the unthinkable.

In the spatial world we look in vain for a place where the deity might be; in the thinkable world we look in vain for a thought that is not a particular mundane object.

In the visible and thinkable world I come to no conclusion, and in this world my thinking cannot be tied down. It proceeds from object to object; but in this process I comprehend neither myself, as self-based, nor the world. Instead, I ask: Whence am I? Yet this transcending question can be answered by no thought that fits its meaning, since everything thinkable will again be part of the world that is to be transcended. The ultimate transcending step of thought can only be to void itself. I come to think: *It is conceivable that there are things which are not conceivable.* This expresses a step which my thinking no sooner takes than it ceases to be thinking. Thinking sets itself a limit it cannot cross—and yet, by thinking it, it appeals for a crossing of the limit.

The self-voiding passion that overcomes my thinking in the face of transcendence will at the same time make me hold on relentlessly to what is really thinkable. The only failures of my thinking are to be the true and necessary ones. For the urge to think clearly and to understand itself is inherent in Existenz; and Existenz will not succumb to the thoughtless inertia of mere feelings that can never truly transcend, nor to the *sacrificium intellectus* in which thought is not voided by transcending but given up altogether.

The utterable propositions that result from such transcending are negations. I reject, as inapplicable to transcendence, whatever I can conceive. I must not define transcendence by any predicate, must not objectify it in any idea, must not conceive it by any inference. Yet all categories may be used to say that transcendent being is neither a quality nor a quantity, neither a relation nor a cause, that it is not singular, not manifold, not being, not nothingness, and so forth.

This transcending of all immanence, even the most sublime, is by no means self-evident. It is an extraordinary effort to refrain from fixing transcendence within the world in some form, especially since a transient form is unavoidable for the appearance of transcendence. Pursuing the mundanization of transcendence into its every hiding place is a task that can never be finished and must always be repeated. Here it is the negations that will lend depth to the transcending thought.

Transcendence is beyond all form. We ascertain the philosophical idea of God as thinking fails us, and what we grasp in this failure is *that* there is a deity, not *what* it is. Our failing thoughts create a space that can—always historically—be fulfilled by a historic Existenz and in reading the ciphers of existence. They elucidate the certainty of transcendence, a certainty whose realization took more than thinking as such; but they give no substance to its being. Hence the rational weakness of this idea of God, and hence its existential power. We find here no personal God of wrath and of grace, no relevance of a life of prayer as religious action, no lasting visuality of the deity for our senses, in symbols as objects of faith.

2. Dialectics of Transcending in Thought

Transcending in thought, seeking to make sure of transcendent being, I want to perform acts of thinking that amount to not thinking. My thought remains in this dialectics as long as I keep it true, as long as I do not either drag transcendent being into the immanence of a conception or lose myself in the mere thoughtless feeling of such a being. It is a somersault that must be constantly renewed here, from thinking to an inability to think—not just a transcending from a conception to the inconceivable, but in that act the very thinking that voids itself: a not thinking that makes me lucid because I am not thinking something and am not thinking nothing either. This self-annihilating dialectics is a specific thinking that means nothing to me as long as objectivity and visuality are my only conditions of meaning; yet it is essential to the elucidation of my philosophical sense of being.

Methodically brought into pure forms, this dialectics might make us try to draw up an analogue of the categories: a list of categories that are self-contradictory and thus self-voiding. But there are no categories other than those of immanence. The transcending in thought which we are talking about will have to be done in those categories or not at all. The *methods* of categorial transcending beyond the categories are as follows.

A single category may be *absolutized,* with transcendence objectively conceived in it for a moment (in the necessity of its being, for example). We understand this thinking as *analogical,* thus depriving the category of its peculiarity (the necessity in our example is neither causal nor logical). This is not a purely formal play on thoughts; it has substance when it is *echoed* by an Existenz that uses it to deepen the single category, to give it a sense which in pure objectivity it does not have (necessity brings peace, for instance). In another example, the category "ground" will turn into my own dark ground in myself, and then, in transcending, into the ground of being in itself. In this way, all categories can be taken as elements into the form of existential consciousness. The attempts made in the philosophy of German idealism, to construe the categories systematically from the I, reflect this connection. But the analogy, as well as the echo from an Existenz seeking transcendence in the category, will transform the meaning of the category. Its qualitative determinacy, the singularity from which we started out, comes to be like a reality in Existenz and transcendence, with the result that our formal transcending will exceed the logical form; but then the definite category is voided by transposition into the indefinite meaning of a last cause and root of all things, forcing us to reverse any cogitative realization. We can put the first dialectics of this kind of thought into words: whichever category may be applied in conceiving transcendence, it is *inapplicable as a definite category, and as one that becomes indefinite it is finally no longer thinkable.*

Another kind of dialectics is the following: since an objectively conceived category remains a definite one, and as such is no more than an untrue absolutization, it must take a form in which any statement will either be voided by a self-contradiction ("Nothingness is being") or annihilated by a tautology ("Truth is truth"). The contradiction is arrived at by positing opposite categories as identical *(coincidentia oppositorum).* In a tautology we define transcendence in the same category in which we stated it, so that the categorial particularity becomes mere appearance, and what remains is the identity of being with itself.

A third kind of dialectics turns the categories—all of which are defined relative to others—into absolutes in the form of *becoming* defined by themselves. Instead of referring to others, they refer to themselves and thus become really meaningless; but for our transcending thought they have a voice because they express the thinking of not thinking (as in *causa sui,* the being that causes itself, or in "the being of being").

3. *Transcending beyond Subject and Object.*

The being I grasp is a definite being. When I ask what it rests upon I find another being. When I ask what it is, another being stands next to it, for comparison. It is always a being among other being in the world.

Yet if I try to aim my thought at the cosmos as being at large, with nothing outside it, I fail. I do encompass being, of course, when I speak of "all being." But this is just a statement of being as the sum of all there is in existence and in thought, a sum that dissolves interminably into endlessness. I can never go all the way through it, and I cannot visualize it as complete. Even if I could, I would be left with a being I cannot conceive as being-in-itself, because it is still an *objective being for a subject.* How it is in itself remains impenetrable.

As any conceived being presupposes the being of a subject, the subject, as subject at large, *presupposes itself.* An object cannot presuppose itself, but a subject to which something else were presupposed would thus turn into an object. Or, the other way round: when I objectify the subject I can inquire into its causes—that is to say, presuppose something for it. But even then there remains the inquiring subject that presupposes itself.

As properly unconditional, the subject is a *free being*. It is truly present as the self-conscious Existenz which in action finds itself in its objectivity but cannot be derived from objective being, no more than that being can be derived from it.

Thus, if I want to advance to being, I do not get there if I mean all things and thoughts in the sense of objective being; nor if I mean subjective being; nor if I aim at the existential subject as free being; nor if I take extant being and free being outwardly together (for they really have nothing in common, nothing I might think of as identical). *Being that is to encompass all being is transcendent.*

Should I wish not only to transcend to being but to try conceiving it as fulfilled, I would have to think of a being not faced with other being, presupposing itself, subjectively free, and yet objectified. I cannot really think any of these things, however. For what has nothing outside it will not become an object for me; what presupposes itself cannot be definite and definable for me; what is free does not exist; and what I objectify is as an object not what it used to be as a potential object.

4. Three Spheres of Transcending along Categorial Lines

When I want to conceive transcendent being I inevitably think of it in definite forms, for any statement of transcending to the unthinkable will be tied to a single category. The statements are as diverse as the categories themselves. To take my thoughts to the brink of being as unthinkable, I must go through all the categories and repeat the same dialectics in the particular form of each one. An order of such thoughts will thus be possible along the order of categories. We distinguish three areas of categories: those of objectivity at large, those of reality, and those of freedom.

In the world of *objectivity* I can ask: Why are there objects for subjects at all? Whence the dichotomy? Why these, and only these, modes of objectivity? Attempts at a metaphysical logic, necessarily deriving all categories from one principle, have sought to provide transcending answers to these questions.

In the face of *reality,* and conceiving it as the cosmos, I can ask: Why is there anything at all? Why not nothing? Mythical tales of occurrences in transcendence before the beginning of time seek parabolical answers to these questions—questions we cannot really think without transcending already.

Conscious of my *freedom,* I can avoid objectifying it and yet arrive at a point of real awareness that I have not created myself—that as I am truly myself I am not all by myself. The question "Whence am I?" goes down to a level that would, in a sense, require me to have attended the Creation to reply from memory.

If I transcend objectivity, reality, and freedom to reach the being upon which such questions founder, I must either perform the last, fulfilling act of thought and stop thinking, or, if I resume conceiving transcendence in an objectified deity after all, the conception will only bring back an intensified form of the same abyss that Kant spoke of: "It is an inescapable thought, but an unbearable one as well, that what we imagine as supreme among all possible beings should say to itself, as it were, 'I am from eternity to eternity; besides myself there is nothing but what I willed to be—yet whence am I?' Here everything sinks beneath us . . ."

The thought that transcends to being must really fail me. The alternative is to continue ad infinitum, in what only seems like transcendence, with the procedure I quite rightly follow in regard to things in the world: wherever I come, to ask anew for a definition of being, and about its ground.

In the world there is no bridging the antitheses of subjective and objective being, of being as thought and being as reality, of free being and extant being, and so forth. Nor can my thinking grasp them in one thought, as possibly one. They must be conceived as overcome, to reach the being where all questions cease, and yet they cannot really be overcome. This limit, this failure of thought, is formal transcending. It is as inevitable for us to look for these thoughts as it is impossible to keep them in the thinkable realm.

The specific feature of formal transcending in categories, shown in an interminable wealth of possible concordant variations, is a cogitative foundering that will be animated only if seized upon by the existential concern with being.

Transcending in Categories of Objectivity at Large

1. Being and Nothingness

I may think of being that is not a definite being covered by a category. In that case, what I think with such indefiniteness is indeed nothing.

To think of something, I must think of something definite. Definite being is a mental conception. Transcendent being is inconceivable and undefinable; it is nothing.

Of nothingness I could think only by not thinking. If I do think of it, I am thinking of *something* as the correlate of nothingness.

To begin with, nothingness is then a definite nothingness, the nothingness of a definite something whose nonbeing I mean. Next, however, it is the nothingness whose correlate would be *being as such*. Measured by the thought of a definite something, this being itself is inconceivable and thus nothing; yet nothing short of it, nothing short of this formal, though wholly indefinite, conception of being can be correlated with the nothingness that would be *absolutely nothing*.

In these thoughts I experience my way to think of nothingness. If a thing's nonbeing is thought of by thinking of the thing, absolute nonbeing cannot be thought of even in this indirect manner because I am incapable of any positive conception of outright being.

As I transcend in the thought of it, absolute nothingness comes to have opposite meanings.

First, it is *indeed nothing*. I step out of the world. The air of existence is throttled off, so to speak. I plummet into the void.

Next, however, nothingness may also be *true being as the nonbeing of any definite something*. For as I transcend from existence to being I can state being only as against existence, which it is not. Time and again, outright being is the nonbeing of something definite. If the nonbeing of being was absolutely nothing, the nonbeing of all definite being is precisely all—the true being.

In transcending we approach this in two steps.

In the first step, nothingness as the nonbeing of anything definite is the superabundance of true being. Being and nothingness become identical. Nothingness is infinite abundance.

The second step takes me to the brink of nothingness as absolute nonbeing. I try to think that there might be no being at all, neither existence nor being proper; and I find not only that this is unthinkable but that the attempt assures me of the impossibility of absolute nonbeing. There can be absolute nothingness only because there can be being, and this very possibility is already the being that dumbfounds me as my attempts to conceive absolute nothingness fail. Whatever exists can be thought out of existence, but I cannot think being out of being —not the still quite indefinite being that is indeed nothing, but as the infinity of possibilities. Silenced, I remain uniquely certain of the impossibility of absolute nonbeing.

The twofold meaning of nothingness—as absolute nothingness and as the identity of being and nothingness—can be stated by contrast as "above-being" and as "nonbeing."

Both are reached by a thinking that transcends in self-voiding thought, in a somersault to *unthinkability*. We do not reach them in the passivity of mere moods, when we do not even set out to think and thus do not experience the failure of thinking, when our vaguely stabilizing thoughts cling to nothingness as if such a thing existed. What unfolds in the conception of being as nothingness is the dialectics between thinking and unthinkability—the elucidative unthinkability in which not to think something does not mean to think nothing. It means to think nothingness, rather, which is either outright nonbeing or above-being.

In the situation of existence, the two meanings of nothingness speak to us in opposite ways.

If my transcending turns nothingness for me into the *nonbeing of all definite, particular being*, it simultaneously makes it a sign of infinite fulfillment in the superabundance above being. Nothingness becomes transcendence; the passion for the void becomes a will to true being. The embodiments of this passion in existence and mundanely real action express the urge to be sublimated in the peace of eternity. But since in existence the phenomena of this transcendence can be grasped as nothingness only by "something," the abundance of the transcendent nothingness depends on the abundance of the Existenz that is so sublimated as it exists in the world. There is nothingness, but in a singular fashion. It is not a statement in words, not an occurrence in the world, not the world entirety—it is, because transcendent being is the fulfillment of returning from the world, but with mundane existence preserved in its negation.

Nothingness is really nothing only if transcending turns it for me into *absolute nonbeing*. If I cannot think of nothingness as above being because of its superabundance, I cannot think of this nonbeing because it is purely and simply nothing. In the face of nothingness as above being, this not thinking will uplift my transcending essence; in the face of nothingness as absolute nonbeing it becomes the horror of the possible transcendent abyss. If in the first case I entered nothingness so as to fade, as finite, into essentiality, the second drops me into a nothingness in which I simply fade out. Nothingness is either true being or ghastly nonbeing.

In between nothingness as above-being and nothingness as nonbeing lies existence, the being defined in categories. There all things are ambiguous. The eye of true being looks at us from existence, as its transcendence, but yawning in the same existence we see the transcendent chasm of true nothingness.

2. Unity and Duality

It is logically impossible to think of something alone without thinking of something else at the same time. Confrontation in dualities is the unavoidable essence of possible thought. What I would like to absolutize as the One is a conception and thus tied instantly to another conception. Being as such leads to the question why it should be, why it should not rather not be; it presupposes the possibility of being. The inception of conscious existence cannot be conceived as an absolute inception, for as consciousness it promptly posits some form of a past from which it came. Revelation illuminates a preexisting darkness. The deity too is a conception and would be simultaneous with the ground of its being—it presupposes its own nature, as Schelling put it. We cannot think of being as simple and immediate, nor of an incipient conciousness, an absolutely incipient revelation, or a simple deity.

Thus being, as purely one, is and is not. Being is for something else, and in something else. As being in existence it is thus conceivable for us by elucidation in antitheses. Plato's *Parmenides* demonstrates this in the most abstract form, on the example of the one and the many: there is neither unity nor multiplicity, but everything is by its antithesis, rather —the one inasmuch as it binds the many, the many inasmuch as they are one. Later, the philosophy of Schelling and Hegel showed in many variations that nothing can be simply by itself. What would be itself alone would not be manifest. It would not be intrinsic. Its selfhood is due solely to something other than itself. How we interpret these antitheses—whether as logical forms of the thinkable, as the painful negativity which in all existence prevents the accomplishment of unity, or as the necessity of duplication in manifestation—does not matter. They are merely different forms of the same nonbeing of unity as such.

The real form of unity lies in self-becoming. I experience myself as one and at the same time not as one; for I confront myself in the formal sense of being I. But as intrinsic self I have my own dark ground like a lucid presence that overcomes the ground in myself. Nothing compares with this being two in one. It is a being-within-myself as every other split is a coming apart, and as—if I allow this inner bond to slacken, if I become either the mere basis of the way I am or the mere light of an empty I—we speak of "being beside myself." The only unity of the self lies in duality. It is the intelligible realm to which the unintelligible is not a limit but its own source. Alien meanings, made meaningful by translation, are taken into the context of my own mind; my being and my will, the necessity of being as I am, and the freedom that will answer for this being—all are taken into one without ending the duality. What we see here is not a polarity on one level but the indissoluble heterogeneity, unique of its kind, that constitutes the essence of self-becoming.

Pure unity, inconceivable in itself and yet formally conceived without fulfillment of the thought, would be what is flatly unknown and does not know of itself. It would be a being that is not, since it is neither for itself nor for anything else.

But duality does not void unity. By itself, as *pure duality* without any unity, it would be equally inconceivable. Conceived as a reality, it would be absolute destruction.

In contrast to the disintegration that results from unrelated dichotomies, all selfhood tends to the unity of becoming and of meaning. In contrast to death, the completion of what is not more than one, it tends to the duality that will reveal it to itself, to the painful experience it needs to become being in existence.

Transcending beyond unity and duality, whether I seek transcendence by way of the one or the other, I get into the inconceivable *identity* of both.

Unity is being without otherness, the absolute One that is not the category of unity, nor the material one facing the other, nor the number one. It is the unthinkable (accordingly called μὴ ὄν by Plotinus, like matter on the other side) which stands above and thus before all thinking and all thinkability, and is the ground of both. This transcendent unity is not the plain one that is not all; in the thought form of this nonbeing it is the being, rather, which we grasp by not thinking and seek in existence. Its closest symbols in existence are the unity of self-being and the One—exclusively grasped in appearance as the form of truth—but they are not this transcendent unity itself. What in existence is split and scattered and intellectually comprehensible only in division, this is what in philosophical transcending will have a present, conscious unity as our thinking fails.

Duality is being to which I transcend in a struggle. The being of transcendence is not *only* being; it is being and its otherness. The otherness is the dark ground, matter, the void. Where the agony of duality is my point of departure and I take one side, so to speak, in the fight between good and evil, there I see true being as a fight that must go to a decision. Transcending in the realm of our senses we speak of a war of the gods, of God and the devil. Yet if unity holds precedence, duality is either not the true, eternal being—so the struggle will end with its destruction and the restoration of the divine kingdom—or the duality itself, as a struggle, is willed and permitted by the deity, the true One and master of all things.

Held fast as thinkable, unity and duality are not transcendent. As transcendent they are no longer thinkable except through their symbols, which are phenomena of relative unity and duality. In transcendence *unity and duality become the same.* As the poet says, "And all our striving, all our struggling, is peace forever in the Lord."

3. Form and Material

The divers modifications of this relationship range from the form of a statue and the marble that is its material to the form of a category and the material of the visuality that fulfills it.

Beyond its logical character, the relationship is laden with an *echo of possible Existenz.* To me as possible Existenz, the material gives a sense of depth and unfathomability, then a sense of formlessness, and finally one of chaos and resistance to form. And the form gives me a sense of lucidity and clarity, of beauty, order, and rationality, then a sense of rigidity, and finally one of insipidity with nothing behind it. Continuing, as far as the material is concerned, is a sense of having it bestowed upon me, of being seduced by it and yielding to it—but yielding to the incomprehensible divine side of its lawlessness as well as to the diffuse and degrading side of matter.

Being goes beyond the antithesis of form and material. While their unity is given for us in existence as the interdependence of all thinkable things, the course of transcending takes us first, via the radical dichotomy, *to pure form and pure material*—reaching neither—so as then to use, not just the solidarity, but the *identity of both* as a conception of the inconceivable transcendence.

If we *void the ambiguity* of the existential echo—if matter comes to be bad, form to be good—a transcending in this dichotomy will tend to look upon the absolutized two sides as nonbeing and above-being, as the plunge into the void and the uplift to being proper. Matter becomes nothingness while pure forms fill the supercelestial regions; existence is the complex product of their mixture. But the price of this unequivocality is a degradation of matter. Matter is robbed of its depth and of its potential. The world and life come to be more harmonious and more transparent than in ambiguity, but they are also enfeebled and become unheroic. This knowledge, ending the risk of decision, makes for a tranquillizing philosophy that would point one true way for all men: upward to forms.

If, on the other hand, form and material are held fast so that we can subject *both of them to negative as well as positive* evaluations, that both will show us the right road and the wrong one, a transcending beyond both roads aims at that unthinkable identity of transcendence in which division, the division that continues even in solidarity, turns into unity. What is properly form becomes matter; what is properly matter becomes form. In this identity, form and material are the same.

4. *Possibility, Reality, Necessity, Chance*

In the world we distinguish the *possibility* that we can think of from the *reality* that we perceive. What turns empirical reality into a possibility is cognition; as a mere perception it is not yet understood as possible, but neither is it definite. All definite being requires us to ask about its possibility. Possibility and reality are interrelated.

Distinguished from *impossibility*, the category of possibility has three modifications. The possible is either *logically* possible, as opposed to that which is impossible because of a contradiction in itself; or it is *really possible* according to the *categories* of empirical reality, as opposed to that which is impossible because it does not become an object in categories of reality; or it is really possible in the sense that there are *forces* and *conditions* favoring it, as opposed to that which is impossible because such forces and conditions do not exist. What is real is possible, but not everything possible is real.

While a category makes immanent sense only with reference to a definite content of being, I transcend in it when I relate it to the whole, to all of being. In the case of the category of possibility, I do this in the following manner.

a. I ask about the possibility of being in the sense found by Kant: How is experience regarding objectivity possible at all? How is a systematic unity of this experience possible? How is autonomous action possible ? How is a perception of beauty possible? How are living creatures possible? These questions are transcending because their point is not to get an understanding of one definite being from other being; rather, it is an understanding of existence itself that each question seeks at the boundary of existence, from principles that do not belong to existence as objects of cognition. Each time the *transcendental possibility* is neither logical nor one of the two real possibilities. It is a possibility, but no longer the category of possibility. Instead, in transcending by way of the category, an overall context of existence is conceived in analogy to something objective in the world. What these thoughts grasp in the possibility is not absolute being; what each of them does is clarify a moment of our existence and thus elucidate the phenomenality of existence in specific fashion. As answered by Kant, each question of possibility touches on the supersensory—on the thing in itself, on the objectivity of the idea, on the intelligible character, on the supersensory substrate of humanity, on the unity of the source of mechanical and teleological legality in the existence of life. But the supersensory itself is not touched upon in Kant's transcending. He stops at the boundary. What his transcending in thoughts of possibility clarifies, together with the mode of our existence, is its phenomenality as an expression of our assurance of intrinsic being.

There is a circle in this transcending, because I use *one category* (possibility) *to conceive the condition of all categories.* I must let possibility cease to be a definite category—and then I cease to think in definite terms. Or I must let possibility become the definite category again —and then I am no longer transcending at the bounds of all existence but am back in existence.

b. Secondly, the question of the possibility of being can be raised transcendently, about being itself. I ask: How is being possible? But absolute being can have nothing outside it and thus cannot be preceded by a possibility; so my transcending puts the possibility into absolute being itself. This is thinkable, but it not only splits absolute being, it also takes me right back into existence, and I have lost being. Or my transcending identifies the possibility of being with its reality—for what our thinking compels us to separate in the world cannot be separate in absolute being; in that being, whatever is possible is also real. That every real thing is also possible—this "also" is not difficult for us to think, but that every possible thing should always be real also is an impossibility in our existence. Trying to entertain this thought as we transcend, we find that we cannot hold on to the "also"—we cannot think, for instance, that in infinite space there is room for everything possible, and that therefore the availability of infinite space means that every possibility must be realized somewhere. We thus retain the split and speak of being that is particular even though piling up endlessly. We have not come to transcendence at all; as a matter of fact, we have never left existence. The only door to transcendence is here the unthinkable thought that possibility and reality are identical, that the opposites are so entwined that there can be no split. Unable to conceive this identity, we think of being as the source in which "possible" and "real" are inseparable because each one is the other. Possibility and reality are no longer what they are as categories in existence; they are symbols, and the light of being shines through their identity. In the presence of such transcending it is moot to reflect on the choice between several worlds as possible forms of being. The thought that something else would also be possible does not apply any more. For being is a reality which cognition cannot turn back into possibility, like an empirical reality.

In existence the realization of the possible depends on *chances,* whether I understand these as causal chains meeting in space or as acts of an arbitrary will. Unlike both, *necessary* is what cannot be otherwise —which is why that transcendent being in which possibility and reality are identical is also called "necessary being." The thought of downright necessary being seems to answer our puzzlement that there is being at all. But again, in this transcending thought the category of necessity is used to transform and to void it.

In categorially defined thinking, necessary is what must be on account of something else, according to rules of causality or cognition. An accidental being of reality is as such merely possible, but the causality of something else makes it necessary under the given conditions. What is due to something else, however, is not necessary in the absolute sense.

If I transcend to the absolute as the necessary being, this being is *not necessitated by something else but by itself.* Yet this means that it is absolute chance at the same time. To conceive transcendence as necessary, I must conceive it in the *identity of necessity and chance,* once again foundering on an unthinkable identity.

If I say that a possibility that has been realized is necessary, this necessity is in existence the definite one of a causal connection of something with something else. Yet the absolute reality of being, as distinct from existence, is not possible first and necessary later; its necessity is an inability to be otherwise, not caused by anything else. Necessity as a statement about absolute being is the designation of the origin where we can no longer ask about any precedent possibility. It is no longer the necessity in existence of which we think in the category; it is transcendent necessity, freed from possibility by its identity with that which in existence would be chance. This transcending to necessity, beyond the category of chance, leaves us totally without insight into that unquestioned necessity. If I could think of necessity and chance as really identical, I would have transcendent being as an object. Because I cannot, this identity on which my thinking founders is simply a possible transcending ascertainment of being in thought.

5. Cause

Every particular thing that exists makes me ask for its cause, and so I want to ask once more for the cause of all existence. In this question I transcend from existence to being (*via causalitatis*). This road, however, will yield no result if I expect an answer in the category of cause, by drawing inferences from existence on being. I would come only to hypotheses such as occur in the natural sciences; I would not get beyond the purely immanent sense of something underneath.

Transcending in the category of cause is something else. It is to ask about the cause of being, with the answer that when I get to *the beginning, being and its cause are one and the same.* The thought of a *causa sui* is one I cannot conceive, because it is self-contradictory. Either I have been thinking of two—in which case neither one is being, and both together are not conceived as one—or I have been thinking of one, and thus not of a cause. To be "its own cause" is an impossibility for our intellect, a thought without an object. It means that in the case of an ultimate being the questions "whence" and "why" are foreclosed, something which the intellect can never admit. The intellect will either deny the object or, if the object exists, ask about its cause. Once again our cogitative foundering on the objectless identity of being and cause is an appearance of being in an unthinkable thought.

6. Universal and Individual

We ask for the *principium individuationis*: if being is conceived as general and entire, where does individualization come from? And if being is conceived as the plurality of individual beings, where does the universal come from?

We conceive individualization as having come about after the being of the universal, due to a second principle, that of matter in space and time. Or we think of the universal as unreal, as having no being at all except in the abstract thought of individuals. But the universal does not help us understand that individualization, and its timeless validity detaches it from all individuality. It is something extant which individuality on its part cannot make us understand.

In the world there remains the disjointness, the universal and the individual in the particular categories that mutually repel each other. If I transcend this immanent being in which neither one will let me understand the other, I must conceive an *absolute individual* that is *identical with the universal*. It would be a universal with the unique character of a simultaneous individuality, and an individual of a sort that would be general at the same time, in every definition.

7. Meaning

There seems to be a meaning to existence. But this meaning is only partly there—in order, in construction, in realizations that are passed on, in the existence which man creates for himself, and which he intends. Meaning in existence is always relative and has an end. Contrary to it are dissolution, death, lawlessness, crime, insanity, suicide, indifference, haphazardness; contrary to it is not only absurdity but unmeaningness.

If I conclude that the meaning of the whole can thus not be of a kind with the meaning we conceive, which always proves to be singular, it seems possible to raise a hypothetical question: how must the world be conceived if it has meaning? Everything absurd and meaningless in the world must then be considered a fact, and the meaning of the whole must be such as to make each fact meaningful.

In this question "meaning," a particular category, is posited as absolute. What exists in particularity, however, can never be understood otherwise than in the world, on grounds of definite existence in the world. Addressed to the cosmos, to cover transcendence, our hypothetical question about its meaning is an impossibility; for while we would expect a meaningful answer, the very question would be forcing transcendence into a particular category, thus missing it in fact. Where transcendence is concerned, no kind of meaning could fail to be delimiting and constrictive.

In my transcending I cannot draw conclusions on any meaning, and I cannot explore being as if it existed in the world. All that I can do is to search for the unthinkable transcendent being in the *identity of meaning and absurdity*. No thought has access to this identity. It becomes accessible only as the absurd thought fails, and only if it has been animated by a historic, existential fulfillment.

What remains for us, instead of false, rationalistic answers to the question what being means, is to read the ciphers in existence. Being is such as to make this existence possible.

Transcending in Categories of Reality

Reality in time and space is existence. It is what exists as matter, as life, as the soul.

A peculiar temptation is inherent in the categories of reality: in consciousness at large, and as creatures of the senses with merely vital concerns, we are tempted to view the existence given in these categories as if it were being as such. Yet if we make an absolute of reality, we void transcendence.

A transcendence conceived in categories of reality—even as otherness—would in fact be no more than another reality, a second existence to which the categories are transferred. For our insight such a duplication of the world would be untenable for lack of empirical confirmation; it would be superfluous because it reveals no true being; and it would be deceptive because it conceals transcendence.

On the other hand, if in transcending we ignore reality as if it were nothing, as if transcendence alone had being, we end up in a void.

Transcending in the categories of reality has thus the same form as all categorial transcending: for our thoughts to fail truly, we must attempt to conceive an identity of things we cannot possibly think of as identical. We cannot circumvent the rigor of existence; we can only grasp transcendence in it.

1. Time

By itself, time is nothing. It is the form in which all reality exists, in modifications not to be derived from one another.

As *physical time* it is an objectivity rooted in the determination of measurable time units, and it remains the skeleton of all other real time.

As *psychological time* it can be examined in the phenomenology of the time sense—describing the original features of our way to experience time—and also in the psychology of estimates of and delusions about time, comparing a subjective view of time with an objective time.

As *existential time* it can be elucidated in decisions and in the moment, in the sense of irreversibility, in dealings with beginning and end.

As *historical time* it is chronology, based on a skeleton of objectively measurable time. In that sense it is the possibility of appeals to Existenz by a decision, an epoch, a crisis, a fulfillment; it is the time that always has an inner structure, a beginning, a middle, and an end, and is not just a quantitative sequence.

These desultorily separated modifications of time belong together because they are due to each other; they clarify each other for us, but they are not enclosed within a definable time at large that each of them would be. Nor does their sum total—time in its modifications as a form of reality and a form of Existenz—encompass all of being. Even in immanent experience *there are limits to time*. In an objective view, of course, I live solely and exclusively in time, but subjectively I can live timelessly in contemplation. I can "forget time," aiming at a world of timelessness and seeming therein to become timeless myself. In acts of original freedom, in all forms of absolute consciousness, in every act of love, on the other hand, my temporality—not forgotten but accentuated, rather, as decision and choice—is simultaneously *broken through to eternity*: existential time as a phenomenon of true being becomes both inexorable time as such and its transcendence in eternity.

Transcending time in thought, we seek this eternity as intrinsic being. We start out from empirical time and end up with paradoxical propositions in which intellectually irreconcilable things are called identical.

"Time is Now," for instance. I no sooner try to grasp time in this manner than it is another Now. I look at that which is no more as the past, and I look at that which is not yet as the future, and while I am looking I have changed the point I am looking from. Gliding incessantly forward, with never a halt, I have a view of time as an endless progression without beginning or end. In either direction this view takes me to another time, and to another, and another. Every start is just a start in the sequence and has others preceding it; every end has other ends following it, so that I cannot think of the end of the future. This progression through the times, this monotonous repetition of the purely negative experience that there is no end and no beginning and that we search for them anyway, will convince the intellect that it cannot realize the endlessness of time, cannot turn time into eternity. If I entrust myself to the intellect I sink into a void.

But the intellect's failure becomes the awakening of Existenz. In the extension of time, athwart its endlessness, lies being. When Existenz breaks through the immanence of consciousness, it conquers time. Standing within the moment, it has the fullness of being revealed to it as transcendence instead of the merely gliding Now as an atom of time.

This transcendence is to Existenz intrinsic being, the cause of its own being. It is the Now that has no Before and no After, the Now that includes its own past and future and is real despite them, the Now that must not be conceived as timeless, therefore, but as temporal at the same time. The presence of this transcendence is not at the end of time. It was not in the past, and it will not be only in the future. It is now, the Now without anything else to come, because nothing is in flux any more and everything is eternal.

It would be untrue to define the eternity of metaphysical time as mere duration. In existence, time is an endlessly reiterated becoming and passing, begetting and devouring, and there is no being in that. Whatever is merely temporal is unfinished and, being temporal, must pass. If it endures it is no longer what it was in time. What had an end, as something definite, is lemurlike if its existence outlasts its end. Endless duration of things past is bound to turn into a matter of indifference. There is no longer a past in it, nor any future; nothing happens; nothing is decided. Duration is not real time but a continuous not-now, a mere diffusion without being, a time that can never be a properly present time because it is always either gone or not here yet. It is as though time had died of itself, being no longer real in its defeat by the moment.

There is something else that we distinguish from the eternal presence of transcendent being in the unthinkable unity of time and timelessness; and that is the lapse of our thinking into an errant pursuit of eternity in the form of timelessness. For timelessness is immanently given: it exists as the lasting validity of the accurate, and it exists as that which is always and at any time, extant under natural laws, with time reduced to a quantitative dimension—in short, it exists as the lifeless object of natural science. To define the eternity of metaphysical time as timelessness would also be untrue. To exclude time would be to create a concept without reality, a being without any present. To Existenz, timelessness is just a means of orientation and a testing measure, but a flatuous, merely possible Existenz clutching at valid objects may clothe timeless knowledge in a sacred aura. The peace of timeless being will give me a moment's support, but soon, drained by my departure from reality, I shall be starting afresh to seek the true road of transcending. Transcending time in thought is not a search for timelessness. What it seeks in the historic temporality of Existenz, moving beyond it, is eternity.

Eternity as transcendence appears in time and encompasses all time. I am aware of it when I no longer see only the endless becoming and passing, when as self-being I see being in all things. In the uplift of transcending I do not see another world through an unreal vision; I see eternity as temporal reality, and time as eternity. I see eternity in the moment, if that moment is existentially present rather than an empty atom of time; but I see nothing unless I am involved as an uplifted Existenz. This uplift alone gives the transcending thought a meaning in which time and timelessness become identical as eternity.

Eternity can be indirectly expressed in thoughts which for a moment falsely turn transcendence into something else—into a separate extant second world to which these thoughts transfer the categories of time. Here are some examples.

a. As objective reality everything is determined by its equally objective past. There is one universal time; but man, as possible Existenz, has *his own time*. He has his beginning, though he cannot grasp it because in every beginning he will promptly posit a new past as his, and he has his end, which is not a boundary with something else beyond it but the horizon that always remains as we approach. Knowing about his birth and his death as a biological creature, man extrapolates the past before his birth as his own, and the entire future as affecting him. Thus he includes in his own time whatever comes into his sight as past and future. His biological limits are objectively and outwardly the ones of his existence, but past and future, both objectively immeasurable, are his real time span, the span that fills his consciousness. The individual's own time is linked with transcendence as the eternity to which it belongs. Eternity can thus be analogically conceived as an intelligible space occupied by every time of an existentially real being. In this space, this universe of times, each time has its proper eternal place.

b. If eternity is called a time, and the mere endless duration of becoming and passing is called a time, I may think that there is *a time before time* and *after time*—an encompassing time in which the empirical time of endless duration is a period.

An eternal past is then conceived as underlying this eternal present—but a past which never was to turn into the present and which is simultaneous with the present because it is eternal. I transfer the form of my consciousness to the eternity of transcendence: to my mind, transcendence can become aware of itself only by positing past and future within its own eternity.

c. Empirical time as the present may be called the *mirage of eternity;* its endlessness is a *semblance of the infinity* of eternity. If I think of encompassing time as fulfilled time, endless time has a beginning in it—not in time, like real things, but in eternity like the cosmos. It is the unthinkable starting point of the endless flow of time, the beginning of something which has no beginning.

In these transcending thoughts I operate with two worlds. I divide what would never be divisible in true transcendence, only to reunite it in contradictory thoughts. I take my categorial material from immanence; and if my thoughts, instead of dissolving as I think them, were to congeal into thinkable objects, they would no longer refer to any transcendence. They express the certainty which Existenz feels of its being, which is neither temporal evanescence nor timeless nonbeing. It belongs, in temporal phenomenality and in the disappearance of that phenomenality, to an eternal realm of transcendence, touched by whatever in temporal reality is more than temporal.

2. Space

Phenomenologically, space is the closed, qualitatively structured field of vision of living creatures. In an *abstracting* visuality—with space conceived as homogeneous, purely quantitative, and endless, but with each step of this cogitative visualization going hand in hand with factual inner visuality—it is the three-dimensional, rationally controlled space we call Euclidean. We also use the word space for structures conceived in a variety of *unvisual mathematical space concepts,* only one of which coincides with the Euclidean. Finally, the word designates the *real space* of physics and astronomy; and while the nature of that space has been settled within the narrow range of our technical activity (there it is Euclidean), the reality of cosmic space may well be of another sort (a curved space, for instance) which we fail to notice only because in the dimensions of our existence the mistakes are infinitesimal. The decision lies here with empirical measurement.

Were I to take *spatial existence for absolute being*, I would be bothered by the question which space I mean—the visually real one I live in, or the Euclidean, or the astronomical one that is yet to be found. What space is cannot be so reduced to a common denominator that all the modes of space might be derived from it. To think, we must choose a definite modification of space. Yet there is no one space pure and simple. This difficulty gives to any absolutization of space a touch of vagueness about what we mean by space—as when it is conceived as the void, as nonbeing, while the spatiality of existence is taken for being proper; or the other way round, when space as immateriality is considered more spiritual than the bodies therein and is accordingly called God's sensorium; or when spaces in space are differentiated as terrestrial ones, inhabited by men, and celestial ones, inhabited by the deity.

Conversely, if I try to conceive *transcendence as spaceless*, I am only saying negatively what it is not. Yet we can no more skip spatiality as the form which all existence has for us than we can skip time. The spatialization of being is its entrance into existence. When I transcend space, I must preserve it even in transcending.

In formal transcending, advancing toward being in the motion of failure, I am *not yet reading the cipher of space* as an expression of transcendence. I come to do this, rather, in a different way. Even in existence, the spatial is faced with the nonspatial (the body with the soul, separateness with inwardness). But even in existence the two are one in the expression of the soul: where the soul is empirically real, it has become spatial and visible as corporeality. In analogy to this unity of spatiality and nonspatiality in psychological expression, transcendence would be the being for which space is a phenomenon of existence, and a symbolic one at that. Endless space would be a parable of infinity. It is one, has nothing outside it, and does not depend on anything. As a symbol the parable is noncontradictory because it lies outside the sphere of exact thought. There is no formal transcending in it any more, but there is the possibility of a historically fulfilled reading of the spatial cipher.

To make an absolute of spatial existence is to deny transcendence; to turn this existence into a cipher is to permit the calm unfolding of contemplative vision. But formal transcending is to seek the unity of space and nonspatiality in the *motion* which does not take me out of the space I am in but allows me to overcome space. Although the spatiality of existence is the most distant and dead opposite of being—which is to me nonspatial and existential, as I am myself—the outward aspect is still the one that can never be denied, the one that is always present. In existence there is no end to the tension of spatiality and nonspatiality.

If I posit both as identical—without bringing them into the quieting and thus resolving relationship of expressions for one another—I transcend in the unthinkable: in the omnipresence of transcendence.

In time I transcend to the unthinkable eternity, which in time extinguishes time because it is the temporality of timelessness; in space I transcend to *vanishing spatiality*. Taken for the unthinkable unity of spatial and nonspatial, it is no longer the rigid space whose dead existence invites transcending solely by its immenseness. It is the spatiality that is no longer pure space, the spatiality that has melted into that which encompasses space but exists only as spatiality.

As I seize upon time in decision, I seize upon space in the fact that the moment's decision is no shriveled point. It is *a world*, rather, which I fulfill because it is not just a world but the presence of transcendent being.

3. Substance, Life, Soul

Dead material in its conformations, living organisms, conscious individuals—these are the three stages of empirical existence whose abstract and general forms are the categories of matter, life, and soul.

Matter is conceived as endless, as permanent, and in all existing things as the lasting substrate for all conformations in spatial existence. When this permanent being turns into the fundament as such, however, when it comes to sustain all existence, it will do so in the category of *substance*, whose modifications are the phenomena. Substance has the massiveness of reality; it has the solid character of resting upon itself, of not only not being born and not dying, but enduring in every respect; there is a soundness about it. But it is also lifeless, a mere thing that is, without being for itself and anything other.

Life is the closed individual existence of an organism as a process—a process that begins and ends, and in which the existing organism relates to outside things that make up its world and undergoes specific metamorphoses of its form and function, according to rules. Life as a category covers this internally structured phenomenon which is infinitely interrelated itself, remains impervious to the intellect, moves teleologically, and changes without rest.

The *soul* is the consciousness of such a life on the part of an individual able to feel well-being and deprivation, an individual directed by drives, effectuating endeavors, and realizing itself in its world. The soul as a category covers the unfathomability of being I, the closed system of inwardness.

There are typical forms which transcendence will assume when we conceive it in these absolutized categories.

Either being is substance: all existence is only an aspect or a single mode of it, in indifferent or evanescent individualization. There really are no such things as motion and antitheses. Being is, and that is all.

Or being is life: whatever is, lives—or else, if lifeless, it is the refuse of life. Being is in infinite motion within itself, an immense organism.

Or being is soul: everything is consciousness, with the individual consciousness merely a specific, narrowed particle.

Yet each of these absolutizations breaks asunder in genuine transcending, in a grasp of transcendence beyond these categories. For now transcendence is that in which substance, life, and soul are as one, in which substance becomes identical with its phenomenal modifications, life with death, and the conscious with the unconscious.

If substance without its modifications were absolutized, it would not be transcendence but the empty chasm in which all things merely vanish; yet the phenomena themselves are substance when we take them up in transcending. Conversely, if we took the phenomena as such for being, they would have nothing to sustain them; they would not be "in being." The unthinkable identity of substance and its modifications, so definitively separated for our thinking, becomes transcendence for the thinking that founders on it.

When life without death is absolutized there is no transcendence in view, only an existence conceived as expanded to the point of endlessness. If death is absolutized, transcendence is veiled because nothing remains but destruction. Yet if life and death become identical—which is absurd for our thinking—the attempt to conceive the identity is a transcending. Death is not what we see in the material that does not live yet and in the corpse that does not live any more; nor is life the visible empirical existence. But both in one are what is more than deathless life and lifeless death. In transcendence, death is the fulfillment of being as the fusion of life and death.

If consciousness becomes being, being is bottomless; if the unconscious becomes being, it is as if it were not at all. In existence we think of consciousness and the unconscious as separates which we only experience as belonging together. But in their unthinkable identity they become a transcendence whose total lucidity combined with the abundance of the unconscious would make it both the one and the other.

We have access to the phenomena, to life, to consciousness, and we let them vanish in substance, in death, in the unconscious. It is where all riches lie for us that they must pass; it is where being seems to be that we see only darkness, as if there were nothing. But when we try and fail to think as one what is downright separate—then we are transcending, not into the dark, but beyond both sides of the antithesis, to being itself.

Transcending in Categories of Freedom

That the deity is not nature but consciousness, not substance but personality, not existence but will—these and other points against a naturalization of transcendence are made by thinkers who want to approach it in categories of freedom.

But we can no more credit transcendence with freedom than with any other category. Freedom too is but a way to something inconceivable.

Freedom, the essence of Existenz in existence, is *possibility* for Existenz, to which a choice is offered while in the world it is dependent, a prey of chance, and has its being in communication with others. Of transcendence, on the other hand, we have seen that it appears not as possibility in the definite sense of free choice, but as a possibility that would be as one with reality and necessity. If I conceive transcendence as free, I make it finite by thinking of it in situations, subject to conditions.

In existence the freedom of a personality remains *tied to nature*. In personality, freedom and nature are not identical but indissoluble. Each of them rests on the other if it is an element of personality, and each disturbs the other and demands a struggle which in time will never cease. Transcending, I would have to conceive freedom and nature as identical, discovering at the same time that for me this identity is neither thinkable nor imaginable. What seems to emerge as perfect freedom if I take the way of approximating an ideal is in fact something flatly, desultorily different—no temporal process any more, not a historic phenomenon, not the self-relation of a free I to its own dark ground that sustains and motivates it and in turn is elucidated and overcome. Identified with nature, this otherness would be transcendence, never transparent for any thought, indeed unthinkable. Through the tension between freedom and nature, the pair I try and fail to conceive as identical, the light of being can shine only as I transcend.

Freedom is in the *intellect* with its valid distinctions and knowledge, its planning and making; it is in the *idea*, that infinite, substantial whole of goal and power of becoming which is also objective as an archetype and a task; it is in *Existenz*, whose historic concretion in the medium of intellect and idea is each individual's decision about his own being.

Absolutized, these categories become statements about transcendence, statements which promptly fall of their own weight and bring transcendence to its true appearance in unthinkability.

We may say that freedom is the intellect. Transcendence, then, becomes the *logos* that orders and destines all things, the master builder who erects the world. As the *logos*, however, transcendence would be no more than a generally valid latticework for articulating all that exists. The conception would turn the sum of all categories into a categorial totality as that which makes it possible for existence to have the character of universal thinkability and order. Like a finite creature in the world, transcendence as the world architect would confront a material which it shapes. As such a master builder it is only a notion without any reality to correspond to it. But it is beyond the reality of finite intellectual creatures engaged in the shaping of matter that we must look for transcendence; what we have to seek in it is the ground of that reality.

Or we may say that freedom is the idea. Transcendence, then, becomes the spirit of entirety, the vinculum that turns all being from endless dispersal into infinite totality to which no plan is adequate. The spirit as an entirety including all the ideas, as the *logos* includes all the categories, would be unthinkable. Ideas lie in the reality of finite creatures whom they animate and guide. They are what in man we call the mind. If this is absolutized into a universal spirit, we do obtain a grandiose picture of transcendence; but transcendence itself has been lost in this immanent conception. Transcendence is the being that makes the ideal entireties possible in existence without any visible or thinkable existence of the idea of one whole.

Or we may say that freedom is Existenz. But transcendence is not Existenz. There is no Existenz unless there is communication, but transcendence is the being that needs nothing else to be itself. The statement "I am myself alone"—an expression of evil for Existenz in existence —would befit a being that is unrelatedly itself. Confinement and dependence, properties of Existenz in existence, cannot be properties of transcendence. Existenz, whose radical self-understanding is that it is not itself alone, relates to transcendence; so transcendence, if it were Existenz, would have to relate not only to itself but to something else which would be *its* transcendence. We cannot identify transcendence with Existenz because Existenz knows it is facing the deity; it does precisely *not* know itself *as* the deity.

The intrinsic being of transcendence is not freedom, as in the case of Existenz. It is the ground of this freedom, the being that makes it possible for Existenz to be free, as well as for the intellect and for the idea. Identical with none, it compels us to transcend them all, only to founder on its unthinkability. The one most apt to be confused with it is Existenz; yet this is the very reality that most strictly keeps its distance, the one that bars an identification with transcendence on its own, and not only to itself but retroactively to the idea and the intellect. For Existenz, whose freedom makes it the last form of true being in existence, must do the least to invite a transcendent transposition. The greatest proximity will here most plainly show the absolute distance.

In existential elucidation, transcending beyond existence and objectively adequate intellectual thinkability, I conceived Existenz as a sign of the certainty of a self-being simultaneously related to its transcendence. Having conceived Existenz as a sign—one that already caused my thoughts to fail, although it stayed within the assurance of present self-being—I transcend beyond this sign to the unthinkable intrinsic being, which the failure of thought brings back to me as a cipher.

The Deity as Formal Transcendence

In formal categorial transcending, the deity will become neither a substantial thought nor a thing I relate to unless these transcending thoughts affect me existentially.

The thought that fails in not thinking does not as such amount to thinking of the unthinkable as the deity. Several of these transcending thoughts have remained identical for thousands of years, almost like mathematical thoughts. Their formality gives them this timeless character, and where they occur as real thoughts, their weight and substance depend on historic Existenz. At certain times, then, certain categories may be preferred for expressing the essentially invariant thought of foundering on the unthinkable.

Formal transcending makes room for the cipher language of transcendence and thereby consciously and systematically prevents its materialization. We want to have the deity in images and in objective thoughts, and not to have these thoughts disappear as mere symbols; in particular, God as a personality with the planning, guiding will of perfect wisdom and goodness is an all but unavoidable conception. But this too is a symbol, a vanishing image, to be voided in transcending thought.

If transcendence springs from absolutization in the three groups of categories, it will be either logicized (in objectivity at large) or naturalized (in categories of reality) or anthropomorphized (in categories of freedom). The choice determines how the unknowable deity will be conceived as known. With these three spheres for its guidelines, theology teaches that God is the light of cognition, the ground of reality, the highest good. From him we get the clear articulation of insight, the cause of existence, the right order of life. He is truth as cognition, being, and action; knowledge, reality, and love; *logos,* nature, and personality; wisdom, omnipotence, and goodness.

This theological cognition of God is not a knowledge, and yet the power of formal transcending is at work in it. I am not done with this transcending when I simply state the unthinkability; it takes a wealth of approaches to find the intrinsic unthinkability and to make sure of it in all its modes.

If the search for the beginning and the source takes me in existence from one thing to another, from the thing to its ground, I never come to an end. I would have to set an arbitrary ultimate and to forbid myself all further questions. I must make a leap, rather, as I transcend from the objective to the nonobjective, from the thinkable to the unthinkable; nothing short of such a leap will without arbitrary fixation take me, if not to cognition of the source, at least to a kind of rumination toward it. The origin is not the first link in a chain of existence, nor is it the whole of existence; the origin does not exist at all. I think it, via the imperfectibility of existence, in the act of not thinking; and I pursue that act in the definite categories in which I make the leap to the place where thinking ends.

The transcendence that comes to appear in this fashion remains indefinite, incognoscible, and unthinkable, and yet it is present in my thinking in the sense *that* it is, not *what* it is. All that we can say about its being is a formal tautological proposition whose possible fulfillment is unfathomable: "It is what it is." Thus Plotinus, in philosophical transcending, expressed what the Old Testament Jew who did not want to make himself any image or likeness had his God say: "I am that I am." The difference is one between cool philosophizing and religious fervor. It shows that even this ultimate tautology will be infiltrated again by the categories and uttered either in the mode of objective being ("it") or in that of free being ("I").

This is why formal transcending keeps the Godhead flatly concealed. Only indirectly—and even then still hidden by distance—does it seem to reveal itself in the historic Existenz that reads the ciphers of existence and thus unveils its present transcendence without comprehending what it is, forever and in generally valid fashion. Transcendence becomes visible in its traces, not as itself, and always ambiguously. It does not become extant in the world. But to Existenz it may mean the perfect peace of being, a superabundant being that has nothing definite about it any more.

Existential Relations to Transcendence

3

There is no present transcendence until an Existenz takes original aim at it in a boundary situation. Then it may be the all-consuming fire or the silence that says everything. And then again it may be as if it were not.

Tied as it is to my own sense of being, transcendence manifests itself in my own attitude toward it. I grasp its being in the inner action that makes me myself; its hand is offered to me as I take it. But it cannot be forced. Where and how it will show remains a question. The activity of holding on to myself, of being ready—which is not the same as being passive—may be as crucial as the tempestuous embrace of my existence in the form of fate.

But my relation to transcendence can never be a planned arrangement. It is life without transcendence, rather, that finds its fulfillment in things I can make, in the purposive bustle that subordinates and dissipates the essence. Life would not be questionable any more if I could really live in utter banality, without any translucence of being.

And yet, when an Existenz looks beyond all existence, at intrinsic being, this being will come in sight in evanescent ciphers only, and it is in those that the Existenz would like to bring transcendence close and to find words for it.

Our discussion, therefore, will proceed, in view of boundary situations, to visualize the existential relations in which the transcendence we experience is considered—the relations in which it is conceived, and thus objectified, only to fade away again.

When my possible Existenz comes to relate to being, the relationship is never unequivocal.

In its dubious existence, an Existenz confronts transcendence in *defiance* or in *surrender*. Arising from the boundary situations that reveal the existing destructiveness is the question why existence is like that. This question leads an Existenz to defy the root of existence or to give itself up to it, trusting to the inconceivable.

An Existenz understands itself as *rising* or *falling*, either tending toward transcendence or departing from it. In its absolute consciousness of descent or ascent, a self-being grasps being itself.

What a rising Existenz is in existence remains indefinite. In its possibility, compliance with *diurnal law and order* appears as the way of rational existence; opposed to it, however, is another way, the way of destructive *nocturnal passion* that claims to stand for a more profound being. It is a phenomenon of awful ambiguity. As Existenz I cannot possibly become self-satisfied as in blind, merely vital existence.

The possibility of truth shows as *the One* that makes me myself when it speaks to me as my transcendence, the One whose betrayal plunges me into the void. Yet this historically determined One in turn is put in doubt by the *diversity* of existing possibilities. In existence there is no such thing as one solid, objectively ascertainable way of Existenz at large. There is an uncertainty of possibility, in which transcendence remains doubtful and ambiguous when I want to know it.

The four existential relations mutually produce each other, granting Existenz no rest in existence. Defiance and surrender, not synthesized in themselves, seem resolved in existential uplifting; yet this will only ensue from decline, in the face of the reality of decline, and is itself equivocal, splintering into the antithesis of diurnal rationality and nihilistic passion. And when the truth in both of these is brought to mind as the One, this One will be qualified by the counterpossibility of multiplicity. Put into words, every transcendent relation lies in alternatives, in factual tensions whose temporary synthesis is an existential reality. To synthesize them in thought would be to understand the incomprehensible being proper as possible Existenz becomes aware of it; yet all that we can do in thought is to elucidate fragments of a whole to which thinking will not give us access.

In each of the four existential relations lies the possibility of an objective visualization of transcendence in the ciphers of myths and speculative thoughts.

Defiance and surrender make me seek a speculative vindication of transcendence in theodicies, or a reason for my defiance in refuting the theodicies.

In his rise and fall, the individual hears transcendence as his genius and his immortality. The process of freedom is mythologically anchored as a possibility in a primal process of supersensory being.

The tension between, on the one hand, life in the legality of rational order and, on the other hand, daemonic passion, compels me to think of two transcendent origins. The God with whom I feel sheltered in obedience and good will is opposed by dark figures, as by subterranean gods. To follow these, sweeps me into an abyss of irrational guilt, but to spurn them exposes me to their vengeance.

Since identification with my present, historically defined One is my only assurance of being phenomenal Existenz, I adopt the idea of one God. But the wealth of existing possibilities propounds its own transcendence: rising against the one God are the many gods.

The existential relations as well as the ciphers of transcendence that appear in them are *antinomical*. The nonobjective being of transcendence comes into present existence in the form of necessarily interdependent antitheses that void each other in objectification. What remains is a spur to our philosophizing; instead of knowingly resolving them, we questioningly see the antitheses break forth anew. Refusing to be fooled by a false knowledge, man is Existenz in the antinomies of his metaphysical views as he is Existenz in boundary situations. In those antinomies he makes the leap beyond revelations and myths. We philosophize in distinction from revelations and myths, in the effort to preserve a substance whose form is for us no longer valid.

If we hypostasize one side of the antinomies, however, that side has become permanent either as a psychological experience or as a mythical object and has lost its life. Only the tension in the antinomies is the true phenomenon of Existenz in relation to its transcendence. To conceive this tension is the way of *metaphysics in the sense of a transcending existential elucidation,* the way we shall try to pursue in this chapter.

Defiance and Surrender

If I hide the boundary situations from myself, stolidly carrying on by force of habit, my life is sheer existence. Transcendence does not enter into a blind soul. But when a boundary situation brings all self-deception to an end, I am close to revolt, to rebelling against the source of existence. The question, then, is whether I find my way back to a surrender to being.

1. Revolt

Consideration of the realities of existence, their examination and appraisal, can give rise to a question: is it good that there are these realities, or would it be better if they did not exist? The course of things seems haphazard; no justice reigns in the world; men of good will and men of malice, highminded men and scoundrels are in luck and out of luck at random. The boundary situations show that all things perish.

Existence seems to be a quagmire. Nothing means anything; one can stand it as long as he will lie to himself. But once it is clear that nothing has true being, that existence is simply frittered away for a while, life becomes unbearable: I do not want to exist as nothing. I refuse to be happy if happiness is just a senseless moment in the tide of perdition. Hating my own, I defy the fact of existence; I do not want to accept it as mine. I revolt against the ground I came from. The possibility of defiant suicide implies an autocratic return of the unwanted gift.

2. The Decision Suspended in the Will to Know

Who am I who can realize this defiance? One whose being would lie in not wanting this existence. But in this sense of unwillingness lies the freedom to see that I am rash: from the boundary of radical renunciation it can urge me to unfold, to go back to experimentation in existence. Defiance, then, takes the form of the original will to know, the will that makes me explore and question relentlessly and reexamine my answers. I no longer judge existence as a whole, but I commit myself to its incessant perambulation in order to experience it. I want by all means to achieve knowledge; my existence has become a cognitive existence. The possibility of either rejecting it or reentering it with an original sense of accord remains open. The defiance in which I rashly believed to have a definitive answer has become a *constant question*.

This posture of wanting to know comes to be an indispensable condition of being human. The questioner is a self-being that seems to itself as though severed from a whole. His freedom is the ability to explore and the faculty of resolving to act on his own. The whole has become inaccessible; not even a possibility of the whole can be validly, clearly, objectively conceived. What I feel as my free being in curiosity and action is simultaneously experienced as a self-sundering self-will.

3. Defiance in Our Human Will to Know

Prometheus is guilty because he brought consciousness, knowledge, and technology to derelict mankind, which Zeus wants to ruin. What makes man human, what makes his unlimited evolution possible, is this origin in the revolt of Prometheus, the rebel who remains himself even in shackles, chained to the rock in the immeasurable agony of impotence —the heartrending accuser who nonetheless refuses to bow to force until the deity's own change moves him to surrender and reconciliation.

It is the myth of an immemorial guilt of becoming human, comparable only in this origin to the biblical fall of man. Knowledge drives Adam out of paradise, the knowledge that makes man really human and hands him all the possibilities of his active future. The Old Testament God, too, takes fright at Adam's menacing rise ("Behold, the man is become as one of us") and by expelling him does not undo the continuing effect of what has happened. The primal guilt of nascent freedom is at the same time the primal guilt of divine violence.

Thus man has become part of the divine world. What he has understood in these myths is his sense of freedom, that indelible consciousness which is the sole truth of his possible Existenz and yet not truth pure and simple but an incomprehensible guilt. Man's worth and greatness lie in autocratic defiance. In the religion of almost all other nations it is impotence, fear of the deity's superior power, that determines the surrender of man who wants well-being and salvation; seldom would he see his heroism enter into divine being as a parable of his own. The biblical fall merely hints at this; the Greeks accomplished it fully. Piously, from the reality of their gods, they managed to draw an experience and conception of what they themselves were in fact, and the result was awareness of a human dignity that has since become man's measure of his capacities and his demands upon himself. True, in their Moira the Greeks removed transcendence farther than the gods, to a new boundary all but beyond human contact; but for defiance and surrender, it was they who wrote the imperishable signs.

This culpable breakaway in self-will, in the will to know without limits, to know every possibility, is an original, extradivine and antidivine development of the free self-being of human Existenz; but the initial will to break away is divine. It does not follow an accidental course but comes back to the self-transforming deity. For if there could be nothing divine about man's being, about whatever he does *against* the deity, such action would be capricious, indeed impossible unless the deity itself were in some sense at work in it or let it happen. But for our conception the mythological world alone provides the proper dimensions in which we can think of action counter to the divine will as an impossibility, in line with the principle of *nemo contra deum nisi deus ipse.*

4. The Defiant Will to Truth as an Appeal to the Deity

I know, in cognition, what I cannot bear in reality. Truth, then, cannot be that which, if it were, would be all-destructive. But if I have the unreserved will to find the truth, I cannot but admit reality as it is—this, and the fact that I never know it wholly and definitively, spurs me on to ceaseless questioning. *The relentless consistency of truthfulness itself becomes my relation to transcendence.*

But if truths proclaimed in the name of a deity will not stand up before cogent empirical reality and rational insight—notably if positive claims of a factual, albeit hidden, justice fly in the face of the injustice prevailing in all existence—then, as in Job's case, the will to be truthful puts man at odds with this form of the deity; for he knows that his free, passionate quest of truth accords with his God. The deity doubles itself in dialectical motion. Trusting in the deity to which truthfulness makes him yield, Job lives in the assurance that this deity will justify him with the deity he defies.

5. The Rift in Volition

There is a rift in the will to truth. As the self-will of mere existence it is indeed without pathos, a nonentity of instincts and, if purposely embraced, of evil; but as a risk freely taken, the rift in self-being qualifies the pathos of autonomous being proper. In the rift, defiance is an origin of Existenz: its potential unconditionality. Arising in the rift, obscure to myself, is the tension that will once enable me to grasp transcendence because I have been in earnest about being. The road to transcendence is still blocked; defiance is a kind of accumulation. It is at the brink of voiding itself in transcendence, but it stays at the brink. Defiant, I am possibility.

Defiance is like a clenched fist that must not be unclenched and cannot strike a blow. If I unclench it before historic communication has made me a positive Existenz in existence, I betray the existential relationship in which defiance conserves what I am to realize in active being and doing; it is not by renouncing defiance that I can truthfully void its possibility, only by the historic realization of my Existenz in existence. Yet if the fist were to strike, as if to hit the deity, defiance would be nothing but the despair in which my blind lunge at the void turns from a possibility into a negative reality. The guilt of a defiance which no longer conserves anything will consume itself in the No of a ruinous, deceptively conclusive knowledge. The No of conservative defiance seeks the Yes and prepares for it—initially by discovering that in the rising tension all being is obscured.

6. Surrender

In the vigor of defiance lies the chance of its reversal. Nothing can force this reversal, of course; no insight shows that it is necessary. But *self-being tends to agree with its seeming adversary*. What I cannot forget in my autonomous freedom—that I am not self-made, that therefore I must not be the ultimate—is the disquieting thought and the threat in my defiance.

Defiance, not to be voided on general grounds, can be voided only on its own ground. The deity grants me the freedom to become myself, and only the deity will let me overcome defiance by self-being—not by some miraculous supersensory act, however, but by tying myself in existence to the One with which I shall remain historically, unconditionally linked. It is with this alone that, yielding to it, I become myself. I yield in the world, the intermediary outside of which there is no road to transcendence.

For transcendence wants me to yield in the reality of existence. If in defiance I spurned fortune as fleeting and delusive, surrender makes me feel that what everyone is to receive in due time must not be disdained. If in defiance I scorned misfortune, if it made me loathe all existence, surrender demands that I stand the trial: this was laid upon me; I must bear it and I will, until I perish. But what I experience in yielding is not the blind luck of existence but one of conquered defiance, a luck still beclouded by possible and imminent calamities and thus of a depth that is alien to mere existence. And neither is it simply wretched suffering, but a suffering as deep as the defiance that was overcome, so that the sufferer may still see a reflection of the radiant bliss possible in existence otherwise. In its place all being is existence; I ought not to withdraw from mine. Surrender is a readiness to live, no matter how, to accept life whatever happens.

7. Theodicy

Yielding, we want to know why. Knowledge, sprung from the defiant will to know and nourishing this defiance, is to serve our submissive desire to make everything explicable by the deity. Theodicies are answers to the question raised by the ills of existence, by the inevitability of guilt, by evil: how could God in his omnipotence create this world so that these ills and injustices are permitted, so that evil exists? Or, framed in the broadest sense: how can we understand the value-negative in existence? Whenever the frustration of each hope makes it appear self-deceptive to expect a happy progeny to requite us for present ills (as in Jewish messianism or in socialist utopias)—whenever the imaginary character of requital in a beyond (of the rewards and punishments of a supernal judgment, for instance) comes to mind—at any such time the question of the need for recompense will force itself newly upon us. And what we seek in that question is not a calculation that will satisfy an observer: its goal is the possibility to rise above existence, in a surrender which the answer will make individually recognizable in the shadow of a universal.

The Indians conceived an impersonal world law in their *karma* doctrine. In metempsychosis, which may bring the soul of man into all forms of a scaled realm of life, his manner of rebirth and his particular fate reward or punish him for the good or evil he has done in previous existence. An automatic continuum of moral retribution governs all that exists, though the successive forms are not linked by conscious remembrance. Everyone made his own fate and will make his future fate. Moral action aims at a better rebirth and ultimately at deliverance from the metempsychotic "wheel" as the rebirths have an end.

By its concept of temporal extension, this doctrine stresses the eternal import of each existential act. It is a sensory cipher, a rationally unequivocal expression of the sense of all evil. Theodicy becomes a moot question, since there is no almighty deity—only the law of existence and the inconceivable pursuit of nonbeing.

Zarathustra, the Manicheans, and the Gnostics taught a *dualism*: God is not almighty; he confronts an evil power. Two principles are locked in combat, with physical and moral evil ensuing from a partial victory of the dark forces that becloud the luminous divine being. The world is the battleground, or it may actually be the work of an evil creator whose misdeed was a revolt against the pure deity. Although the good gods are sure to triumph in the end, the world process is full of suffering and absurdity. It is in this process that the scattered bearers of light will be freed from their shrouds, step by step, and will return to the point of definitive separation of good and evil powers. The dichotomy of good and evil is recognizable in purity and impurity, in light and darkness, in all value contrasts.

Dualism is the intellectually simple solution by a duplication in the primal ground of existence. Fixed, crude, undialectical, it does not permit existence to be thought through any further, except in continuing by means of all possible evaluations to subsume things over and over. Once dualism is dialectically developed, however, its simplicity makes it an impressive cipher for the transcendent basis of the struggle of existence. Man may be defiant and yielding in either direction; he may experience the ambivalence of both postures in the reversals of their possible phenomenality as diurnal law and nocturnal passion.

In the doctrine of *predestination,* the hidden God (*deus absconditus*) stands beyond all moral claims and human intelligibility. His decrees are as settled as they are inscrutable. They have determined every individual's fate on earth and in eternity. No standard of earthly justice can be applied to them, since they infinitely transcend any such limited meaning. The point of what I am and do on earth is not that by any merit of mine I might affect God's decree and thus alter my fate; it is to scrutinize my being and doing for signs of my election or damnation.

Originally, the doctrine of predestination is a statement of the insolubility of the theodicy problem. What makes it quickly more than such a statement is the definite knowledge implied, the argumentative, rational, ratiocinating kind of formulas that turn incomprehension into the positive understanding of an extensive theology. Decision in time is voided, destroying the possibility of choice: freedom no longer exists as a formula, only in the factual action that will be taken on the basis of these thoughts.

Speculation about the three doctrines shows that for human reason the theodicy question can no more be cogently answered than the question whether God exists. We try in vain to make a formula generally valid. These rational forms have had a life-molding import for great nations; and for moments, perhaps, we too may use them as forms of expression. So, in our present historic situation, we try to get deeper by way of a knowledge of not knowing. The existential vigor of the people who lived believing in those doctrines demonstrates their historic truth, but it does not prove that the doctrines are true for us. What we must try instead, after the doctrines' failure, is to *understand that we cannot understand them.* We are no longer living presently, securely, by the unknown depth of a whole. Our consciousness is no longer an unquestioned part of a historic substance with its mythical contents of faith, and there is no limit to the questions that strike us. The free possible Existenz in our consciousness will doubt its own freedom along with its transcendence, and in reflecting, in staggering dialectically between defiance and surrender, it will experience the utter *impossibility of knowing a solution*—whereas in mythical theodicy the solution was believed, not known.

If insight could solve the questions of guilt and struggle, of all evils and their origin, there would be no more boundary situations. Possible Existenz would have lost its original experience. That for pure knowledge there is no solution is the very reason why, starting from the boundary character of our situations, we must seek our individual, invariably historic uplifting in communication. The failure of every theodicy is an appeal to the activity of our freedom, which keeps us capable of defiance and surrender.

In surrender I dispense with knowledge and put my trust in the ground of being. I truly yield myself only when I do not know, when my existence is sublimated in being, both voided and sheltered in being, although I cannot know that there is being. Whenever I would knowingly justify it, my surrender becomes untruthful. But as not knowing, as acquiescing in active trust, it is a glimpse of transcendence.

Defiance shows in negativity. When it makes me try to convince myself scientifically that there is no God, for instance, that there is nothing but the blind law of nature and the sum of finite things, I may say disdainfully, on the strength of my knowledge, that "God helps those who help themselves." But surrender makes me reply that I do not know: divine gifts are indeed bestowed only on the active; they also come only via freedom; I certainly am called upon to help myself—but if I do, I may be yielding and trustful. This trust does not rest on any knowledge, though I stake my life on it.

If surrender should make me go on, then, to speak of a harmony of the whole and to justify physical and moral evil, I would get lost in illusions. I would be using them to shroud the source of the defiance which alone can make me yield truly, without pulling back from any knowledge.

8. The Hidden Deity a Cause of Tension in Temporal Existence

If divine transcendence were speaking an audible language, man could do nothing but submit and fade away. Any question would cease. Prostrate before a phenomenal omnipotence that has come out of hiding, I would have lost my freedom. There could be neither defiance nor surrender. For both aim at the hidden deity, in questions answered at a risk of possible Existenz.

We are still in temporal existence. As long as the deity stays hidden, does not answer, leaves every cipher ambiguous, man is cast back upon his freedom. His fate is the tension of having to dare what he would live by; in his search for truth he has no other way to find it. The deity does not want him to yield blindly; it wants him free to defy it, and from defiance to come to a true surrender.

This is why the tension remains unresolved. Surrender will keep springing from defiance; trust will not put an end to the asking of questions. There can be no definitive synthesis in temporal existence; it would be an untrue anticipation. It is only out of this tension, in historic phenomenality, that an Existenz can find its own truth. I trust in being, then, on grounds of trusting myself—that is, I come to surrender by way of defiance. But I come equally to trust myself on grounds of trust in being—that is, I find my defiant independence in surrender.

Because defiance in its negativity aims at God from the outset, to deny God does not make me indifferent; rather, it is the negative expression of my relation to transcendence. In defiance, whether denying or cursing God, I am enthralled by transcendence; it may go deeper than an unquestioning faith. To chide God is to seek God. My every No is a plea for a Yes, but for a true, honest Yes. To be true, surrender must spring from a defiance that has been overcome.

9. Fatal Enhancement in Isolating the Poles

If either pole of the tension is exaggerated in mundane existence, the resulting perfection will be grandiose, perhaps, but impossible for an Existenz that remains in time.

In titanic defiance, a self-sustained Existenz seeks in the world, in a world that it regards as its creation, to realize itself by means of its own freedom, without God or against God. The question whether the world is worth anything or nothing does not make sense any more. What matters is that I am worth something, that my creations make sense: I am what is, or else there is nothing.

Heroic surrender, on the other hand, is true in the self-destruction of a martyr. There is dignity in this will to be destroyed. It realizes the absolute dedication of a mundanely indifferent life to the transcendent truth grasped in that life.

But the perfection into which both autocratic titan and dedicated saint step from mundane existence makes them communicatively inaccessible. They become possible objects of admiration or indices of possibilities.

10. Vacuous Decline in Isolating the Poles

If I isolate myself at either pole, rejecting the possibilities of being myself and seeking merely to exist, I am bound to lapse into nonentity.

Defiance, then, turns into a mode of wanting to "live my own life." As long as it lasts, I want to enjoy it without scruples. I want power, the delight of destroying and ruling; what makes me want it is hate and vindictiveness against any existence that impairs my own. This is no longer the free revolt of a defiant self-being but the license of determined subjectivity.

In feebler forms defiance may stick fast, as it were, instead of remaining suspended. Instead of a struggle for the deity as the pure picture of transcendence, it may become the last stage of an empty nihilism. There is a touch of destructive glee in it: Now you can see what the world is like. To show the deity by his own kind of existence how things are all over, a man becomes a vulgarian. This defiance is due to resentment. It remains shallow.

Surrender, on the other hand, may decline into passivity. Chiding God is then no longer possible; the temporal phenomenon of Existenz has been enfeebled. An existing harmony has been carried over into time—but in time, as existence, such harmony is impossible. In this passivity I have abandoned my freedom; I find myself submitting piously to earthly authorities.

11. Surrender without Trust; Godforsakenness; Godlessness

Defiance and surrender coincide when self-being is lost in a sense of reprobation, of knowing oneself destroyed in the eyes of transcendence. It is the despair of surrender without trust. Man not only feels himself quake in his relation to transcendence; he is without hope. He feels helplessly crushed in eternity. He is reduced to sheer dread in view of the consuming power. Surrender—which did, after all, include trust— has given way to total dependence. An affirmative self-being, on the other hand, shudders at the uncanny antagonism of overpowering transcendence.

Godforsakenness is not defiance. It involves a sense of distance, a lack of faith that makes me unable to be either defiant or yielding. It is not the unconscious state preceding my awakening in boundary situations; it is the consciousness, rather, of having known but lost defiance and surrender. It is not the indifference of no longer really wanting anything, the inability to rejoice and to suffer because nothing is serious to me any more; it is an empty waiting for transcendence to come to me. Godforsakenness may rise to the point of feeling: God is dead. This is no longer defiance but consternation—an attitude which, like defiance, contains possibilities. Only a dull, indifferently continuing life without questions and without despair makes every possibility trickle away.

Defiance ceases where man might be really, unquestioningly godless. There are reports that "at the Christianization of Scandinavia one found people who believed in nothing but relied upon their strength." Taken literally, this would characterize an unconscious existence without foresight and reflection, lived wholly in the present, without a boundary situation and thus still without defiance. And yet, such a fiercely independent existence would have an unparalleled potential for defiance— that is to say, for a passionate search for God.

12. The Ultimate Question

By objectifying a knowledge in order to resolve the tension of defiance and surrender, an Existenz chokes off its own historic freedom. It remains Existenz in temporal existence.

Defiance is the properly human reaction. Any man who keeps his eyes open, who looks at facts and asks questions, will find himself saying No. The trust I feel in yielding cannot be an imperturbable prejudgment that would give me peace; it can only be a feeling I have acquired in the face of the dreadful hopelessness of real existence. It must have withstood the Gorgon's petrifying gaze.

Only he who really enters into the horror and stands the test can know about trust. It cannot be forced on anyone. It goes with a sense of lacking merit. Its possession does not add to the possessor's worth. It remains tied to wondering whether one is entitled to it.

I do not know what is to last and to live, and what is to perish; neither one ever has precedence, to my knowledge, and I know in general that it is not the best of things that last—frequently, indeed, the ones that merely last will be the worst. *It is never in the outcome of events, in the success of action, that I hear the deity's answer.* Downfall may mean rejection, and it may mean consecration. Victory may be a challenge or a curse.

The least rudiment of a notion that I might expect the deity to turn things a certain way because thus, and only thus, would they make sense; or that this noble life, this amount of good will, this commitment of the best could not be in vain; or that there is something I do or do not deserve, and might therefore expect or need not fear—all this puts me into a confusing position. Either I try to gain access to the inaccessible, to catch a glimpse of the intrinsic being from which Providence springs, or, no matter how righteous the thoughts I use, I secretly seek to sway Providence, if not to coerce it. In such thinking lies a sublimated magic, a desire to steer the deity, not by witchcraft but by my being and works.

Existence comprises not just Existenz and idea but the whole vast, overwhelming world, as well as the otherness that may inwardly wither or outwardly destroy the possibility of Existenz. Since flatly *everything is possible* that would be impossible by the standards of sense, of justice, of goodness, the tensions in defiance and surrender remain. Hence there is as much existential failure in despair at senseless foundering as in the pride and contentment of success. But in success and in failure, in the absurd and in the meaningful, trust in transcendence can be true if both are kept open to question.

When I ask if the deity is also with the smug, with the arrogant, the intolerant, the narrowminded, the blind, I dare not deny it. My deity is not in those; I know that I must fight them with all my strength;

but I cannot expect to emerge victorious. When the hidden deity speaks indirectly to me, it never speaks wholly to me. It comes to meet me in something which to me is not its self, but to which it grants existence and self-preservation, and I may have to witness the triumph and the permanence of what I strove against as being bad and evil.

Rise and Fall

I do not relate to transcendence by thinking of it, nor by dealing with it in the sort of action that might be repeated according to rules. I am soaring toward it or declining from it. Existentially I cannot experience the one except through the other: my rise depends upon my possible and real fall, and vice versa. For thousands of years, man's rise and fall have been transcendently narrated in primal thoughts.

1. I Myself in Rise and Fall

In absolute consciousness I am sure of being, but not of a calmly perfect being that might last in time. Rather, I always find myself in the possibility of coming to myself or losing myself—either scattered in diversity or concentrated in the essence, either distracted in fears and sorrows and self-oblivious in pleasure, or else in the presence of my self. I know the desolate nonbeing of my intrinsic self, and I know the ascent from this existent nonbeing.

All of the phrasings used for existential decline cover the sense of this peril in which I keep experiencing myself.

a. The origin in absolute consciousness may be viewed as active motion in self-becoming. The decline occurs in the direction of pure, *fixed objectivity,* whether timelessly extant or as regular, passive motion.

Or we see the origin in fulfilled substance. Then the decline lies in clinging to empty form, in *formalization* and *mechanization.*

Or the origin is the historic continuity of Existenz. The decline, then, goes to what is *arbitrary,* and to what is *purposively fabricated* without being grounded any longer in something that encompasses and animates it.

What has happened in the decline, in each case, is that something purely objective was taken for being although it can be true only as a function of Existenz. Fixation, formalization, and fabrication are one and the same.

b. The origin in absolute consciousness may be found in the *decisive order* of substantial *rank.* The decline, then, is the perversion of making the unconditional conditioned, and the conditioned unconditional.

c. The origin in absolute consciousness may be *genuine* in the identity of essence and appearance, subsequently manifested as fidelity in holding on with a persistence adequate to the moment of founding. The decline goes to *spurious* experiences and gestures that are purely subjective, real at the moment, yet untrue because their point remains illusory; or it goes to the spuriousness of professing, acknowledging, admitting contents which I no longer allow to work in myself.

d. We may hold the origin in absolute consciousness to be self-related, and thus fulfilled, as present *infinity*. We decline, then, to the *endlessness* of mere repetition, which is no longer the fidelity of ever-new and present self-reproduction.

2. I Become the Way I Judge

Nothing simply exists for me in the process of my rise and fall; everything is subject to possible evaluation. I judge my actions, my inner posture, the existence from which the other comes to meet me in communication, and whatever else occurs to me. I am—and I become—the way I judge. I keep rising if I hold on to my judgments, if I test and surmount them; but if I lose touch with the appraisals that had only just been true for me, I fall.

Appraisals derive a clear definition only from definable normative concepts, from finite standards that allow us to evaluate things from a particular point of view. The intellect clearly conceives and distinguishes reductions in performance by unfavorable dispositions, by diseases, by all the dysteleologies of life. Opposed to such cogent appraisals that can be gained by distinct concepts of purpose and norm, our judgment of historic experience is an *indistinct*, noncompelling, but evident *sight of rank* in the physiognomic character of all things. This sight is processual and not definitive; it does not work by subsumption, but by original elucidation; it lacks knowledge but has an intuitive proximity; it is not demonstrable, but it can be made plain. Definitive normative concepts yield a multifarious hierarchy of existing things from many points of view, to which definite orders of rank are only relatively attached as generally valid. From Existenz, however, we get an eye for the unconditional, never-conclusive orders of rank of each singular physiognomy.

Although these existential appraisals are merely becoming in time, they do tend to be objectified. Having seen the rank in historic situations and choices, we have only one road to an elucidative knowledge of what we really do: the rationalization of that rank into general values. This rationalization can be sought without limits and always lays the ground for the future historicity of Existenz, and yet it remains relative, never penetrating all the way to the absolute historic consciousness of Existenz itself. For the objectified order of rank can no more be identified with the originally comprehensible orders than can evaluation by a definable purpose.

Cogent evaluation is thus only relatively possible, if normative concepts are presupposed. And the other cognition of rank—indistinct, but penetrating to the depths, because it intends the real essence—this becomes deceptive if definitively objectified and presumed to be objectively valid for all men. It is most intimately linked with the sense of my own rise and fall that finds expression in the activity of this appraisal. As in my judgment I see descents and ascents everywhere, I am already taking part in them. The orders of rank become untrue unless I *commit my own essence*. The following are ways of decline in the form of appraisal.

a. When I truly evaluate something, I either *love it or I hate it because I would like to love it*. For I am in possible communication with it, appraising it not just as an extant being but together with its nascent potentiality. I am involved, because true appraisal is potentially a loving struggle, never a mere determination. I become untrue, on the other hand, when I isolate myself and pass supposedly valid judgments on something that exists, as if it did not concern me. These untrue appraisals, in which my own being declines to that of a rigid observer presuming to be a judge, signify my fall into uncommunicativeness.

b. True evaluation is part of my own rise, in a *continuity* that I cannot adequately define with rationalistic consistency, and yet I manifest it as I prove myself, as I am faithful rather than forgetful. Decline, on the other hand, is the arbitrary judging and condemning on grounds of purely rationalistic thoughts, and of the momentary, evanescent affections for which a man does not stand up, which he himself forgets and deems accidental.

c. A true evaluation is one in which I am *wholly with the thing I judge*. If my judgments and appraisals are merely put forward to cover different motives, I decline by fooling others and myself about my real ends. I may enthusiastically praise a man, for instance, not because I love him, but because I want to hurt others. Or I may hate and spurn the phenomenon of an Existenz because I do not want to test myself by possibly ensuing standards. If I want something minimized, or if I want it admired, there are endless arguments which somewhere seem to appeal to possible judgments—but these judgments are inadequate, especially the ones offered by the current average of the opaque, if seemingly concurrent, human mass.

d. A true judgment is one that objectifies in quest of clarity about oneself. Objectifications are always necessary means of self-elucidation; standards and sets of values belong to the realm of Existenz. But in the *tranquillity of a schematic order of values* as such, I am declining. Instead of infinitely immersing myself in my historic adversary, to discover his values in him and, with him, in my own ascent—instead of this communication in open, unarmed struggle I simply finish off all individuality by filing it in given, general pigeonholes. To congeal is to fall. Every order of rank conceived by man has had a historic origin that will not permit unconditional decisions to be shifted into valid objectivity. The evaluation is possible only where I consciously retain the possibility of rising and falling, the possibility that encompasses all objectification and will not let me come to rest.

3. Self-becoming in Dependence

In active self-reflection I always collide with the being I already am. I cannot have the direct will to be what I would like to be.

I see, for instance, that I am *dependent on my body*. Were I to take the results of its exploration for myself, however, I would be turning myself into a thing—a thing which in a utopian perspective would resolve itself into the outcome of causal processes that might enable me, by technical arrangements, to make of myself what I wish. My inner posture, my sense of intrinsic being, would be producible.

The senselessness of this notion becomes clear when we ask about the I that makes these arrangements, the I that has the will to achieve a particular desired mode of self-being. For the I that has this will cannot be conceived as producible any more, because we have now reached the origin, the source of all our exploring, willing, and producing. Positively, too, I am aware of my freedom in the daily effort of breaking loose. There are, of course, conditions of existence without which freedom has an end; but there are no such conditions that might produce freedom itself and help to steer its substance. Here lies the point to which no merely passive experience has access, the point where I depend upon myself. Rise and fall are processes that launch themselves, and their source is freedom.

Yet rise and fall are *tied to their antecedents*. I cannot change at any time, without premises. I have always laid a foundation, have become, am still en route and thus desultory—in leaps, each of which has its moment, I am advancing or relapsing, imperceptibly growing or declining in constant activity.

As by myself I have already become a historically determined being, I am *dependent on the world I live in*. But my true freedom attains its depth where the factual, present existence of my world is seized upon, adopted, and transformed. Whatever is definite in this present human world existence, in particular constellations and situations I have encountered—this I can only try to evade in the direction of a worldless freedom that will always be disturbed by something else, or I can accept it as part of me, as my own responsibility.

Dependent on myself, tied to my own ground and to the world, I make myself rise or fall. But however sure this self-dependence may make me feel of *a direction* which I formally elucidate in thinking of my declines, *I know nothing of its whence and whither.* I can know concretely what I want now, when I uplift myself; but I do not know what the direction is in general.

4. Transcendent Basis and Uncertain Direction

Since I do not know whither I am bound as I fall or rise—since in both cases I am inescapably bound up, rather, with my inconclusive world —I have my only support in the transcendence I sight in the process of rising and falling. Only where an Existenz believes itself rooted in its transcendence does the process radically show what it is to be in existence. There alone will Existenz combine true resolution with an open mind for things other than itself. Its absolute consciousness of the presence of the occult must be flagging before Existenz will also grow less sure, and thus less free, in action—whether in dishonest violence or in the honest whirl of not knowing what to do. Unable to will my relation to transcendence, I can only hold on to a readiness for it, once I have heard the transcendent voice in myself.

Yet even though my essential goals are *transcendently related,* this does not make them *transcendently set.* I can name such goals: purity of soul; historic appearance of the substance of my being; responsible action based on the historic determinacy of the entire circle of existence that I can fulfill. But all of these trickle away when I mean them as such rather than as signs. Stated like that, they are as if nothing had been said. There is no objective form in which the transcendent goal of my life will become visible. It cannot be conceived for all time, nor identically for all men.

Suppose—conceiving the inconceivable in empty thoughts—I wished to know whether I am rising, and I could see through the point of being before I begin to act. I would end up unexistential and unhistoric. Every purpose is particular, and none, as such, suffices to uplift me; but the point of the whole, as a known final purpose, would void the reality of historic action. At bottom, all things would have to come to an end. Nothing need happen any more; temporality would be superfluous. If the sense of knowledge were eventually to lead me to definitive cognition of the final purpose and thus of the whole, the growth of my knowledge of the possible, of that which can be causally realized and can accord with the sense of knowledge, would bring me closer to this unreality—instead of doing the very opposite: following the course of historic experience into the boundless realm that defies anticipation. And if I carried the intellectual emptying of my knowledge to the point of treating it as complete, the remaining posture would be: no matter what happens, everything is possible and everything makes sense—or the other way round: since there is nothing for which reasons cannot be found, everything is really senseless, every definition is an illusion, every thought a lie, every resolute volition an act of partisanship; confusion is the nature of all.

Or, a supposed knowledge whither I am rising may make me fall as I think I know the one way to rise, excluding others. I unify my being in the peace of self-satisfaction, but I lose the tension of the antinomy. Existentially, ascent is tied to decline, to real and possible falling. While there is temporal existence, there is no definitive possession of the transcendent relationship. Unless contentment with myself takes the form of simultaneous demands upon myself and of a sense of failure, it means I am already lost in the indifference of a habitual existence. What may be permissible in old age, as contemplation of a life about to be rounded out, is at each previous moment a fall into lack of tension.

5. I Myself as Process and as Entirety

Since rise and fall are a process in temporal existence, I am already falling when I withdraw from the process, to extant tranquillity, and yet continue to exist in time. This does not mean, however, that my *being whole* ought to be flatly spurned in favor of the mere process. In the process I transcend beyond the process, to the being from which the process gets its direction. Transcendence, my only possible support, includes for me my own entirety as well. In existence I am the *will to become whole;* I could *be whole* in transcendence only.

Death as a fact is indeed a mere cessation of my existence in time. But death as a boundary situation points me toward myself: *whether I am a whole,* and *not merely finished.* Death is not only the end of the process; as my death it inexorably conjures up the question of my being whole: what am I, now that my life has become and has been, with the future no longer a process?

In temporal existence, however, my rise and fall are not definitively settled. They alternate. I do not get to be a whole; all seeming perfection fails. I can transcend the irremovable boundary only to a possibility of deliverance, of being whole. While my life remains a ruptured entirety, ruptured in guilt and ruin, my death is to sublimate the disruption in the unknown.

To live in temporal existence without entirety, to live philosophically at his own peril, is the fate of one who knows that he ought to be free. The eeriness of an existence without entirety overcomes him like a thing dropped out of being, in the question that dares voice the horror of the possibility of downright nothingness. Here I stand, unsheltered, in the hand of—what? I do not know. I see myself cast back upon myself: it is only in the resolution, where I am most strictly myself and yet not quite myself, that I see it is possible for me to be uplifted or lost.

Entirety comes into my existence *mythically*—the more clearly felt, the more firmly I enter into the process—as my guiding genius; and it comes into my existence as immortality, which I enter as intrinsic being. In my genius I am reconciled with myself as one who can become whole. In the thought of my immortality I am to my existing self the shadow I cast as I appear in the process, in rising and falling: as such, elucidated in self-being, obscured in existence, I am to myself the possible entirety of a transcending Existenz.

6. Genius and Daemon

People appeal to each other by the phenomena of their uplifted being, attained in the process of existence. Yet however deep this communication, which covers the being in existence, I also remain alone. Without rigorous self-being I would become diffuse and thus incapable of real communication. Alone with myself, I am doubled: I talk to myself and I hear myself. In solitude I am not alone. What happens there is another communication.

We can make a banality of this by psychological interpretation; but in such an approach we miss the substance whereby a monologue makes transcendent reality felt with the binding force of a mythical objectivity.

In the motion of monologue, genius or daemon are like forms of my intrinsic self. They are close to me, like friends who share a long history with me, and they assume the form of enemies who challenge or tempt and enchant me. They do not leave me in peace. It is only when I succumb to mere existence, to its opaque instinctiveness and rationality, that both of them have left me.

My genius leads to lucidity; he is the source of my loyalty, of the part of me that wants realization and permanence. He knows law and order in the bright realm of a man-made world. He shows me this world, allows my reason to hold sway in it, chides me where I do not heed my reason, and dissuades me, at the bounds of reason, from attempted forays into another realm.

My daemon shows a depth that fills me with fear. He seeks to lead me into a worldless being. He may counsel destruction. He brings me not only to an understanding of failure but to its direct accomplishment. He regards as potentially positive what used to be negative at other times. He may thus be the ruin of loyalty, legality, and lucidity.

My genius may be the one God, who can still be revealed to me in this form while his essence is so far removed that as himself he cannot become familiar. My daemon is like a power both divine and antidivine, a power whose obscurity bars definition. He is not the same as evil; he is the invisible possibility on the course steered by my genius. While the genius gives me certainty, the daemon is unfathomably ambiguous. The genius seems to speak in a firm, distinct voice; the daemon, in his secretly coercive indistinctness, makes me feel at the same time as if he were not there.

Genius and daemon are like a split in one and the same thing: in the entirety of my own self, which is imperfectible in my existence and speaks to me only in its mythical objectification. In existence they are the guides of my soul on the path of existential self-manifestation, signposts that stay veiled themselves—or else they are anticipations, in which case I must not trust them. On my path I come up against limits of transparency, limits which are never fixed, but which keep reemerging in ever-different forms; and it is at those limits that genius and daemon make their voices heard without being wholly and definitively revealed to me in temporal existence.

Here, as always in the mythical realm, the untruth lies in *perpetuation*, from fanciful superstition to the hallucinatory delusions of a split personality. If I live merely from day to day, such things simply do not exist. They are—without existing—a form of self-elucidation at the existential moment, articulations of the ascertainment of Existenz, the mythical objectifications of the fact that there is no Existenz except in communicative struggle, including the struggle with oneself.

7. Immortality

I fall with the dark consciousness of sliding into the void; I rise as I become aware of being.

Far from necessary as a result of temporal life, immortality is a metaphysical certainty that does not lie in the future, as another kind of being. It is an already present being in eternity. It is not extant, but I enter into it as Existenz. An uplifted self-being is assured of immortality by its uplift, not by any insight. There is no way to prove immortality. No general reflection can do anything but disprove it.

If an Existenz in the boundary situation musters its courage and transforms the boundary into a depth, the place of its faith in a life after death will be taken by a sense of immortality in soaring. Our sensorily vital instinct is always just to go on living, but precisely this instinct of ours is hopelessly mortal. It regards duration in time as the point of our immortality. There is no immortality for that instinct—only for possible Existenz, which no longer needs a sense of endless duration in time to be sure of being.

And if this assurance of being is elucidated in ideas that are identical with those of a sensory, temporal immortality, it does suggest a fixation of such ideas, produced by the unbelief of mere existence. Their truth content may have the suspended character of symbolic substitution, its powerful and real meanings along with its void and vanishing appearance—as, for example, in the notion of eternally, lovingly seeing each other in perfect clarity, or of a limitless continuation of our activity in new forms, or of a fusion of the ideas of death and renascence.

Any concession to this symbolism, in the sense of a real continuation in time, is impossible in philosophical thinking; but acknowledging the symbolism will make sense as long as, rather than placating a sensuous craving for life, it serves to ascertain an existential substance. It is only when questions and doubts have arisen that the philosophical thought is inexorably justified. Being, then, lies not in time beyond death, but in the depth of present existence, as eternity.

If immortality is the metaphysical expression for the uplifting of Existenz, falling means really dying. That is to say: if Existenz is not void, it cannot be mere existence.

Existing, I cannot, of course, disregard my existence. Death, as the void, makes me shudder. But as uplifted Existenz, when I am sure of being, I can disregard existence and look at the void without congealing. This is why in the enthusiasm of lofty moments men have been able to go to their deaths despite a sure knowledge of the mortality of their sensory existence in space and time. The young, with their soaring Existenz not yet inculpated by finite worries, have often found dying easier than have the old. For the survivor, the pain of sensory parting could be surmountable for a moment by the light of the immortal soul; he could be granted a peace that does not affect the infinite longing for the presence of the departed, because not even in the transcendent glow of memory can existence ever be whole.

But when I talk of immortality—when I do not keep silent, rather—I must objectify; and that I cannot do except in time, as if I endured in time even though I must die as existence. If I then let this objectification vanish in a symbol, the reality of immortality does not cease even if it crumbles as existence. For I cannot claim that Existenz is vanishing in death, in its last moment, because it ceases to have an existence. I can neither objectify nor deny eternity. Thus, if I say I can be pure existence,

I am saying neither that there is something else—something I still cannot conceive otherwise than as existing—nor that death would reduce me to nothing. Objectively, the metaphysical thought of immortality is indeed always conceived as existence in time, and yet in the sense of immortality this cipher fades into a certainty of present reality.

If there is no getting around the pain of death, not for the dying and not for the survivor, it can be eclipsed only by existentially uplifting realities: by the risk of action, by the heroism of commitment, by the high-minded swan song of farewell—and by plain loyalty.

What we hear in the uplift, when all our knowledge deserts us, is a challenge: if death does end everything, to bear this boundary, and in our love to trust that the absolute ground of our transcendence sublimates the no-longer-being of all things. In the final analysis, stern silence shields the truth of the sense of immortality.

8. I Myself and the World Entirety

As Existenz in its historicity cannot see itself as a whole, neither can it see the way of the whole to which it belongs as existence. Yet the possibility of its own rise and fall makes it ask about the way of the whole. After all, Existenz itself is not an isolated individuality; it is in its encompassing, in that which for the consciousness of Existenz expands without limits, as though still advancing its frontiers—as though it would be reached only in the world entirety, if that were accessible. Here lies the source of mythical notions of the origin and the last things, of the world process and of mankind's history.

Because Existenz is in existence, inseparable from existence, it cannot be indifferent to anything that exists. Since the world is its stage, its material, its condition, its encompassing and, in time, ultimately conquering reality, the world's being is to Existenz as its own being.

The existence of the world concerns me everywhere, and yet I cannot at all identify with it. I fight it as the alien thing that threatens me; but it may serve me as well. It is a being of its own. I segregate myself from one part of it by taking hold of the other part in which I include myself as existence. With this, my own objectivity, I have become one. Beyond that which belongs to me, however, I feel more closely linked with the other as the heart of my Existenz opens in adopting existence. The deeper I go, the greater my solidarity with initially alien things; my isolation strikes me as more culpable as the alien comes to seem less necessarily and absolutely alien. In a utopian lucidity I might perhaps rediscover myself in all things, and what the world is would be my fate also.

It is only with my existence that there is a world for me, and I am not without the world's existence. When I become aware of it, beyond all particular world images and perspectives, I can as Existenz in the boundary situation put the question of this existence in a form that will simultaneously raise the question of my own existence. I do not think in nihilistic impotence of smashing the world, attempting to reverse it, so to speak, nor do I destroy myself. Instead, I call existence and, *in it*, my own existence into question. I thus see the whole as a process that does not passively take its course, but in which I actively participate. On its own ground, existence is unquestionable; questioning it has now a source outside its immanence, in Existenz. From there alone comes the question, expressing an active entrance into existence. The process is experienced only in action, and without the original reach, it would come to a standstill. It is *in its own rise and fall* that possible Existenz comes to *see a whole* in which its existence is entwined. I treat this whole as though it were rising and falling itself. Once it is clear to me that all things are subject to evaluation, I look on the possible rise and fall of existence from the viewpoint of my own being.

9. The World Process

Even so, the whole of existence remains inaccessible, and a cognitive determination of its rise and fall, impossible. It is only in myths and speculations that ideas of the world process materialize for Existenz.

In the medium of consciousness at large Existenz cannot get beyond world orientation, in which every anticipated world entirety is abandoned so as to attain the basic posture of cogent cognition: the conquest of the most concrete, always particular knowledge in an inconclusive existence. There is no getting out of this posture of true factuality; if Existenz transcends it in quest of a world entirety, no kind of mundane cognition will result from cipher ideas of a whole that is always mythical—but these ideas will express what can be existentially experienced in existence when transcendence seems to be our guide. Rise and fall, then, will not seem to be possible in myself alone.

For world orientation the final horizon is matter, which moves from endlessness to endlessness and precedes every beginning of a particular existence. In an existential view of existence, on the other hand, we ask existence about its source and its ground. Can we tell how the world came to be? There are several possibilities.

I may see the world in ever-repeated cycles, growing and sinking back into chaos, from which it will spring anew. It has no ground because it has always been.

Or I may imagine the world as existence, which need not have arisen. It is due to an error of transcendence, an apostasy from its own ground.

The world were better not, but a lust of becoming led to mundane existence. One would wish it were reversible and there were nothing but transcendence, felicitous in itself.

Or the decision was the creative will of the deity that wished its power, its goodness, its love to be revealed; it needed negativity in order to void it, and thus to achieve the greatest possible realization of the divine essence.

Or the world's existence is a link in the eternal, present circulation of the one being, always rising and falling at once, always becoming, eternally at the goal.

These myths are so questionable in concretion that we are soon surfeited. And yet, to us they are not utterly alien: they lend a voice, a symbolic expression, to the unfathomability of existence as a matter of crucial concern to us, in our proximity to things and at a distance, when we rejoice at life and when it makes us shudder.

None of these thoughts is still possible for us as an insight, or as faith with such definite contents.

Existentially our thoughts of the world entirety have opposite meanings. In thinking of the one world process in which decisions still depend upon what happens, the stress on the moment creates the highest tension in the self-being faced with a choice: nothing can be undone; I have one chance only; the One is the crux; there is but one God; there is no metempsychosis, only immortality and death; rise and fall decide definitively.

On the other hand, thoughts in which the eternal presence of being is conceived as encompassing, as the presence of a being which has always already reached the goal, give us contemplative peace in a trust without tension.

This antinomy—of the decision yet to be made at the moment and the eternal present we cannot lose—is transcended by an Existenz capable of uniting both in its existence: the tension of the decision to be made in soaring with the composed view of the decision itself as a phenomenon of eternal being. The contradictory becomes existentially possible. Yet this is precisely what excludes a knowledge of this unity, and then of the being of transcendence, in a noncontradictory form.

This attitude toward transcendence keeps my mind *open for the historicity of the world entirety.* The world, of course, is not one of several possibilities, as if on the whole it might also be different. Possibility is included in the world, but the world is not a possibility itself, in a way that would be comprehensible to consciousness at large and Existenz. "Nobody can lay another ground than has been laid in the beginning"—thus Schelling, mythicizing logically, could still express the respect for reality as such, for what really happens, that we owe throughout to its transcendent historicity, without relaxing the existential tension of our possible rise and fall.

10. Rise and Fall in History

In looking at the world entirety, I was transcending the realm of existence which I can *affect* as possible Existenz. I was transcending it not just quantitatively, but qualitatively.

As a historic being I am real only in the situation of my limited world. I see possibilities that are possible only on ground of my knowledge; the more strictly I act on this knowledge, the more clearly will its limits show the incalculability. I am with other individuals in the process of manifestation; the more resolutely I enter into this communication, the more do I come to feel the overwhelming lack of communication with everything outside. Fulfilling my intelligible world, I am in an all-encompassing one that is not yet understood and unintelligible.

Yet my knowledge and my searching spread beyond the limits of the world that is accessible to my understanding and my intervention; and their way of spreading to the world entirety differs from the way they spread to history—to the human existence that concerns me more closely because it has produced and is still producing my existence, and because its realities and decisions show my own potential at the same time.

What is mythically conceived in the world entirety is either the being of nature as downright otherness or something which from the outset refers to the history of man. The beginning of the world—of our world, in which we are—is then the origin of consciousness and knowledge, the birth of the world which man makes for himself as his habitat, his language, his field of action. Therefore, though intended to bring closer the otherness that is inaccessible and yet indistinctly appealing to us as being, that which the myths conceived as the world entirety was the very presence of a realm *beyond our influence and responsibility,* even if its power and infinite abundance concern and enthrall us.

In history, on the other hand, we are in the *realm of our own capacities.* Here, rise and fall are modes of being of the reality I am myself. Yet as I find myself only an ephemeral link in the human chain, as even in myself I find no unequivocal uplifting, rise and fall are simultaneously in me and in the whole. They are like events to which I am indeed an impotent prey—not as to nature, however, but as to a reality that is always also up to man, and thus up to me.

When man is acting historically, he cannot lucidly know his own will, nor can his will be unconditional, unless his absolute consciousness pervades events and anchors them in transcendence. Otherwise he would be arbitrarily and unsurely pursuing merely rationalistic final goals; or he would be left with nothing but the sureness of his vital instinct: to stay afloat on the sea of events as this individual, in any case and for as long as possible.

Only if a man relates to transcendence will he be able in cases of conflict to risk perdition as existence because something has to be *settled*. To live unclearly, to endure essentially by compromises, is to decline. For reality's sake—that is, for the sake of a chance to rise out of such existing unreality—man is *driven to his limit* and made to say what he is in essence. However, since in existence he must live in relativity, by compromises, there is no telling objectively where things should be settled and where they need not be. The will to a decision is existential, not impelled by the impatience and discontent of those who seek nothing but movement, excitement, change, or self-destruction. Rather, the impulse behind that will is the sense that *reality should be true*. Whether a social or personal status quo deserves protection, whether a mode of conceiving truth ought to be left unassailed—what ultimately manifests all this to each deciding Existenz is solely its own transcendent relation. It is an untrue phrase that from time to time everything must be destroyed and begun all over. In historic existence it is truthful to maintain the tension between tradition, preserving what is extant, and the boundless risk of destruction. But no decision is to be derived from mere experience and from definable ends. The roots of all original decisions lie in transcendence as the presence of rise and fall. Hence, at each moment when I see historical and present existence in transparence rather than simply on the endless plane of empirical reality, this existence will be arranged in being that rises and being that falls.

Historical rise and fall are what we feel in a *philosophical reading* of history and what becomes real to us *in our own action*, in the joint action we call political.

Reading history as a cipher of transcendence is the contemplative complement of the activity of present action. The affected philosopher reads a cipher of the supersensory into the human history which he tells as a myth, although with elements drawn from empirical reality. The last of these myths was Hegel's. But this view makes of history a *myth in reality*, as distinct from the purely supersensory myths of the cosmogonies. I experience it not by devising a process outside the world, but by immersing myself in reality. If I come so close that it may seem as if I myself were living in history, I am involved in a communication that is now real too, albeit one-sided. History moves into the present, then, in the sense that the past can come to be again as if it were still in the future. Once again it comes into the suspension of possibility, only to bring us to a more resolute acceptance of its definitive elements as absolutely historic. This is the source of the respect for reality as such that has its depth in relating to transcendence. This way of reading history is philosophy of history, a temporal voiding of time.

When history is so understood, rise and fall in it are indeterminate. My immediate reading seems to show them over and over, in ever-varying forms: history is an appeal that points to both. But then again it is ambiguous, and in the sequence of periods everything seems to go both up and down.

The consciousness of rising and falling throws a possible Existenz back on its *present action*. This is fulfilled, in the realm of viewed and adopted history, if every echo of the past in me serves to make sure of that consciousness and to spur decisive action now. Yet the tension between reading history and rebounding into the present situation remains: the two are not in the same perspective unless the transcendent One unites them from another source. The reading means that for a moment I will shield my eyes against the present, and the present means I can forget the past—for a present that is still subject to intervention remains detached from history. When I get into a real situation I am concretely affected, whereas the most thorough understanding of past situations is never more than a thought in the realm of possibility.

Purposive action is action only *in* the world; it is not a creation and transformation, as if the world itself were either an object or a goal of planning. Not for one moment, therefore, can the passing glow of universal power let us deem the world encompassed by a single consciousness, as if it were to be shaped as a whole. The strongest action still accords with awe of that entirety; and along with the most concrete historical knowledge goes an aversion to abstract statements about the whole of the world's course. Man intervenes in history, but he does not make it. In his impotence he does retain a sense that all things need not be the way they are, and that they might come to be different—but unfathomably so, in the ground once laid, which is reality itself.

The whole, however, is neither the entire past nor the future. Rise and fall are real, each time, *in the present*. The transcendent relation not only turns history as a cipher into the eternal present; it also stands for the *pure present,* against a pure future and against the pure past. No time can be relativized in favor of another, and none can be absolutized as the sole fulfillment of eternity. For an active Existenz, therefore, the only possible phenomenon of true being is each present time. The truth, for such an Existenz, does not lie at an eye-catching place in the past, nor does it lie in the future as a final goal whose expectation and pursuit makes the present an empty transition. The truth lies in realization at the moment, which alone enables it to be a future reality for its given time span also. The vindication of present failure by the claim that it will bring about a better future is a deceptive practice. Referring to the future is relatively valid in specific technical measures for the preservation and expansion of existence (learning, training, saving, building); but if such references are presumed to extend to existence as a whole, they become evasions of the reality of self-being. The present is itself when it is the eternal present into which all history is received.

Rise and fall are the ways of this intrinsic being. Echoing out of history, which was a substantial present, they are experienced and acted out on our own responsibility. The fact that I do not know the one world plan adds to the weight of my actions: I cannot deduce them as right from any general knowledge, yet they make me part of the world plan as I win or lose the being I must freely realize in my historicity.

11. Rise and Fall Completed in the Whole

Forced upon us by the world process and mankind's history is the question of the end. Mythical answers to this are given in a doctrine of the last things, of the perfection or definitive destruction of existence.

The question of the end can be put in unmythical terms. We can ask about the future, how it might be and how it will probably be. Taking a long enough period, we can say of whatever had a beginning that it will perish as all things end in time. The possibilities preceding this end are incalculable. Whether we believe in an indefinite progress in the evolution of the human race; whether we conceive a final goal of the order of human existence on a pacified planet; whether we vaguely assume and desire an infinite, aimless motion—in each case we mean the end or the endlessness as a future reality in the world, to be lived by generations to come. We are not transcendingly searching for the end of all things.

That kind of search was undertaken in the myths, which combined temporal reality with supersensory fantasies. Their content goes beyond happenings conceived solely in time. Whoever took them for empirical prognoses and started awaiting the world's end at a definite time was bound to be disappointed by its nonoccurrence. Once the impossibility of the sensory-temporal side of the idea is recognized, however, the point is no longer to drag the end into time but to grasp it in transcending: what remains as the eschatological myths grow pale is their intentional reference to being proper, which in ascent stands before our eyes as the cipher of final perfection, in decline as the cipher of total annihilation.

For, in time, the inaccessible being appears through the antinomy of rise and fall. What is eternal must, as temporal existence, come to itself by way of decision. If this decision is temporal, the end lies in the future; if the decision is a phenomenon of being, the end is perfection in present eternity. In temporal existence, therefore, I can never be directly with transcendence; I can only approach it as I rise, and lose it as I fall. If I were with transcendence, all motion would cease; perfection would have been attained; time would be at an end. In time, the moment of perfect absolute consciousness must instantly turn back into the movement of tension.

Diurnal Law and Nocturnal Passion

In defiance and fall there was something negative confronting something positive. At times it seems to be a nonentity's imminent dissolution into nonbeing, and then again the very premise of positivity, the articulation of the movement in whose tension we realize our relation to transcendence. Eventually, however, the negative may come in the antinomy to be an annihilation that is positivity itself: what previously seemed sheer negation turns into truth, comes bewilderingly to be not just a temptation but a claim—and it becomes a new fall to evade this truth. Our being seems in existence as though relating to two powers. We call their existential phenomena "diurnal law" and "nocturnal passion."

1. The Antinomy of Day and Night

The *diurnal law* regulates our existence, demands clarity, consistency, and loyalty, binds us to reason and to the idea, to the One and to ourselves. It demands realization in the world, construction in time, the perfection of existence along a way that is infinite.

Speaking at the limits of the day is something else, however. Having spurned it, we cannot find peace. *Nocturnal passion* will disrupt all orders. It plunges us into the timeless abyss of nothingness, dragging everything into its whirl. All of the building we do in time, as a historic phenomenon, looks to this passion like a superficial mirage. Nothing essential can be clear to it; oblivious of itself, it will indeed seek out obscurity as the timeless darkness of intrinsic being. An incomprehensible compulsion that does not even seek a chance to be vindicated makes it unbelieving and unfaithful to the day. No tasks, no goals speak for it; its is the urge to ruin myself in the world to gain perfection in the depth of worldlessness.

The diurnal law knows about death as a limit, but at bottom, when uplifted Existenz makes sure of its immortality, it does not believe in death. In action I think of life, not of death. Aimed at the historic continuity of constructive being in existence, I think of this existence even as I die; I think of working on it as if death did not face me. The law of the day will let me risk death, not seek it. I have the courage to die, but to me death is neither friend nor foe. In nocturnal passion, on the other hand, I have a loving and shuddering relationship with death as my friendly enemy. I long for it, just as I strive to put it off; it speaks to me, and I associate with it. In painful existence, living without possibility, and in the worldless joy of life—in both these products of the night I love death. Passion knows exaltation in death; the last trickle of this exaltation is the sense of a longed-for peace of the grave after so much erring and suffering. Every instance of this passion is an act of treason against life, of unfaithfulness to all reality and visibility. Its home, its real habitat, will be the realm of shadows.

If originally I am not a stranger to existence, not averse to reason and constructiveness, the realm of night will be a world that grows on me later in life if I choose the day. I come to be at home in it even if today it is still distant; and at the end, when I have aged and retired from a world of existence grown strange, the realm of night receives me as the memory of life. The diurnal law may lose its substance for me as I exhaust it. My being in existence may grow weary, and nocturnal passion may be the end.

In the sure stride of a historic being in existence I am guided by the will to become manifest. A self-secluding defiance resists manifestation. But nocturnal passion *cannot manifest itself* even though it wants to. It makes me embrace the fate I see, the fate I want and do not want, and which thus appears both necessary and free. Nocturnal passion can make me say "A god did it" as well as "I did it." It shrinks from no risk, not only in the purposive world of existence but precisely where it seems to ruin Existenz itself by violating rules, fidelity, and self-being. Its goal is the depth of being that puts man outside existence and brings him to naught. It is man's plunge into senselessness. The fear of being driven to his fate looks like the end of choice and deliberation, and yet, it all seems unsurpassably chosen and deliberate. Nothing seems to match the resolve of this passion—a resolve that stays invisible to others, secluding all movement in the individual himself. Destructiveness comes to possess the whole of man; whatever constructive will remains is pressed into its service, seeming to effect the opposite of the apparent volition.

There is an original obscurity about passion. This is its agony, but it is also its mystery, beyond any charm of the forbidden and concealed. It makes me seek to discover, to clarify everything so as to get a pure view of the true, undiscoverable mystery—as distinct from the self-will that manufactures secrets artificially and, by beclouding, prevents the disclosure of banal, empirical facts. This passion is obscure, yet wholly certain. It puts me in fear, but in an infinite fear of the fateful need to break faith and be unclearly driven to my death by the absolute mystery.

It is in embracing the nocturnal passion, sure of its being in the void, blessed and damned at once, that in existence I atone by dying for the betrayals I committed, and for the havoc I wrought. It is only when I want to die that I know the truth of my passion, and that it will be true even for one who was not personally swept into its transcendence.

2. Attempts at a More Concrete Description

Concrete descriptions of the phenomenon of nocturnal passion fail because every definite statement moves into the light of day, belongs to the day, and is subject to its law. In thought, the day has primacy. Clarification would avoid an obscurity that is a source of its own. In description, every concrete phenomenon of nocturnal passion will be artificial and banal; drawn into the sphere of possible justification, it seems to dissolve. For the day is loath to acknowledge that nocturnal world. The day cannot want it, or even admit that it is possible. It is so far removed from cogent intelligibility that the day can declare to be flatly void, senseless and untrue, what the night regards as its transcendent substance.

Out of the night I have come to myself. *Soil, mother, blood kinship, race*—these make up the dark ground that encompasses me and is transformed by the light of day. As mother love and love of my mother, as love of home and family feeling and love of country they are received into the diurnal sense of historicity. But the ground remains a dark power. The pride and defiance of this subterranean proximity, so to speak, may turn against the spiritual task of friendship, of being-for-each-other, that confronts an Existenz that has met another. The subterranean power will not be relativized; eventually it comes to boast of itself. I am to take myself back into that which gave birth to me, instead of seeking truth in diurnal existential communication, which occurs on grounds of truth.

Eroticism is a shackle incomprehensible in itself. The diurnal law turns the erotic reality into an expression of existential proximity, into its sensory symbolism, and thus makes it relative. Yet in the consuming surrender to passion I betray everything; I want only the passion itself. Once I acknowledge the dark Eros as absolute, I care nothing for existence as such. This is not blind sexuality, the polygamous instinct that lacks passion and is thus existentially powerless; it is the tie, enforced without existential communication, to the present sex creature in its singularity, its own intrinsic being. I skip reality and Existenz, as if the encounter in which self-being dissolves were instantly and solely in transcendence. Without a way of understanding, this passion is unconditional all the same. Without elucidation of their rational being, two who meet, or one of them, will plunge into the transcendence that destroys them. To them, the process of communicative manifestation, with its challenge to realize oneself, becomes an untrue, self-limiting absolutization. Their own submergence, though experienced as guilt, is the deeper truth.

An existential dependence on life and loyalty will move erotic passion into the realm of day; conversely, it may consummate itself in holding sway over lovers who sell out their love to death. Their betrayal of diurnal love, of loyalty, amounts to a self-betrayal, to betraying the intrinsic self of each. Not knowing why and to what end, they feel and passionately seize upon an eternity which in this world, because of the betrayal, calls for instant death. If an Existenz does not find death—but did commit the betrayal—its existence in this world is now damned and desolate.

In the "love death" a choice would be made between two possibilities: love as a process of self-becoming in manifestation, and love as the consummation of dark unphenomenality. Selling out to passion, which need but have faced me as a possibility to throw everything else into question, will not appear to be a moral lapse, then, but an eternal betrayal. Where this seems real, however, it leaves me not just silently put out but in awe of something incomprehensible—because this betrayal itself seems to have its transcendence, whose possibility excludes self-righteousness on the part of any happy lovers in the world.

For, though at first the diurnal law confers a sense of incomparable happiness in communication, in living by ideas, in challenge, idea, and realization, what we hear at the end of this bright world—given true lucidity—is the call of daemons we have spurned.

The night to which I yielded, wide awake, is not nothing. It is not evil as such. Beyond good and evil—which apply where decisions remain—night seems evil only to the day, and yet the day feels that it is not everything. When I trust the day and withhold myself from the night,

I do not have the absolute consciousness of guiltless truth. I know I evaded a claim on me, and a challenge. In embracing the day, and fidelity, I disobeyed a transcendence.

The day's communication is lucid and a process; the night's is the moment of union in common destruction, when darkness is unveiled only to fold its wings and sweep us into itself. What happened remains cloaked in the devouring night. If there are lovers who faced each other in this possibility and disobeyed the daemon, they would not know it— for what has been put into words is not what has been. They obeyed the diurnal law; they obeyed themselves. But in their world, now, consciousness will not stop wavering. The firmest assurance of the right path shies away from expression. It is as if something were out of order, something that will never be in order. The very achievement of the good seems to involve a guilt toward another world.

The demands of night are everywhere and can never be taken into the day as adequately justifiable. Lying for my country, perjuring myself for a woman—these are still surveyable acts contrary to particular moral and legal rules. But tearing a bond once given, so as to expand one's own creative life—as Goethe did to Friederike Brion—is an act he himself was never able to elucidate and vindicate. Thus Cromwell, for the power of his state, took inhumanity upon himself with a conscience that was never fully eased. In situations of this kind the historic realization, the very day himself, rests on the violation of diurnal orders. The scope of the nocturnal claim shows up here, in the will of men who act politically, if in case of failure they choose to go down themselves: they are putting so much real historic existence at stake, are sacrificing so many human lives to that existence, that their own, bound up with the cause and goal of their actions, will strike them as forfeit.

3. Confusions

Instinct, lust, curiosity, intoxication may be phenomena of night, but they do not make out its depth. Nor does self-destructive defiance or the unreadiness of secluding myself from another; and neither does self-will, which isolates me from the universal and entire, or the vacuous nihilism that would give itself weight as destructive judgment. By existing in the mass, these declines into *unsubstantial negativity* conceal the true world of night, or they let it stand as pure evil, as dissipation, as particular and momentary passion and sheer arbitrariness. Yet substantial night is the way of vanishing in the abyss that is not simply nothing. Death is its law which makes the day's world disintegrate. He who radically violated the diurnal law on principle, for the night's sake, cannot go on really living—that is to say, living constructively and with a chance to be happy. Forever broken by his own betrayal, he is no longer capable of any unconditionality if he stays alive. There is an intimate relationship between true passion and all the orders it breaks. If it does not lead us straight to our deaths, therefore, it is a living parable of death, a lifelong blight in which the choice of life seems to eclipse fidelity. We do not know this passion when it grips us, but those in loving proximity to us can know about it. It is a loyalty to night, the unreflective self-torture of Existenz in the process of asking without getting answers. This passion seems like a reversal of Existenz, but one far distant from the loss of Existenz in lust and intoxication, in autocratic defiance or complaisant yielding. These may be its transitory media, but with an unbreakable core that looks as though on the brink of being broken.

The nocturnal world is timeless, whether man goes to his death or lives in the analogue of death, as the sort of Existenz which in all its reality is unreal. The diurnal world, however, is historically constructive, self-producing, and accordingly temporal. The mere *counterblow to night,* the defense that seeks to destroy it, shows therefore that if it becomes timeless, like night itself, it succumbs to the night's own law without coming to the day of historic Existenz. Asceticism, for example —freeing from all bonds, from family, soil, and possessions, diabolizing eroticism and all the joy of life, growing spiritual only in the sense of being tied to nothing—is not the world of day. It destroys the historicity in building the spiritual existence of Existenz because it would obliterate the nocturnal ground of that existence, because it knows only an either-or, an abstract all-or-nothing. Its spirituality is unearthy, and yet it seeks to realize true being in the world, wholly and at once, as being right and universal. While historicity is a hard, free becoming in an impervious material, asceticism cuts it off from its ground, so as to have a timeless truth on hand. This counterblow is bound to become mere destruction and to plunge into the night it was meant to combat. What may happen to it as it ruins existence is that a sudden turnabout will let it once more blindly serve the ground that was its target. Then, utterly in thrall to earth, it will become the most confused self-deception.

The ruthless *vital will to exist* lies on a different plane. Its perspective is narrow but lets us see exactly what can give us power, pleasure, and prestige in the world. With this will we want nothing but ourselves. We violently push aside what gets in our way. The goal achieved, we start to reinterpret. Brutalities that established our existence are silently passed over and forgotten. A mother's blind urge for her children, that of husband and wife for each other, that of man for his bare existence and erotic satisfaction—in an opaque barbarism these may be the blank wall that shatters any will to communicate, the deaf, furious violence that is not night because it has no transcendence.

Opposed to the blind will to exist is the lucid realm of man whose world makes him transparent to himself. In the very throes of passion he is marked by clarity and circumspection. The I that speaks out of him will never be impossible to communicate with. There is dependability in him, which means he will be around again as the one who always met me. He shows the tension of constant self-disentanglement in the peril of falling and rising; but his is also the calm serenity of well-founded self-assurance. He listens to questions and arguments and recognizes in their medium an unconditional law, albeit one that eludes all definitive substantial phrasing. He seems unbreakable and yet infinitely flexible. There is no point in him that must not be touched, but there is readiness without reserve. To him the diurnal law grows lucid, and he understands the possibility of truth in another's night.

4. The Doubtful Basic Premises of the Day

The basic premise of diurnal life seems to be that limitless manifestation will give transcendent fulfillment to a man of good will, and a pure sense of his true being. This premise grows doubtful, however, once the nocturnal world has caught our eye.

In the day, good will is the final purpose of our existence; nothing else has value except in relation to it. Yet for all his good will, man cannot act without transgressing. He is prey to the boundary situation of unavoidable guilt. The question is always what his good will makes him will in the concrete historic situation. There is no good will as a general form; it is only together with its fulfillment—and in that, if it is more deeply understood, it will impinge upon the world of others. When we wish our good will to be self-fulfilling, we can feel its limits. And if in transcending along those limits our good will comes to question itself, it remains absolute only as the phenomenon of its existence, as the diurnal law that bounds upon the night. As a creature of the day I have a good conscience in doing right. But the right founders on guilt, its link with night.

In the day I see existence as the abundance of the beautiful world; I know the enjoyment of life that is mirrored in the image of my existence, in the structure of the world, in the grandeur of classic perfection and tragic destruction, in the fullness of appearance put into form. But it is only when I am their mirror that nature and men are that grandiose. It is a beautiful surface, proffered to the point of view of man who sees and celebrates. Viewed only in this way, the world is a suspended fancy. The act of yielding to it, wholly and definitively, detaches from existential reality in favor of pictorial representation. By this act, in an abrupt turnabout, the observer himself is handed over to the nocturnal despair that seemed behind him.

Day is tied to night, because the day itself is not without *true foundering at the end.* Day does presuppose the idea of positive construction in historic growth, the will that extant things be relatively enduring; but night teaches the ruin of whatever comes to be. It is not only the course of the world in time that nothing can last; it is like a wil that nothing intrinsic should be permanent, Foundering is what we call our experience—one we can no more anticipate than we can avoid it—that perfection is also disappearance. Realization to the end of genuine foundering is the ultimate possibility of temporal existence. It will sink into the night that laid its ground.

If the day is sufficient unto itself, its not foundering will be less and less substantial until eventually it founders on the outside, on something alien. The day, of course, cannot have the will to founder. But it is not fulfilled unless the unwanted experience becomes part of it, as a known inner necessity.

If I take the day to be *bounded* by night, I can neither realize the substance of historic Existenz in mere law and order and formal fidelity nor plunge into the world of night, at whose borders I must stand to experience transcendence. It remains a question, of course, whether hopelessness before the nocturnal mystery is not what brings the last transcendence to the soul. No thought can decide this question, and the individual never decides it in general, and never for others. Diurnal Existenz will approach it with awe, shunning proud self-assurance and any boast of its own happiness.

5. *The Possible Guilt*

Existenz wants to maintain its possibility. Its holding back from realization is an original strength where it means self-preservation for the proper moment; it is weakness when it bespeaks a reluctance to take hold. Hence it is only in my youth that I truly live in pure possibility. Existenz does not want to waste itself at random, but to squander its existence for the essence. Only when the decision ripens, when I might realize myself in a historic grasp and yet keep clinging fearfully to my general possibility, which now grows dubious—only then do I slip away from myself in this refusal to enter into my diurnal fate. If I shrink from every irrevocable fixation, from every professional, marital, contractual bond, I prevent my own realization; eventually, what might have been an origin in me will trickle off into the void as I remain a merely possible Existenz. Nor, having thus missed the hour, do I plunge into the abyss of night. By holding back I deny myself to the day as well as to the night; I do not come to live or die.

I only imagine that my life in the boundless possibility preceding realization is spacious, human, and free, superior to everything narrow. In fact, I am living emptily, pretentiously, in playful contemplation. An existential will seeks limitations and bonds in existence. It thrusts toward situations where a decision is called for: from the possibility of all things springs the uniquely One. This thrust is not an unequivocal activity. To realize myself in limiting my possibilities is a struggle in which I keep my self-becoming at arm's length, as if it were hostile to me. I let myself wrest my fate from myself, whether I enter into the day or surrender to night. I am guilty if I *avoid reality.*

But then, each time, there is the deeper guilt of *rejecting the other possibility.* The self-abandonment of yielding to passion is the road to perdition, and he who takes it denies himself to constructive, life-embracing love. Yet in building he denies himself to the surrender to death.

Existenz as such is guilt-conscious. In diurnal law, guilt lies at the boundary where something else is revealed: the radical question raised by the rejected possibility. And passion involves guilt as an original part of it; in its depths we know guilt without being able to say it, and we know penance without acts we might define.

The way to elucidate guilt is not an untrue justification of passion, or of the day—for as principles, both stand in unconditionality, beyond all justification. Even less is it the sentimentality of making allowance for whatever lives in self-torment. The elucidation of guilt does derive from shuddering at passion; it is the knowledge of the possibility of passion and goes together with the guilt-consciousness of the self-limiting and defensive world of day. In night, however, there is no philosophizing.

6. Genius and Daemon Fighting for Existenz

The daemon's magic sweeps me to a love akin to night; not daring to touch it, I am led by my genius to the loving enthusiasm of uplifted lucidity. In enchanted love I do not know what to do; stripped of each earthly medium, this love grows wholly transcendent; it seeks fulfillment in destruction. Love under the clear guidance of the genius knows it is en route, has a dependable communicative accord with the other's rational nature, and wants to live in the world.

The daemon lets the phenomenon of Existenz dissolve in its transcendence. It will not look for its fate. Even a child can both perceive and exude the painful charm whose later transformations will in maturity be neither denied nor affirmed but uncomprehendingly accepted. If Existenz follows the daemon, the course of its fate will unwittingly and unwillingly lead it to cruelty and callousness. It experiences inexorable necessity, suffering it as much as acting under its compulsion. It may find itself, its form of existence, in lovingly protecting others and observing all rules, though otherwise beholden to the daemon. From the child, that magic in the face of fate is hidden, shrouded in wildness and play; but some day, if the guarding geni s confines the daemon, the magic turns into the kind of indulgence, of clear-eyed love, that stays remote even in close proximity.

The manifest diurnal Existenz, on the other hand, led by its genius, finds a clear phenomenal expression of its reality in time. It is the same inwardly and outwardly. It thinks what it says, and it agrees with itself because it loves itself on this road to lucidity. It is also at odds with itself because, subjecting everything to investigation and criticism, it must doubt everything—because it can listen to everything and put itself into everyone else's place. It seeks the validity, the form, the general effability in all things conveyed to man as such. It knows it is free, and it actively takes up its fate with the idea that there is a way of possible comprehension. Such an Existenz is stern in clarity, tender in aid. It seeks the struggle, because struggle is the medium in which it comes to itself. It is due to itself, which makes it feel strong; it is also due to something else, and in calling on its genius it can feel itself quake at the sight of the daemon entering its circle. It is dependable, and as a person living wholly in this world, it becomes a true companion of the other's fate. Fidelity is its essence; losing that, it loses itself. It lives only by the active undertaking of tasks in the world, because they are its own and because they are essential.

No matter how the polarity of day and night may be schematized, its conception is the utmost possible enhancement of the dubiousness of existence in regard to its transcendence. I do not know what is. As a diurnal creature, I trust in my God, but I do so in fear of strange powers beyond my understanding. In thrall to night, I give myself up to depths in which the night destroys me, but as it does, it turns into a truth that is both consuming and fulfilling.

7. *The Question of a Synthesis of Both Worlds*

The two worlds are interrelated. Their division is only an elucidative schema and is itself in dialectical motion. What seemed to be diurnal law is reversed into a nocturnal abyss when the One—which to the day is crucial—rises against universal lucidity and becomes lawless itself. And what seemed to be night turns into the ground of day when the human bondage to night is transformed into a building whose dark foundation is known, but whose architect is now rejecting and fighting the very thing that once gave rise to the edifice.

We would like to conceive a synthesis of both worlds. But there is no Existenz in which that will happen. What may succeed at a time, in historic singularity, is not just objectively imperfect but subjectively fractured. Not even the idea of a synthesis is possible; for in the world of diversity, being as the phenomenal existence of each Existenz lies in the distinctness of the individual whose final import is ineffable and inimitable. The synthesis as a generally possible conception is a question, not a task. Both worlds are themselves only when they are unconditional. To which of them I pledge myself appears to me in the continuity of concrete action, if I can interpret the action as deciding to which world I gave absolute precedence and which I would only admit relatively to the other. Night can tolerate relative order and purposiveness and even heed them as long as this does not require allowing itself to be touched. The day permits adventure; it permits limited and disciplined intoxication as a noncommittal experiment devoid of unconditional seriousness; it permits us to look down into the abyss.

The seeming happiness of a synthesis is either flawed or it involves betrayal. The flaw of evading the abyss will somewhere deprive Existenz of its footing in the day. And in betrayals of the diurnal law, of the human individual, of the building of existence, of all loyalties, the night will be darkened by unrevealed guilt. The superficial result, on the other hand, would be the inconsistency which supposedly realizes everything and is truly nothing. Existenz has depth only where it knows its fate. Either I know I am not among the initiates, not having touched the gates of death and the nocturnal law—or I know: my life is forfeit, for I followed night and broke the law of day. The desire to be diurnal life and nocturnal depth at the same time is a delusion. The ultimate truths are a diffident respect for the other and the pain of guilt.

Decisions come in existential crises only. In those there are two opposite possibilities: either to leave the day and to substitute a love of death for the will to live and work, or to return from night to day, making night itself the foundation. But when and how it is possible to decide, where an eternal decision has already been made and where there is still a way back—this is not known in any sort of knowledge, only to the individual in his historicity, and never so that he might definitely say it of himself. For there are not even two ways I might know, two ways to choose from. Such a choice would be no longer existential, and what enabled me to make it would be a decline from elucidative discussion to the objective fixation of a schema. The two worlds are a polarity that is never clarified; each one enkindles the other. I can confront them in elucidation, but I cannot know their being in thought.

8. *Mythical Elucidation*

The mythical elucidation also occurs in a pictorial objectification of two powers. But the objective form of that incomprehensibility is not tied to the simplifying polarity of two. Rather it tends first to many gods, is then concentrated in a duality of the deity and an antidivine power, and finally moves into the deity itself, to be experienced as its wrath.

Polytheism is the world that keeps the One in the background. By serving many gods, I can allow for any power in life. If I do all things in their time and place, without asking whether they can coexist, I consecrate each in its own way as divine, permit every possible thing to be realized, but remain ignorant of eternal decision. Here the passion for night may find a realization that is positive but limited. Its conflict with the diurnal powers may come in sight, but it will not be a matter of principle to the same extent as an eternal struggle in transcendence. The chthonian deities take their place beside the celestial gods. Bound to their localities, obscure in their abysses, they make an absolute of earth for moments at a time. The gods of intoxication hallow self-oblivion; the cult of night becomes a transient reality in mythical ecstasy or in bacchantic rage. There is Shiva, the dancing destroyer, in whose cult nocturnal passion seems to give itself a sense of truth.

In polytheism the nocturnal positivity is naïvely accepted, so to speak. When the antithesis of day and night comes to be a form of conscious transcending, however, night becomes an antidivine power—the deity, but the untrue one. In the *dualism* of transcendence, one of all conceivable antitheses is always posited as negative. In the battle of these antitheses man takes his stand on one side—with God against the anti-God, with light, with heaven, with the good, with constructive action, against night, earth, evil, and destruction. Night lives on as the devil where men have ceased to believe in it as an absolute principle.

Yet our experience in dualistic thinking is that *in transcendence no antithesis can be held fast.* Either the clearly conceived opposites turn into opposites in the diurnal world, such as good and evil—and we are left with the task of couching the other in a new antithesis, whose lucidity will make it slide back to day in the same fashion—or the pairs of opposites (self-preservation and self-abandonment, mind and soul, being and nonbeing) reverse their meaning. What had been indicative of night becomes a sign of the day, and vice versa.

Hence the last mode of pictorial transcending, which places *night into the deity itself*. The deity remains the One, but an unfathomable One whose decrees have meanings we can never understand and whose ways are never ours. It will only seem to be possible to grasp the "wrath of God" as retribution. It is considered an outburst of the deity that visits the iniquities of men upon their children and their children's children and reveals its wrath in catastrophes affecting entire nations and the world. Man ponders ways to assuage the divine wrath by means of magic, and then, antimagically, by a sinless life. Experience shows him that such a life is impossible, or that the wrath will strike him even though he believes himself to be unaware of any specific misdeed. Thus the sensory picture of the divine wrath must be abandoned. It fits neither the mood of an ogre nor the legalistic justice meted out by a judge who requires an eye for an eye, a tooth for a tooth. These images pale into mere signs of the most profound inconceivability—signs which a transcending consciousness was able to formulate, but not to elucidate, in the thought that God himself creates and predestines the "vessels" of his wrath: what I am as a nocturnal being I was made by God in his wrath; where I abandon myself to nocturnal passion, God's wrath willed it so. This thought is bound to fall by its own weight, leaving nothing but the power of the word "the wrath of God."

The Wealth of Diversity and the One

The One has many meanings. In logic it is the unity of being thinkable. In the world, in nature as in history, it is the unity of reality. To Existenz, it is the One in which Existenz has its being; to Existenz, the One is everything.

In metaphysics we are seeking the One—whether in transcending *beyond* the thinkable unity or in embracing the mundane one or in transcending *out of* the unity of the existential One, out of the unconditionality of historic self-being. The ways cut across one another and may meet in a common perspective, but initially they are by themselves.

1. The Existential Origin of the One

In existential elucidation, what makes us feel the unconditionality of action is the identity of a self-being with the One it takes up in existence.

I am not really myself unless there is to me one thing that matters. Just as the formal unity of the object is the condition of its being thinkable for a self-conscious mind, the substantial One is the phenomenon of unconditionality for a self-being. However, while thinkability belongs in the context of one generally valid truth, the existential One is the truth that has other truths beside it, truths which it is not. There is no knowable whole to sublimate them all, only the boundless possible communication of these existing truths in a being that will never be entire, a being that is not even thinkable from outside.

Existential unity is, first, limitation. Whatever a man will identify with himself, with an exclusiveness that shows the depth of his being, is *historically definite*. In existence, of course, an Existenz may want one thing and also another. It shifts and experiments. It fails and makes new experiments. But all this belongs only in existence, where I myself am not involved in it; I merely put it to use. Where I am myself, I am myself *only in identity* with a reality that is limited, seen from outside. It is only where I turn from a possible Existenz into a historic one, where I immerse myself in existence, that I am. The decline goes to the *scattering* of diversity. If everything might as well be different, I am not myself. If I want all, I want nothing; if I experience all, I am diffused in endlessness without coming to be.

Unity is, second, the whole as an *idea*. What relates to ideas as totalities has its unity in the relative whole of this idea; without it, it would be mere accidental multiplicity. The decline from unity in this sense goes to the part and to its absolutization, hence to the split into random embattled antitheses without direction or goal.

Between existential unity, which prevents dispersal, and unity of the idea, whose entirety preserves from endless multiplicity, there is not coincidence but tension. Ideas are carried by many an Existenz, but the unity of Existenz will break through an idea that has flagged or grown rigid. Conceived as a cosmos of the mind, ideas give a picture of the world of the mind; but then the varied Existenz without which this world would not be real will disappear before the seeming totality. I myself am not the picture of the world of the mind, once that picture has come into the free suspension of ideal entireties. As a possibility it is indeed more than I, but as a reality it is less.

Unity is, third, that of the existential origin: of *decision by choice*. The decline goes to indecision and reluctance to decide. I do not come to be, and I do not come to be aware of myself, in a vacillation that merely protects my existence, with decisions made about me instead of me becoming a decisive factor.

Thus original unity means historic definition, ideal totality, and decisiveness. The decline goes to dispersal, to isolating absolutization, to indecisiveness.

When I, as a historically defined being filled with ideas, have decisively identified with something that exists, it becomes absolute for me, but not *qua* existence. What is encountered in historicity, at the moment of becoming existential, is the transcendence of historicity. The existing One becomes the road to that transcendence; the secrecy of the One becomes a certainty of relating to it. For just as no reasons can be given for the One, no statements can be made about it either. Any statement will cover only an external unity; it will be a finite objectification. The statement, as a mere objectivity in numerical unity, may be devoid of the One: it may lay down something finite to which I tie the knot by force, without transcendence. The One is the heart that beats in finite existence, the ray of the one unknown light—each man has only his own, which will light up for him in communication. Metaphorically speaking, all rays come from the one deity, yet it is not for all men that the one God becomes an objective transcendence. He is never more than the One pulsing for the Existenz that transcends in this One.

Only a man whom the One never touches, who takes the positivity of diverse existence for the absolute, who sees possibility in the fact that all things are replaceable, and forgets death over it—only such a man would be able to call it useful in life not to attach one's whole heart to one person or thing, but to develop a broadly based love for many people and many things. For, so the reasoning goes, if the whole were jeopardized by an individual loss, one's own existence would be too greatly affected, indeed annihilated, by the death and destruction of others. Distributing one's love and loving nothing too much is advocated as a sensible precaution.

This way of thinking immanently, by the standards of utility in existence, is the most direct contrast to experiencing transcendence in the One with which existing Existenz identifies as encompassing existence.

2. Unity in the World

Since world orientation gives me access only to what I can grasp as an inwardly coherent One, disparateness, that which cannot be brought into the context of a unity, remains uncomprehended. The standard we apply to cognition, as distinct from a mere endless gathering of knowledge, is a demand for systematic unity. To a scientist, unity is the directive power that guards all his divisions—without which it would not be possible—from leading him into quicksand.

Only because there are unity, entirety, and form in the world can there be systematic cognition of the world; and yet none of these unities is as such the One of transcendence. The mundane unities are either relativized into methodical viewpoints or else substantialized as themselves by their relation to the transcendent One.

Unity in the world cannot, therefore, become really true either as a scientific viewpoint or as a spatial network in the interaction of all things; nor as the community of understanding each other in rational transparency; nor as an order of human affairs in a universal body politic; nor in professing an objective unity of religious faith. It can become true only by its own transcendent relation. Every other unity is relative for itself, and as an outward unity it is deceptive.

3. Unity in Logic

When I think of unity, it is first the *numerical One* that enables me to count the many. Then it is the unity in which a diversity of objects is a *whole* that makes the diversity comprehensible. Third, it is the *unity of consciousness* in the self-related personality. Transcendence is not appropriately conceived in any of these unities; we seek it as the One beyond them all, but in such a way that these mundane unities remain its vanishing aspect.

a. The deity is not numerically one—for then there would instantly be the conceivable possibility of there being not one God only. For the numerical One confronts the many; but neither as one nor as many can the deity, in principle, be subject to a count. The unity of a number remains a formal, and thus always superficial, unity.

On the other hand, if we were to conceive transcendence as both one and many, the definite figure would have to round itself out so as to be several and one at once, in a sense that would encompass countability. That our conceptions operate inevitably with numerical unity and multiplicity—that in transcending, therefore, the absurdity of conceiving them as identical cannot but break them both down—this is what lets us feel that applying numerical unity to the deity is as inadequate as applying numerical multiplicity. What is intended, beyond any one and many, in transcending to the transcendent One has to lie deeper than a number can express.

b. A multiplicity has unity not only as a sum but qualitatively, as multiplicity that has achieved unity as *entirety* or *form*. This unity is only due to multiplicity, and this self-related multiplicity lies only in the unity. In the world it is the unity of each object as this one thing—of a tool, for instance, of a living thing as this particular organism, of a work of art. Such unities are those of structures I can see objectively before me. To the extent to which they are more than finitely surveyable, they may, as beauty, make us seem carried away to a transcendent

One. But the deity itself cannot be this unity. If it were, it would have become the mere image of an objectivity—however grand—to which my relation is that of an admiring spectator. I would be at peace in the splendor of that objectivity, but would miss what disturbs unity in existence: the realities that touch my heart and destroy me. For what shows in this unity is no longer the transcendence to which I relate in such insoluble antinomies as defiance and surrender, fall and rise, diurnal law and nocturnal passion.

c. Numerical unity and unity of a whole are for a subject that sees and conceives them, but they are not for themselves. They have no effect on themselves, no sense of referring to themselves. Consciousness, *self-consciousness*, and personality make out the *unity that we can be* but can no longer conceive as an object, in a logically adequate manner.

No unity in which transcendence can appear to us is more inadequate than the unity we can be ourselves. Personality is the very minimum that would have to appertain to divine unity; but we are personalities only with other personalities, whereas the deity is not with its kind. Personality is Existenz, not yet transcendence. It is precisely that for which alone there is transcendence.

The unity of personality, the unity which is both present and unfathomable, is the medium of transcending. This is what lends to this unity the weight of its being and the shimmer of an encompassing import, but it does not make a personality of transcendence.

4. Transcending to the One

If we look back upon the forms of unity accessible to us, we see in each a possible relation to transcendence. Our metaphysical grasp on the One itself is rooted in the *existential* One. Our relation to transcendence has room to exist in the *mundane and historical* One. And the *logical* forms of the One are means of expression, which make rational sense even without transcendence.

The One is not the one world; it is not the one truth for all; it is not what unites all men; and it is not the one spirit in which we understand each other. To make metaphysical sense of the validity of the One in logic and world orientation, and then of our transcending in these unities, takes the One of Existenz.

The question is this: why is there such magic in the one deity, and why is the One a matter of course, as if it could not be different? Why is it like being impaired, like being lost, if divine transcendence were not one? It is because in the transcendent One I find my true self-being, and because self-being fades only before the one transcendence and does not truthfully fade anywhere else.

If the One with which I identify to come to myself is revealed to me as possible Existenz in existence, its appearance brings me to the inconceivable One of the one God. While all unities manifest their relativity, the existential One in its unconditionality remains the cause of seeing God as the one ground of all historic Existenz. The extent of my unconditional grasp of the One in life is the measure of my ability to believe in the one God. My existential transcending to the One in the historic reality of my life is a condition for transcending to the one deity. Conversely, the fact that after this last leap I live with an assurance of the one God is the cause of an equally unconditional attitude toward the One in my world. For me there is only so much transcendence as there is the One in the continuity of my existence.

It is thus by virtue of the existential One that the one God is always *my* God. Only as an exclusive One is he near me. I do not have him in the community of all men. The nearness of the One is the aspect of my transcending; but even the most assured presence is objectively no more than a possibility, a reaching down to me, the only way in which he can be One for me. This proximity voids nothing that comes to approach me from the world, no alien faith, no other gods of others. Yet when I am looking at this world, the One is *far* from me and downright inaccessible. When the one deity makes itself felt in the One of Existenz, it is either in the nontransferable, incommunicable proximity of this historic moment or in the most abstract and unattainable distance. It never comes to be identical with me. In the closest proximity it maintains absolute detachment. And yet its proximity is like a presence. The distance, on the other hand, lies beyond the task that must be accomplished at the outset: in my transcending to penetrate mundane existence in its inconclusiveness, disjointness, diversity, and ungovernability. It is only beyond the aspects of the powers whose forms compete as transcendence in mundane existence that the one God might be found.

As in existence the urge to the whole comes up against otherness, so, in transcendence, does the urge to unity come up against the deity which does not show the same features to all men. When I act against others, strengthened by my vision of the One, it would be *hubris* to take my God for the only one. The nearby God cannot make truthful Existenz lose sight of the far-away God. Even in combat it will see the other's link with God. God is my enemy's as well as mine. Tolerance grows positive in the will to boundless communication—and, that failing, in the sense of a struggle ordained by fate: there has to be a decision.

Near or far, the one deity flatly *defies cognition*. It is a boundary, and it is absolute only as the One. If we take the diverse figures, the variegation of the cipher language, to be the deity, we fall into an arbitrary posture: the many gods will somehow justify whatever I would like. I move at random from one to the other; but the One, splintered into the small coin of the many, is no longer unconditional. Faced with the multiplicity of transcendence, I always know that I produce it myself. But the One as a boundary is the being I am not at all, the being to which I relate, rather, in my relations with my own intrinsic self. If this being did not differ from me, my relation would not be with transcendence; I would be relating only to myself, yet without being myself. Only my being, the reality of the existential One that depends on me, can make me receptive for the One which I am not.

In esthetic multiplicity, unconditionality is lost along with unity. Although in a beautiful picture multiplicity is curbed and brought at least into objective unity, I am promptly shown many other beautiful pictures. No more than the temporarily exclusive existential One becomes objectively definable for the intellect is the one God accessible as objectively One. Objectification of the One is precisely what we must avoid in order to preserve the One without betrayal. The wealth of existence and of ciphers is there to be known and looked upon, but it remains a façade and a game unless it becomes a historical form of the One in the concrete present.

I am sure of the things I experience and do: of my factual community with people; of my inner action, my factual conduct toward myself; of my outward actions. I shall never know what God is; what makes me sure of him is what I am.

The transcendent One is not a general one for all men, nor does it remain the absolutely incommunicable one of the isolated individual. Rather, it comes to be the source of the deepest communication, though not of universal communication. To Existenz, defining the true deity as that which can universally unite mankind makes a banality of transcendence. The most intensive communication is possible in closely confined circles only. There alone will transcendence reveal its depth, always in historic form. It is no longer the deity that links all men nowadays; it is concerns of existence and technology, the rationalism of the generally valid intellect and the lowest level of generally human drives, the violence of a utopian unity or the negative unity of a readiness to be tolerant in the coexistence of essentially different people who do not concern each other. To live in the utmost universality as if that were transcendence means to lose transcendence. In fact, the One becomes a phenomenon in existence by exclusion only. The visions of one world and one transcendence for all crumble under the real strength of

Existenz in boundary situations of struggle—the strength with which an Existenz must first make transcendence its own, so that then, in genuine communication, it may reach out for the historic expanse of possible unity with all men.

5. Polytheism and the One God

Multiplicity will have its due. Originally there is polytheism every-where. The sense it makes is beyond voiding in existence; to Existenz in existence, transcendence can appear in ever-vanishing and thus vastly varying forms. Yet equally original as polytheism has been the concept of the deity as One—not in everyday life and not in a cult, only in the background, and without existentially relating to it as to a present deity. The mythical All-father of the primitives; the Greek *theion*, the divine at large, underlying all personifications and definitions, encompassing them and merely represented by them; the combination of gods into unified groups, into a divine state with a chief god; finally the one God who is not just the chief, not just the one god alongside the other gods of other nations, but the unique, all-governing God: the one deity of Greek philosophy, conceived by philosophical reason, and the God of the Hebrew prophets, originally experienced in the loneliness of the soul, without any philosophy—these are historical forms of this One in the historic process of freeing itself from polytheism.

In stated form, the simple ideas of the One God I turn to—whether he reveals himself to me or hides—are naïve again. The idea becomes a definite one of the deity as omnipotent, omnipresent, omniscient, as loving and angry, as just and merciful, and so forth. Without an idea or a thought, however, the deity is not even for our not-knowing. If it is true that not-knowing expresses an existential relation to the deity, it is true also that to Existenz the deity comes to appear in the form of vanishing ideas and thoughts.

Yet the thought, obviously, cannot stop with the conception of the one God as the *absolutely one* who rests in himself and has nothing out-side himself, nothing that he is not—for there is the world and there am I, free to choose between the possibilities of defiance and surrender, of falling and rising; I experience transcendence not only in the diurnal law but in nocturnal darkness; and the many rise against the One, the diverse world of existence against the unity of human history. But it is just as impossible to turn multiplicity as such into being. *Multiplicity is received into the deity itself*, so that the antinomy may let us find the uplift to true being.

This is the point of origin for concepts and ideas that become sheer absurdities when they are clearly thought through, yet whose historic concretion has made them signs of the most profound, most unknowable mystery. The one deity is to enter, so to speak, into a process of becoming and to admit multiplicity without impairing its unity. The *trinitarian* doctrine conceives God in the differentiation of his independent persons; it conceives the three persons as equal despite the Son's dependence on the Father, and the Holy Spirit's dependence on both of them; it conceives being as eternal despite the Son's being begotten, despite the becoming of the Spirit. Conceived on the inadequate numerical plane, the idea requires us to believe that one equals three. The absurdity is not removed by the parable of personal self-consciousness—in which I split myself and return to myself, promptly split myself again and have my existence in a circular process, in constant unrest amid restful self-conclusion, with myself one of the three—for in this parable we add the unity of self-consciousness as a way of transcending. But this consciousness is only with other self-consciousness, and the absurdity remains: one person is supposed to be three persons, and three independent persons are supposed to be one.

These ponderings may be true as long as we are transcending in impossibilities, but they become untrue when we stabilize them as tenets of faith.

6. Transcendence of the One Deity

As a concept, the one God necessarily leads to absurdities which are to make me feel him as I transcend them; but in an existential sense he is the hand that answers me wherever I am really and truly myself. He is the nearby God who justifies me with the distant one. A childlike piety skips all the problems and ciphers; destructible by neither, it implies trust and an end of questioning—where I am uplifted, where I follow the diurnal law, where I stay in the world, and where I assent to what the deity sends me.

This God can teach me how to bear mortality by the mere sense of his being. Let immortality remain in transformation, as a sense of uplifted being; the agony that all I love in the world is unqualifiedly mortal, as I am—this agony will be acknowledged and accepted without delusions. The strength it takes is possible in view of the one eternal God. He *is*, for all his hiding in inaccessibility.

Despair at the nonentity of human life will then be resolved in its uplift. That there is the being of the One suffices. What *my* being is, the being which passes away as existence, does not matter if only I keep soaring while I live. In the world there is no real and true consolation that would make my transiency and that of all things appear compre-

hensible to me, and bearable. Instead of comfort, there is the sense of
being in the certainty of the One.

Sure of the One, man knows that the One *wants truth*. The world-
wide terrors spread by human fear and by its priestly exegesis, the dread
of hellfire because of offending God, perhaps—these fall by the wayside
when I am truly truthful. God wants no deception. Whatever appears
in this world, even if it pretends to be God's vicar, is subject to questioning: how it really is, how it came to be, what it is doing and how.
I do not offend God by a relentless scrutiny of any of God's works—if
for a moment we apply this term to everything mundane. As a childlike
notion (for he who remains truly human remains a child) the one God
is in the background of my naïve consciousness whenever I find God
doubtful in the world, whenever I defy him, whenever I grasp his
wrath in the dark of nocturnal passion. The truth remains that God as
the One is not knowable in our dubious, disjoint world. In this world he
shows so many aspects I truthfully have to acknowledge that time and
again the One seems to sink out of sight.

The one God pales when I think of him. As a concept he is anything
but compelling. Everything speaks against him. We grasp him only as
though in an anticipation, skipping all the intermediate links. This is
why only the childlike conception fits: it is the one least liable to be
taken for a sensory reality, for something deceptively objective.

But it is on the ground of the one God that after all my doubts I find
an echo for my good will, for my diurnal being. It is he who comes close
in my loneliness, and yet he is never there.

When I can feel him as a boundary, he stands above everything
relative and underlies all genuine communication. For himself he seems
to ask nothing but what a true Existenz is for itself as it soars in communication with other Existenz—no price, no cult, no propaganda. In the
world I meet nothing but Existenz. God as himself is not in the world.

Prayer is an invasion of the mystery, an importunity which man may
dare in his greatest loneliness and need; but as a daily habit and developed custom it is a dubious fixation to which philosophy will not
lend itself. An everyday assurance of God's proximity would deprive
the relation to God of the depth it has in doubt; what would be gained,
at the cost of the supramundane character, is a peace and contentment
which an Existenz finds wanting. For God's concealment seems to call
for men to agonize in doubt and in distress.

Existentially, God's help has not the character of bringing something
to pass, or preventing it, at my prayer. This help shows in the cipher and
stays hidden all the same. The cipher in which it shows most directly
and clearly is my own action. But prayer as the ascertainment of abso-

lute consciousness in its transcendent relation—this is an incommunicable and unobjectifiable existential presence, an always historic, always singular uplifting to the One.

Even such words go too far if understood as expressions of definitive peace. In being uplifted to the One, I would be sheltered, then, leaving the world of existence in its endless diversity, uncertainty, and ambiguity behind; I would break faith with the world and withdraw from reality to a facilitating harmony. For the transcendent One is *like a deity that enters this world as a stranger,* to help me if the existential One makes me feel in accord with it. But it seems to come to me from another world, and over its proximity I must not forget its distance, which makes this world in its disjointness what it is.

The transcendent One, that supreme and final refuge, may come to pose an existential peril unless approached from reality and in the full tension of possible Existenz. It is true only on the ground that brought me to it: unconditionality of the One in the existence of Existenz. It never turns into a lasting peace that would overcome all that has gone before. In existence I cannot remain in accord with my transcendence; I must make my way back to defiance, to the possibilities of falling and of night, and to the many—this way will have to be repeated as long as I am in temporal existence, for any peace turns swiftly into the pursuit of happiness by one who merely exists and does not wish to be disturbed.

The Reading
of Ciphers

We call the metaphysical objectivity a cipher because it is the language of transcendence, not transcendence itself. It is not a language to be understood or even heard in consciousness at large. This kind of language and the manner in which it accosts us are for possible Existenz alone.

The Three Languages

It is only in the absolute consciousness of Existenz that a *direct language of transcendence* is truly, substantially present. It will be heard by an individual, at a singular historic moment.

What is *conveyed* in this language, however, is conveyed by way of generalization; even the man who heard it originally will understand it only in generalized form. This *second language,* that of palpable transmission from Existenz to Existenz, detaches the content from the original hearing and makes transferable—as a narrative, an image, a form, a gesture—what had seemed to be incommunicable. What was originally a transcendent language comes to be shared, and as this second language is passed on, it may be replenished by relating back to its source.

Finally, when our thinking takes aim at this merely palpable language and penetrates it to the source, the result, in the form of metaphysical speculation, is an incognoscible but cogitative *third language*: the language of *philosophical communication*.

1. The First Language: The Direct Language of Transcendence

We experience being in the ciphers of existence; it takes reality to reveal transcendence. About transcendence we can know nothing in general; we can hear it only historically, in reality. Experience is the font of transcendent ascertainment as it is the font of empirical knowledge.

Experience as "sense perception" is to have a thing before me as an object in space and time. Experience as "living" is my existence as I become aware of it. A "cognitive experience" is the current outcome of methodically developed, deductive-inductive research; it is a trying out of what I can make and what I can predict. The experience of "thinking" is the consequence for my consciousness of the execution of thought movements. An "intuitive experience" is a sensing of the whole of a present reality in its situations, with my ability to hit on what is crucial for myself and others as the criterion. It takes all these experiences to give rise to the metaphysical experience. There I face the abyss and feel the desperate shortcoming when the experience remains simply one in existence. But there, too, I find present fulfillment when the experience becomes transparent, when it turns into a cipher.

This metaphysical experience is the reading of the first language. Its reading is not an understanding, not a key to what lies underneath, but a real, personal involvement. Nor is it just rational ascertainment. It goes beyond that: it makes being transparent in existence, beginning in the most primitive existential immediacy; and even when this transparency is conveyed in the most sublime thoughts, it is never a thought but a thought-conveyed new immediacy.

There is nothing demonstrable about a metaphysical experience, nothing that might make it valid for everyone. It becomes a delusion when I treat it as knowledge, when I think I can produce it at will and have it in consciousness at large. But it also becomes a delusion when I treat it lightly, as a mere subjective feeling. It puts me into a mode of being other than a purely positive existence. It implies a translation of being from mere existence into eternity, which is beyond knowing.

If a not-knowing was the negative limit of my experience of mundane things, of life and thought as such, this becomes now a fulfilled not-knowing as I return to present sensory reality—not to reality as a content of existence, however, but to reality as a cipher. In my search for transcendent being I therefore want all possible experience to be tangible, an experience I can realize myself, in order that it may reveal transcendence. The urge to see whatever is visible, to do whatever is possible—existentially this curiosity is still blind, but it is the impulse to find the road to being. When I enter into the world by assuming the tasks of realization, of tying myself to responsibility, I go beyond the diversity of knowable things. No demonstrable final goal can ever be sufficient reason for this entrance; what drives me to it is the deeper impulse to attain my own experience of true being, whether in embracing it or in abstention and limitation. I want to touch reality, to void possibility. Full of possibilities, I proceed to reality, turning myself into a limited individual; I want to get to the point where there is no more possibility, nothing but the clear-cut reality caused solely by outright being. In temporal existence I can never meet being itself, but reading its cipher comes to be the point of whatever else I may do and may experience.

Reading the first language *demands an experience*. It is not the abstract thought but the cipher in historic, present particularity that reveals being. What shows it to me is not a metaphysical hypothesis in which I infer and calculate what being might be; it is the tangibility of the cipher. I do not think beyond the cipher, for its glow is that of being. What an experience is, however—this is ambiguous. The a priori thought itself becomes an experience. The call for an experience goes only against the empty thought, not against the factually performed substantial thought that is the cipher in which I experience my being.

Our experience of transcendence pales in generalization; it becomes more forthright as it climbs toward the peak of something fulfilled only here and now. Our experience of nature, for instance, becomes a reading of ciphers as its wholly individual side grows more and more distinct, as the most concrete knowledge of minute realities is acquired in the presence of a world entirety.

2. The Second Language: Generalization in Communication

It is in the echo of that transcendent language—audible only in the immediacy of the present moment—that languages are created, images and thoughts intended to convey what has been heard. The language of man takes its place beside the language of being.

The objectifications of language with a metaphysical content appear in three palpable forms: as "discrete myths," as "revelations of a beyond," and as "mythical realities."

a. The Greek gods are not transcendent; they are still in reality. Only philosophical transcending, from Xenophanes to Plotinus, goes beyond the world and these gods. Yet as myths in reality, the gods differ from the rest of reality. Man may meet them in the world, for their figures are a reality alongside empirical reality. The real sea is to us the cipher of something unfathomable; in the form of sea gods as speaking symbols it becomes a *discrete myth*.

Myths relate events said to have determined the ground and the essence of existence. They serve to resolve existential tensions, not by rational cognition, but by telling a story. Myths unveil by veiling things anew, and their figures, the anonymous creations of scores of centuries, continue to be effective. In a superhuman world man sees what he is. He beholds, as an act of divinity, what he does not yet reflect upon as his own being and doing, although in fact he regards his being and doing as determined by that which he beheld. The myth changes its meaning. It is no unequivocal logical structure, nor will exegesis exhaust it. It is always historic, yet its eternal truth remains even if it is recognized and distinguished as a myth. What the myths mean, however, is revealed only to one who keeps believing in the truth to which they lent the peculiar form of vanishing as truth. Whenever myths are interpreted, the result is a false simplification; their historic content is lost, and the interpretation becomes an inversion: what looks in it like knowable necessity is not supposed to be known as necessary in the myths at all.

b. The myth of a *world in the beyond* devalues empirical reality into mere sensory contents, into essential nonbeing. But the beyond appears in the myth, gives signs, and works wonders. A supersensory entirety opens up. Instead of familiarizing itself in reality with the divine character of reality, an Existenz enters into something "beyond reality," into another world of being proper, conveyed to the Existenz by *revelation*. Either the revelation is fixed in history, not repeated, but happening as a singular, comprehensive world drama—a sequence of unique acts that occur when the time is fulfilled, until the revelations in divine words and deeds are complete and the world can come to an end—or there are repeated revelations; the world drama is not arranged in the economy of a whole, and endless world periods succeed one another. The way to emerge definitively from existence has been opened, but when and whether everything works for all men remains obscure.

c. If *reality* itself is simultaneously *mythical*, it is neither devalued nor complemented by a discrete objectivity. It is seen as such, and at the same time it is seen in the significance conferred on it by transcendence. It is not the simple empirical reality of things we can explore— rather, its reality encompasses everything explorable—nor is it transcendence without empirical reality. To van Gogh the landscape, things, people in their factual presence have a mythical quality at the same time; hence the unique power of his paintings.

A curious yearning awakens if as Existenz, living in the sensory present, I do not simultaneously live in it as a transcendence. The yearning is curious because, after all, that which it seeks is right here. It does not urge me beyond things, into another country; I must regard such pursuit of a beyond as a betrayal, rather, because in the present I have failed to do what I existentially can. This yearning is not the nervous phenomenon of inability to grasp things as real, to comprehend myself as existing, to experience the moment as the real Now. A mythical Now would content the yearning; what it consists in, precisely despite the full sensory presence of mere empirical reality, is a vitally fulfilled sense of existence. What torments me in this yearning is not lack of reality but lack of transcendence.

Communication with another, aimed at myself and at him as phenomena of original self-being, brings me closer and closer—and my yearning grows, finding fulfillment only in those moments when death is no more. To be empirically close to a person, and thus only to intensify my longing, to quench it not until our empirical proximity will serve as a transcendent link between us, without an imaginary beyond—this is metaphysical love; and for that love there is mythical reality.

3. The Third Language: Speculative Language

When a thinker interprets the cipher language for himself, he obviously cannot know transcendence as the Other. Nor can he, in existence, expand world orientation as the knowledge of existence. However, obeying his own formal law, he thinks necessarily in objectivities. He *reads the original cipher script by writing a new one*: he conceives transcendence *in analogy* to his palpably and logically present mundane existence. His thought itself is a mere symbol, a language that has now become communicable. It can be spoken in many different ways.

One way is to keep my eye on reality as such. I ask everywhere: why is this? But my question is not the rationalistic one of world orientation, searching for a cause; it is the transcending question that does not require an answer, because I know there can be none. My question seeks to make reality a full existential presence, to pervade it, as it were: *that's how existence is, so this can occur in it—that's how being is, so this can exist*. In wonder, in hate, in trepidation and despair, in love and in uplifting I see the same: *that's the way it is*. It is a way to deal with being in existence, a way essentially different from cognitive, scientific world orientation, and yet impossible except in the material of world orientation. The communication of that way, moving exclusively in the real realm, can of course be understood without transcendence—the description of nature, for instance, as a representation of occurrences in space, and the presentation of history as a summary form of conveying empirical researches on the human past. But when they voice the language of a transcending comprehension, they are media of metaphysical communication. For the intellect there is no telling whether they are; only a transcending Existenz can hear it.

Another way is to speak expressly of the real being of transcendence. I conceived it in analogy to being that exists, to self-being, to historic being. A whole is rounded into a thought picture. But even when it is elaborated into a *metaphysical system*, the thought is just a thought symbol, not cognition of transcendence. The thought itself is a cipher, a possibility of being read, and thus not identical with itself. Only in current adoption is the thought itself.

A third way to speak the speculative language is to go by my existence, by myself in my world, to find the way to the being of transcendence. In trains of thought that are still taught under the name of "proofs" of God, I make sure of being in a factual correlation with my own substance; it is from this correlation that the thoughts—in themselves cognitively irrelevant and apt to deteriorate into games played with logic—acquire an existential power of conviction which they utterly lack as objective proofs.

A fourth way is to transcend in reminiscence and foresight, pondering the origin and the end.

These and other modes of conceiving transcendence analogically, in the cipher of thought symbols, are what we call *speculation*: neither cognition of an object nor appeals to freedom by existentially elucidative reflections, neither a categorial transcending that liberates but does not comprehend anything nor an interpretation of existential relations to transcendence. They are a contemplative self-immersion to the point of contact with transcendence, in a self-invented, pondered, formed cipher script that brings transcendence to mind as a metaphysical objectivity.

Speculation is a kind of thinking that attempts a contemplative being with transcendence; this is why Hegel called it "divine service." Since it remains without cognitive results, however, F. A. Lange characterized it as "conceptual poetry." It is indeed essentially different from all other thinking—which it presupposes, employs, and dissolves. It lets the other thinking evaporate in its own thought movements, in which no object remains solid. In the place of ever-vanishing objectivity, speculation puts a nonobjective function; its intrinsic involvement is a realization of the thinker's absolute consciousness. It is not yet in acts of intellectual thinking, therefore, that we understand speculation; we understand it only as we go through those acts, as the absolute that can be gained in them will come to mind. Speculation is a thinking that drives us to think the unthinkable. It is mysticism to the intellect that wants cognition, but it is lucidity to a self-being that transcends in it.

Yet it is wrong to call speculation divine service. Speculation is not a cult, only the philosophical analogue of a cult. Too much would be attributed to it by the term "divine service," for speculation comes only to ciphers, not to a real relation to the deity which real cults address in prayer. The term would shroud the leap that lies between cults and the cogitative play of metaphysics.

Still, the term "conceptual poetry" does not fit either, if we take it to mean the noncommittal nature of such play. What would correspond to noncommittal esthetic art, to an art for art's sake, is the equally noncommittal metaphysics of world hypotheses—a metaphysics in pursuit of purely rational accuracy and estimable probability, just as the art of a supposedly self-sustained esthetic sphere will pursue a proper form. But even art, if genuine, is not noncommittal. Rather, its own voice is that of a cipher. Despite the analogy between speculation and art as another language of transcendence, "conceptual poetry" is a misnomer since it confuses the specific traits of both: the *visual* elucidation of absolute consciousness on the one hand, and its *cogitative* elucidation on the other.

As speculation never gets beyond the cipher, it can see transcendence in no form of being as such. In its symbols it is only *nearer* to transcendence *and farther* from it. Its world, expressed in the cipher script, does not lie on an even plane. The positive factuality which it accentuates is a remote spur of being, in an existence alien to me; it is nearer as that which decisively affects me from outside; it comes closest in my own action. The regions of being in existence—the regions we can survey in the categories—are not all equally relevant to the analogical thought of speculation. As a cipher, none of them fits being in the same way as any other; none of them fits it intrinsically and entirely.

4. Immanence and Transcendence

There is being for us if it has a voice in existence. A pure beyond is empty; it is as if it were not. Hence the possibility of experiencing being proper requires an *immanent transcendence*.

Yet this immanence is patently paradoxical in character. Immanent (precisely as distinct from transcendent) is that which can be concurrently experienced by everyone in consciousness at large. In other words: the world is immanent. Also immanent is the existential certainty of being oneself (a certainty not accessible in any consciousness at large but present in the respective self-being, as distinct from transcendent being—in other words, from that which to Existenz is the essence it relates to). When transcendent being comes into the presence of an Existenz, however, it does not do so as itself, for there is no identity of Existenz and transcendence. It comes to mind as a *cipher,* and even then not as an object that is this object, but *athwart all objectivity,* so to speak. Immanent transcendence is an immanence that has instantly vanished again, and it is a transcendence that has come to exist as the language of a cipher. As in consciousness at large it is the experiment that mediates between subject and object, so it is the cipher that mediates between Existenz and transcendence.

The cipher is what brings transcendence to mind without obliging transcendence to become an objective being, and without obliging Existenz to become a subjective being. It is a decline from the original genuine presence into the sphere of consciousness at large when exegesis of a cipher makes of transcendence an object, something we know, or when subjective modes of conduct are conceived and bred as organs for the perception and production of the metaphysical experience.

In both cases the unfathomable dialectics of cipher being would be voided. We would be left with a beyond, another world of transcendence, and with the empirical living of this world. Objectively, God and the world would face each other as strangers. The split would open an abyss between unrelated separates. A dead chasm would separate out-and-out otherness. Initially, in playful fantasizing, the chasm could be filled ad infinitum with intermediate links; but since the world alone has an existence, it would soon permit deletion of the deity and of all fantasies that have been interjected. There is only one world, an inconclusive one without entirety, in which we have the infinite experience of being as extant existence. Once immanence and transcendence have become completely heterogeneous, we drop transcendence. With transcendence and immanence conceived as downright otherness for one another, they must—if transcendence is not to go down—evolve their own present dialectics for us in the cipher, as immanent transcendence.

The cipher motion shifts from language to language.

The original, present reading of the cipher script is without method, not volitive, not to be produced according to plan. It is like a gift from the source of being. As a mundane ascertainment of transcendence it seeks out the light from the root of possible Existenz, and its content is not an advancement of knowledge but the historic truth of transparent existence.

Method is the mark, not of the original experience, but of its communication in the second language. In myths and revelations, this communication proceeds by translating the original cipher into the specific objectivity of personifications and visions, of visionary history and dogmatic definitions; as a language of parables it is not lost when the original reality ceases to be attainable in this form. Another way is to let reality speak *as reality*, in such a form and with such an emphasis that as reality it will become a cipher. Transcendent experiences will then be conveyed by immanent facts—conveyed indirectly, hidden from me as long as I see only empirically real things, but manifest to an Existenz that hears what is truly at issue. Truth would be lost if its transformation into something universal and identical for all were to deprive it of its indirect language.

The diversity of symbols is not the world entirety of a closed system. Each symbol already contains totality and unity as phenomena of transcendence. In the symbol I become one with that to which, cast back upon myself, I relate at the same time. Thus there are differences of proximity and distance, but every symbol remains one sole aspect of transcendence. While existence is extant and grasped in relations from one to the other—with systematic cognition accordingly the same as cognition of existence—symbolic being cuts across existence. To perceive it means to break through the tangled web of empirical realities and cogent validities in order to stand directly before the unknown.

Beginning with the first language, to which each subsequent one refers as its fulfillment, the world and transcendence are one without being identical. In the third language, when our thought seeks to make them understood, it begins as intellect. The intellect at large, unable to conceive even transcendence otherwise than as existence on the same plane with the world, can see two possibilities: either the world is everything, the world is God, or there are the world and transcendence —in which case they are two, and transcendence is that other existence in the beyond that is not here. This alternative between pantheism and a transcendence in the beyond is intellectually valid; but when an Existenz assures itself of transcendence, it can find it only in unity with the world—in a unity which at the same time maintains the downright otherness of transcendence vis-à-vis existence, so that transcendence can be seen neither as merely mundane nor as purely transcendent. To a transcending Existenz *the intellectual alternative is a decline,* whether to a pantheistic immanence without transcendence or to the worldless transcendence in a beyond. What happens in genuine transcending is the deepest possible affirmation of the world, performed toward mundane existence as a cipher language because that language transfigures the world, and what we secretly hear in it is the voice of transcendence. In the split, however, there could be no affirmation of the world without delusion, for an opaque existence has no satisfaction in itself.

This is why believers use the third language to overcome the intellect —which either absolutizes the difference between the world and transcendence or denies it altogether—and to try to objectify the dialectics that are originally present in the cipher script but speculatively accessible only in the form of a thought voided by its own motion.

5. Reality in the Ciphers

In the medium of the second language a child can experience transcendent being as unquestioned reality. In his own life, seeing and acting, he grows into the world of which he is aware as the one truth—clearly and happily aware with his entire being, though only with a vague knowledge. Then the experience of existence dims his early view. He no longer sees all men in the same relation to God; his eye is sharpened for human limitations, for abuse and destructiveness. He has to fight for the being that threatens to elude him, for the being he may lose.

For the child in his original awakening there is no historical objectivity, nothing but the pure present of reality and truth. It is only in retrospect, in the decomposing consciousness of a knowledge about to part with reality, that what used to be true being pure and simple becomes known to him as the inherited tradition of his particular historicity. The original consciousness is transformed into a historic one. The reality that founds an Existenz looks like a typical chain of events when it is observed as a process.

The objectivity of metaphysical tradition lifts a nascent Existenz up to its own level before dissolving in the Existenz that has come to be. There is something durable about historical objectivity; no meaningful doubt can be cast upon it until the individual Existenz comes to itself. Toward the awakening consciousness, authority was claimed by a stock of traditions; their demand for recognition was met before it could be questioned. As world orientation expands, this claim is opposed by experiences in existence that may drive a person to believe nothing that is not finite and empirical. Later, when this positivism breaks down at its self-perceived limits, it becomes possible to regain the objectivity whose initial existence was purely authoritative. Integrated into the motion of the existential ascertainment of transcendence, it serves now as a function in which the substantial ground comes to mind, for the transcendent objectivity in the ciphers of the second language can neither be invented according to principles nor be arbitrarily conceived *ad hoc;* it can only be historically acquired. First acknowledged in historical tradition, then tested by questioning, finally either rejected or adopted, it helps mold the new Existenz. The metaphysical objectivity that has been handed down is a single, precious, irreplaceable asset, rooted in prehistoric origins and acquired by mankind in its destinies over some thousands of years.

After the great crisis of reflection, the previous reality of the ciphers of the second language, of the myths and revelations, cannot be regained identically. Discrete myth, revelation, and mythical reality are objective contents whose forms seem to be mutually exclusive; and they do fight in fact, but in the individual consciousness in which one of them will address the other even though repelling it. In the crisis they fight with the seriousness of a struggle in which my own self is at stake. The crisis leaves the individual on his own; subjecting the authoritative tradition of myth and revelations to questioning, he is now forced to find his way through mutually exclusive claims. In the end the struggle declines into a defense against the possibility of deceptive concealment, when nothing but mythical reality is still a strictly and undoubtedly transcendent language; by then, revelation and discrete myths may retain the relative significance of historic memories. Contents that have been preserved speak in forms that are past, but in more pallid fashion, no longer in a complete present that has become reality.

A question that becomes urgent, then, is how to distinguish an *idea of transcendence* from *transcendence*. Any cipher language may deteriorate into a dreamlike play with mere ideas; what matters is where the language is reality. The reality of transcendence—a clear-cut reality only in the first language—draws all mere ideas into itself, so to speak. Ideas are fluid, in incessant tranformation; but transcendent reality is without possibility. It is itself in the original cipher, for whose reading the forms of the second and third language serve when they keep their true meaning.

A cipher as such is thus not transcendence. Although its reading leads to mythical figures; although in the growing transparency of natural and historical reality I mythicize ideas into objective powers; although I heroicize many an Existenz—it is still only beyond particular mysticisms and beyond any cipher that I can transcend to the true transcendent abyss and ground of all mythicism, to the ground I cannot mythicize any more.

Ambiguity of Ciphers

If a cipher is that in which transcendence and a mundane being are unified at one time, the unity ends when we think of the cipher as meaning something else. In the cipher script *the symbol is inseparable from that which it symbolizes.* Ciphers bring transcendence to mind, but there is no interpreting them. To interpret, I would have to split what is only in union. I would compare a cipher with transcendence, but transcendence only appears to me in the cipher script; it is not the cipher script. My reading of ciphers would decline into a conception of purely immanent symbol relations. To read the ciphers is to stand in an unconscious symbolism, despite the attendant lucidity of consciousness, and I cannot know this symbolism once again, *qua* symbolism. A conscious symbolism—"having" things in the world through their relationship, through the fact that one relates to the other as something which is otherwise as well, in the sense of signs, of metaphors, comparisons, representations, models—is not a cipher script. This conscious symbolism gets it lucidity precisely from exegesis, but the unconscious symbolism of the ciphers is quite untouched by exegesis: what I comprehend when I interpret them is not the cipher script itself but a cipher script destroyed and denatured into mere symbolism. Interpreted, the cipher would have become as clear as the symbol, which can be shown to mean something that exists elsewhere. But the cipher is what it is; it cannot be clarified again by something else.

The symbolic relationship and our transcending beyond it enable us to make statements about the nature of the metaphysical cipher script, but that script itself is no relationship any more. It is unity in the existence of transcendence. Hence the prerequisite of a clear and undeceptive grasp on the transcendent cipher script is to be clear in our minds about symbolism as such.

1. Expression of Being and Communicative Expression

Possible symbolism pervades all of existence. I meet no one and nothing occurs to me that could not be an expression. This is either silently extant, expressing a being that does not answer when I question it, or else a communicative expression that addresses me and, questioned, will reply. The expression of being is universal; the communicative expression is confined to persons.

In man I perceive an expression of being in his physiognomy and in his involuntary gestures. There is no mutual exchange of speech between the perceived and the perceiver; the expression is a purely unconscious one of a person's nature, without any will to communicate or hold aloof. I perceive myself like this, in my own expression, and I seem like a stranger to me, like somebody else. Only afterwards am I startled because it is myself, and because my appearance, whether it frightened me or received my approval, turns now into an appeal to me.

What is perceptible in this fashion can be enunciated in statements about the character, the mood, the inner posture, or the temperament of a human being. The statements can be verified by observing the respective individual's conduct, and by recalling his life story. What we note in the expression is empirical—if we understand the word to mean not only what can be objectively experienced but what can be explored in contexts and judged according to criteria, as rightly or wrongly viewed. The perception of gesture and physiognomy has something of empirical psychology about it, since it concerns the expression of a being whose existence is accessible in other ways as well.

Yet even this existence, although empirical, is in no way identical at all times and for all men. The perception of a man's expression is not only a perception on the part of consciousness at large; it is a view of a free being by another free being. What is visible here depends on the person itself; when I state it, it is always still a possibility (both as an appeal to the other and as an appeal to myself, to look more deeply as I come to be myself). The empirical existence that is supposed to be grasped and determined in the expression is thus not flatly extant. Insofar as I objectify it into pure existence I restrict my perceptive faculties along with my commitment to an original relationship. I lose the human being and keep nothing but a character schema of extant qualities. Insofar as I truly penetrate, however, there will be a leap in the expression: it becomes possibility in a deeper sense as I get to the freedom I can see as the nobility and rank of a present existence; I get all the way to the ground of a man's being, which is like a past choice that he himself made before the beginning of time. To objective cognition, a thing either does or does not exist, and nothing is nobler than anything else; but in viewing expressions, rank and level qualify every view in him who understands and in him who is understood. The determination of extant existence is only one side of understanding expressions, a side which in truth cannot be isolated and which in the sense of generally valid cognition is always doubtful, too. What we grasp in such understanding, rather, is an extant existence with freedom behind it.

This understanding of *human* expressions covered empirical existence as well as freedom, and neither one without the other. It thus implied empirical verifiability as well as an appeal to freedom, though both within limits. But expression is not an exclusive human trait. *All things* seem to express a being. They seem to speak, in a sense, to have their rank, their peculiar nobility, and their corruptness. We experience this physiognomy of all existence in nature, in a landscape, also in the dark realities of man and his social history; we love it and hate it, adopt it with intensity or reject it in agony. But we cannot verify it as an empirical reality, and we can never encounter it as a being to whose freedom we might appeal. This physiognomy stays mute. A reality is unveiled here, and yet it will never be known, is not the same for every consciousness, and does not remain the same for me in the course of time. It appears transparent, yet there is no nailing it down even though all existence has to me its noble or ignoble rank—even though things impress me as splendid and magnificent or leave me untouched as indifferent or repel me as ugly and mean.

Communicative expression, as distinct from the mere expression of being, intends to convey something. This sort of expression alone is a language in the proper sense of the word, in the sense that allows all other expression to be termed "language" only metaphorically. In this expression lies an intended meaning with transferable contents. Issuing from it are challenges and appeals, questions and answers.

In communicative expression we also seek to *convey our own original perception of symbols.* In communication with myself, the second language makes me understand what in immediacy is real but murky. A symbolism does not really exist until it has become communicative. The echo in the perceiver lends communicability to the general side of the symbolism of all existence. What is original only in immediacy is conscious only in reproduction. The direct symbolism remains the source, but that symbolism is rarely perceived except insofar as it has become language; only in moments of a creative vision of being will language be produced and thus expanded.

The communicative expression is encompassing, since it is the means whereby all other expression too is translated into a communicable language. But the expression of being is encompassing inasmuch as communicative expression will be only an enclave in existence, and inasmuch as the whole existence of communicative expression comes once again to express a being, which it will unconsciously symbolize. Communicative expression is a lucidly intelligible thing which in its turn—when it is genuine rather than detached and dissolving in an empty clarity—continues to express the unintelligibility of being.

2. The Random Interpretability of Symbols

It takes a communicative language to turn the direct expression of being into something like a language. The symbolism that has been created in the echo gives us a grasp on the meaning of the expression; but when we solidify this meaning in a thought, or when we try to define it, we are engaging in the kind of symbol interpretation that happens along outwardly comparable lines in areas as disparate as dream interpretation, astrology, interpretation of myths, physiognomics, psychoanalysis, and metaphysics. The meaning we ask about in each case varies, depending on the symbolism we mean. In the age-old interpretation of dreams, for instance, it is coming events and fates; in astrology it is the individual's past and future, his qualities and occupations, his good and bad luck; in physiognomics it is character types. There are also shifts between these areas. In psychoanalysis it is repressed drives and experiences that show in fantasies, dreams, modes of conduct; in interpretive metaphysics it would be the being of transcendence. What each symbol makes only apparent is meant as itself, not as a phenomenon any more, but as being. Everything is interpreted, the original symbols as well as the symbols of those symbols. As long as men have been living on earth they have been practicing exegesis in a vast variety of forms and thoughts whose one common feature is their endless, random ambiguity.

If we are to state any meaning, an endlessness of random possibilities unfolds before us unless an arbitrary will calls a halt and restrains the interpretive spirit. Whether we are dealing with the dream interpretation of Antiquity or with that of psychoanalysis, with mythological exegesis or with a logical-metaphysical one of the world—what will always be laid down is a set of rules and principles under which simply anything is possible in a particular case. Every counterinterpretation that may occur will be sublimated, and all opposition forestalled by interpreting it and turning it into a building block and proof of one's own true interpretation. As Bayle put it: "Allegorical interpretations are mental eyes that can be multiplied ad infinitum and enable one always to find what he is looking for." The line is borne out as much by mythological exegesis as by psychoanalysis. The champions of such interpretation show a peculiar assurance, because they feel irrefutable but forget that if their principles leave no argument against them immune to use as an argument for them, neither do they have a chance to prove their supposed insights. Of the metaphysical thought systems that might make sense as a cipher script but are applied as a knowledge that seems to understand all things, the most magnificent example is Hegel's logic. His dialectics, his way of permitting each counterargument to be turned into a link of his own truth from the outset, is unique of its kind. Contradiction itself is taken into the system, understood in each of its forms, and overcome; it can no longer come from without. The meanings mean themselves as well as the opposite.

3. Symbolism and Cognition

It is untruthful to take symbolism for cognition. It becomes monotonous to interpret existence in line with a few principles to which auxiliary hypotheses brought up at will seem to give power over all things. The procedure seems to put us in control of our own and the world's bottom grounds, and yet we only move in a self-made circle of formulas that will somehow fit everywhere. Cognitively a symbol is nothing, and this is not altered by the fact that *by convention* a set of symbols may become a sign language, a technical means in greatly varying form. Mathematical symbols, chemical symbols, the models used in physics and other natural sciences, all these have their definable, unequivocal meanings in the service of rational cognition. But they are not cognition itself.

A metaphysical symbol, on the other hand, has the being of a cipher, and in the cipher it is itself. Real being for empirical knowledge is only a being in contexts and dependencies; it is by way of those that it is understood. Genesis and causality show us whether and how a thing exists. No existing thing is itself; everything is in relations. Symbolic being as a cipher of transcendence, on the other hand, is not in any relation; it is only directly for one who can see it. It cuts across reality, so to speak, in a dimension of depth; a man may immerse himself in that dimension, but he cannot step out of it without promptly losing it all.

Symbols, therefore, cannot be researched; they can only be grasped and created. Even research into the language of past and historical views of symbols is possible only if the scientist meets the subjective conditions: if he is able to see a symbol and, before any research, to hold himself open for it.

4. Interpretable and Viewable Symbols

As soon as we trace the process of meaning in thought, separating it from that which is meant, we land in an endless universal symbolism. Everything can mean everything. There is a to and fro, a universal interchangeability; it all depends upon the point of view, from which certain rules and schemata apply. A symbolism that can be interpreted is objective; its sense is soluble. It is a matter of comparisons and designations, solid and lasting only due to conventions, or to habits that are psychologically comprehensible.

We no sooner approach the symbol as a cipher of transcendence, however, than it *can be viewed*. A viewable symbolism permits no separation of the sign from its meaning, but embraces both in one. We do separate them again, to make clear to ourselves what we have comprehended, but we do this in a new symbolism, not in interpreting one by means of the other. We only elucidate what we already had. We return and gaze into new depths. Viewable symbols as sounds of the cipher language are accessible only to such deepening by an Existenz. An interpretable symbolism exists for consciousness at large.

If I ask what symbols ultimately mean, an interpretive symbolism actually tells me such ultimates. A mythological theory will hold, for instance, that events in nature and human actions in agriculture and handicraft are what everything is really all about. Psychoanalysis cites the libido; and Hegelian metaphysics, the dialectical motion of the logical concept. The ultimate may thus be a vapid reality as well as the *logos*. Whatever its kind, its definition is unequivocal. Yet the symbols which mean this unequivocal thing at the end of so much interpretation —these mean everything and thus remain equivocal and indefinite.

A viewable symbolism knows no ultimate. It is not focused from the outset on a being of which it is a phenomenon and which is already known in other ways. Rather, for all its manifestness, for all its openness to the present moment, this symbolism has at the same time an unfathomable depth from which it alone transmits the light of indefinite being.

This viewable, not properly interpretable symbolism can only be the cipher script of transcendence. In it, a thought posing as exegesis becomes a symbol itself. Seeing through the *logos*, the eye that reads the cipher script gets to the ground of the *logos*. All exegesis becomes the voice of a cipher legible for Existenz—for any Existenz that perceives in the cipher the being it believes as its transcendence.

5. *Exegesis in Circles*

Cognitive interpretation of symbols has an endless, random character that makes it incapable of proof or disproof and destroys it as cognition; but to their exegesis in a circle every turn around its axis may give the symbolic character of the third language, the speculative reading of the cipher script. From the cognitive point of view a logical circle is empty, and arguments in it become nonsensical; but in another dimension, when the substance of an Existenz fulfills it, the circle is the present view of transcendence as imparted in the speculative language. It is the viewpoint from which all interpretations that seek to fathom the whole are indeed modes of creating and reading a cipher script.

Claims of cognitive significance for the symbol are scientifically void, but in its cipher character it invites the question whether a possible Existenz sees *its* transcendence in the symbol. Since the criterion of the circle's truth is existential rather than logical, the question at each point is where I am involved, where I am made aware of that truth by my self-being. The question is not, for example, which is right: the psychoanalytical view of being or its dialectical pondering a la Hegel. The question is which one I freely accept—for they are neither right nor wrong; cognitively they are nothing. *What convinces me is not the intellect, nor is it empirical observation; it is what I am and what I want.* My standard is no longer that of a scientific, methodical inquiry with a final result; I ask instead whether a cipher language is existentially true or existentially ruinous. What has collapsed as cognition remains a symbol for the way a self-being knew its transcendence. And I in turn defend or deny the truth of this way by my own reading of the cipher script, which is my experience of transcendence. This reading tells me each time what is the shallow exegesis of simply relating things in the world—a procedure that always takes me back to the ground I know already—and what becomes a cipher of being in which I can immerse myself and not strike bottom.

6. Random Ambiguity and Ambiguity of Ciphers

An *interpretable* symbolism makes each individual case endlessly ambiguous, but the ultimate that is conceived and interpreted in it is unequivocally meaningless. The *viewable* symbolism of the genuine cipher has a different ambiguity.

If exegesis would turn the cipher into a knowledge—in other words, if it is supposed to be objective and valid—the cipher will be existentially uprooted and in that form indeed as ambiguous as all interpretive symbolism. But it does not have this kind of ambiguity if it is not interpreted at all, if its roots are kept intact.

On the other hand, if an original cipher is so interpreted that thinking turns the exegesis back into *another cipher*, the ambiguity, while just as great, is not a random one. It lies in the diversity of possible existential adoptions. Not until an Existenz is historically present will the possibility of adoption become unequivocal for that Existenz, in a way that is nontransferable and unknowable for the Existenz itself. The unequivocality lies in the fact that nothing substitutes for the transcendence that fulfills this Existenz.

In random exegesis as supposed knowledge the *point of departure* is always *definite*, the *interpretation* is *endless*, and the *goal of interpretation* is a *finite being*.

In interpreting the cipher script, the point of departure is the *infinite presence of transcendence*, the *cipher* is *finite and definite*, and the goal of interpretation is that *indefinite*, already present infinity.

Exegesis in quest of a knowledge starts with the finite; it is from the finite that we vainly seek a way to master the infinite by endless interpretation. The interpretation never really happens; it only seems to happen in formulas that do no more than accumulate or repeat themselves, formulas that will in no way master the facts. When we interpret symbolism as cognition, all things grow stale because they are purely finite. The infinite is lost in unwilling obeisance to the finite. When we take up the cipher script, on the other hand, we start with the infinite; it is the infinite presence of transcendence that turns finite things into ciphers.

The *unequivocality* of the infinite presence of transcendence is a current completion, a peak in the temporal existence of Existenz. Yet wherever the cipher acquires a general side, wherever I find it communicable and encounter it in the manner in which those peaks later speak to me, there is *ambiguity*, due to the varied possibilities of existential adoption and realization.

For the metaphysical posture of questioning, there is thus nothing definitive about the cipher script. There are ciphers wherever they freely bring transcendence to mind, and there is always some other way to read them. They never contain a conclusion about transcendence, as if this had now been figured out. *From where I stand*, the cipher remains permanently ambiguous—which means, speaking from the standpoint of transcendence, that transcendence *has other ways yet to convey itself*. No cipher script could come to be definitive in temporal existence. It would not remain a possibility, then, and unequivocal perfection would take its place. Now a realm that does not yet commit us, a realm that may possibly commit us, and then a commitment for this specific Existenz, it would remain neither the one nor the other; it would not be a cipher script any more but would become the sole being of transcendence. Now always particular, without any chance to become a whole, it would cancel itself in totality. Now evanescent and historic, it would become extant and absolute.

The infinite ambiguity of all ciphers shows in temporal existence as their nature. There is no end to the interpretation of ciphers by other ciphers, of visual ones by speculative ones, of real ones by artificial ones—this sort of exegesis is the medium in which Existenz would like to assure itself of its transcendence and preparatorily to create its own possibilities. A system of ciphers is an impossibility, because they would enter into such a system only as finite things, not as carriers of transcendence. Their infinite ambiguity bars a system of possible ciphers. A system may itself be a cipher, but it can never be a draft that meaningfully covers the authentic ciphers.

Existenz as the Place of Reading Ciphers

1. Reading Ciphers by Self-being

Reading ciphers is so unlike comprehending a being independent of me that it is quite impossible unless I am myself. Transcendent being in itself is independent of me but inaccessible as such; only things in the world have the mode of accessibility. About transcendence I learn only so much as I become myself. Its presence—constant in itself—is dimmed by my flagging; my extinction, my reduction to the existence of pure consciousness at large, makes it disappear. Seized upon, it is to me the only being there is, the being that remains what it is without me.

Just as our sense organs must be intact for us to perceive the realities of the world, so must the self-being of possible Existenz be present to be affected by transcendence. If I am existentially deaf, I cannot hear the transcendent language in the object.

It is not yet by scientific insight, therefore, that I penetrate the cipher script, by the collection and rationalistic adoption of material. I penetrate it, with the help of that material, only in the motion of an existential life. The experience of the first language instantly *calls for possible Existenz to commit itself.* It is not an experience that can be gathered and identically demonstrated to everyone, for it takes freedom to gain. It is not the random immediacy of a lived experience, but the echo of being in the cipher.

If all things may become ciphers, the being of ciphers seems a random thing. If it has truth and reality, it must be *verifiable.* In world orientation I verify by making something perceptible or logically compelling, by producing and achieving something. In existential elucidation I verify by my way of dealing with myself and with another, of being assured of myself by the unconditionality of my actions; I verify by the motions I experience inwardly as I am uplifted, as I love and hate, as I seclude myself and as I fail. But I cannot directly verify the truth of the cipher, for when I state it objectively, it is a game that does not claim to be valid and thus does not need to be justified. To myself, however, it is not just a game.

When I am reading ciphers, I am responsible, because I read them only through my self-being whose possibility and veracity appears to me in the way I read the ciphers. I verify by my self-being—without having another yardstick than this very self-being, which I recognize by the transcendence of the cipher.

The reading of ciphers is thus performed in inner action. I try to tear myself out of my constant decline; I take myself in hand and experience the decision that comes from me; but this process of self-becoming is as one with listening for transcendence, without which it would not be. In my actions—in resistance, success, failure and loss, finally in my thinking which conceives all of that and qualifies it again—I have the experiences in which I hear the cipher. What happens, and what I do in it, is like question and answer. I hear from what happens to me, by reacting to it. My wrestling with myself and with things is a wrestling for transcendence, which appears to me solely in this immanent form, as a cipher. I am driven to the sensory presence of factual mundane experience, to real action in victory and defeat, because there alone is the field where I can hear what is.

It is foolish to think of being as that which everyone might know. What men have been: what made them sure of transcendence; how transcendence fulfilled them; which reality was *the* reality for them; to what inner life this brought them; what they loved—all this will never be presently grasped by one individual. There is no way of being for everyone. All things stay dark to him who is not himself.

What I grasp in reading ciphers of transcendence is thus a being I hear by *struggling* for it. It is indeed only with transcendent being that I have a sense of being proper; there alone do I find peace. But I am always back in the restless struggle, am forsaken and like someone lost; I lose myself when I lose contact with being.

Never to approach the hidden God directly is the fate which a philosophical Existenz must bear. Only the ciphers speak, if I am ready. Philosophizing, I remain suspended between straining to realize my potential and receiving the gift of my reality. I am somehow consorting with myself and with transcendence, but only seldom will an eye seem to look at me in the dark. Day in, day out, it is as if there were nothing. In his eerie abandonment man seeks a more direct access, objective guarantees, and firm support; he takes God's hand in prayer, so to speak, turns to authority, and sees the Godhead in personal form—and only in this form is it God at all, while as the Godhead it maintains its undefinable distance.

2. Existential Contemplation

Left to us, in philosophical abandonment, is the existential contemplation of absolute consciousness. This is not prayer—prayer, which delimits philosophizing, is philosophically inaccessible, hence dubious—but as *imagination* it is the eye of possible Existenz, committed to its active struggle, lighting and fulfilling its way.

In consciousness at large we dissolved the reality of existence into objects of world orientation. But imagination lets us see being in the reality that has not been rationally dissolved, and again in its very dissolution—not, however, as if there were a factual being hidden behind existence and now fantastically deduced from it. To our imagination, being is visibly present in the cipher.

I cannot know what being is, the way I know existence. I can read the cipher of existence only if I do not go beyond its symbolic character. In world orientation I know existence by concepts, but the being in existence can be read only by imagination; it is the paradox that no matter what exists, an Existenz cannot take it for all of being. To preserve itself in transcendence, Existenz detaches itself from all existing certainties as such. Our philosophical imagination does employ symbols also, but not as building blocks for a structure of existence; because in that imagination we do not mean the concepts as themselves, they turn into ciphers for us, as does everything else. This transparent view of existence is like a physiognomic viewing—but not like the bad physiognomy aimed at a form of knowledge, with inferences drawn, from signs, on something underneath; it is like the true physiognomy whose "knowledge" is all in the viewing. In the cipher I confront, as being, what has to do with the root of my own being and yet will not become one with me. I am truthful by being myself in the cipher, without pursuing ends or serving interests of my existence.

The reality of the ciphers of being that are comparable to a physiognomic image is *given* as well as *made*. It is given because it is not invented, not derived from empty subjectivity, but speaking in existence only. And it is made, because it does not exist as a cogent, generally valid object identical for everyone; the cipher reality exists on the basis of Existenz and its imaginative view of its own closeness to being. The cipher is neither psychologically comprehensible as a product of the soul nor objectively explorable by sciences as a reality. It is objective as the voice of a being and subjective as a mirror of the self—but of that self whose roots are linked with the being that appears as the cipher.

I *abide* in the cipher. I do not come to know it, but I steep myself in it. Its entire truth lies in the concrete vision, in each historic fulfillment it brings. In nature, this being reveals itself to me only if I let the wholly singular configurations touch me as intimacies on the part of whatever exists like that right here, defying any generalization.

In reading ciphers I aim at *existence in time*. I must not let this existence evaporate, for then, along with reality, I would miss being. Nor may I turn existence into something fixed and extant, as does scientific world orientation, for along with freedom, which I do not meet in existence, I would lose my way to transcendence. Rather, the point of my existential imagination is to grasp all being as saturated with freedom. To read ciphers means to know about being in a sense that makes existent being and free being identical, so that in the deepest view of my imagination there will, so to speak, be neither the one nor the other, but the ground of both.

The speculative thought is a cipher script that has become communicable. I interpret, but my interpretation is no understanding of being; rather, in understanding I touch upon that which in the substance of being is essentially incapable of being understood. A speculative thought which I merely understand is thus not really understood unless it *brings me up against the unintelligible being* by which, and with which, I really am. The cogitative language is the medium of my understanding; it permits me to make intelligible to myself just where I met up with the unintelligible. But this understanding is not a better insight into things which an infinite process would eventually make quite intelligible; it is a clearer visualization of what lies beyond the antithesis of intelligible and unintelligible, of the being which in intelligibility makes an evanescent appearance. In understanding, Existenz encounters that which cannot be understood, and in both it encounters being. Comprehension becomes a decline when we take comprehensibility for being, and a turn toward incomprehensibility becomes a decline when the language of comprehension is destroyed and that which is simply, brutally given is accepted and done without question, as incomprehensible.

As consciousness at large I see nothing but sheer existence. Antinomies are built into my existential relations to transcendence; through these relations there is as yet no completion in time. But the eye of Existenz, contemplative imagination, makes it possible for me as I read the ciphers to have a sense of completion, of temporal fulfillment, for a vanishing moment. Imagination lets an Existenz find peace in being; the cipher transfigures the world. All existence becomes a phenomenon of transcendence; in this loving imagination whatever exists is viewed as a being for its own sake. No usefulness, no purpose, no causal genesis defines its being for me. No matter what it is: as a phenomenon it will be beautiful because it is a cipher.

There are no ciphers for a dull consciousness to which all is still one and the same, neither self-being nor nonself-being. Possibility, along with divisions, will arise only in a lucid consciousness. Now all existence will acquire, first, the positivity of empirical reality and the rationality of validity; it will cease to be transparent and to delude us in fantasies and dreams. But this does not make it a cipher script. Ciphers have to reveal themselves first, in a new leap; they are manifest when a self-being has firmly seized upon that positivity and rationality, so its transcending gaze may pierce them without confusion.

In time we are left with the ambiguity of contemplation. When we take a contemplative view of being in existence, its reality—as a merely contemplative one—will quickly turn noncommittal. Contemplation is a mode of Existenz that involves commitment only when it is transposed into the strictest unity with Existenz in its temporal reality. As a division into two spheres of life between which I shuttle, an ideal one of transcendence and a real one of existence, contemplation becomes untrue.

Conversely, *Existenz without the eye of imagination is without lucidity in itself*. It remains confined to a narrow, positive existence. Without reading ciphers, an Existenz lives blind.

Because of the constant proximity of decline I must, if I do not want to succumb to it, surmount it consciously in self-elucidation. To move in the world of symbols, to be gripped by that world, is initially no more than to live a possibility. I prepare myself in it, but I fool myself if vivid emotions lead me to mistake this possibility for the reality of the historic moment, the reality in which transcendence originally manifests itself to me.

What will speak as a cipher depends upon the Existenz that hears. Potentially ciphers speak everywhere, but they are not received everywhere. Embracing a cipher is a free choice made by the man who reads it. In the choice I convince myself that I have this kind of being because I have this kind of will—although my choice produces flatly nothing and I only receive what I choose.

What is a cipher does not lie all on one plane. What touches me distantly or strikes right at my heart; in which rank of being proper I hear the language; whether in the worst straits as in utter bliss I turn to nature or to man—this, through myself, defines my being.

3. Faith in Ciphers

All ciphers vanish for an Existenz that comprehends itself in its freedom to rise and to fall, in the freedom in which Existenz is not isolated but belongs in solidarity with others to something uncomprehended and encompassing. The existential origin of my grasp on transcendence comes to be understood in those unfixed, unfixable mythical and speculative forms whose rigid possession would prevent my uplifting. Uplifting demands their free adoption by an Existenz that will dare commit itself unreservedly in factual reality; it does not permit holding on to an extant objectivity that need only be acknowledged and agreed to.

If I am asked: "Do you really believe in your genius? Do you believe in immortality? Do you believe in the one transcendence?" I should have to answer as follows.

If the question issues from a consciousness at large, all this does not exist, for we cannot find it anywhere. If the question is addressed by an Existenz to my possible Existenz, however, I cannot reply in general statements, only in the motion of existential communication and factual conduct. If that motion does not demonstrate faith to an Existenz, there is no faith. A statement of its content is existentially questionable, because it is the first step in evading the challenge by way of objectivity.

I can no more state a faith objectively than I can promise things that happen only if they are due to the freedom of an Existenz. An expressed tenet of faith and a substantial, definite promise are both outwardly intelligible and therefore finite. Making no promises is a far surer ground of our being in existence, if it springs from a reluctance to anticipate what can be realized only by a free act—and if it happens with the sense of an inner commitment beyond all that can be promised. Likewise, it is in the nature of faith that in all statements its content will be simultaneously suspended if the believer is committed to his faith, by being sure of his transcendence.

Hence the answer: I do not know whether I believe. But when I philosophize, I communicate in thought movements that serve as modes of indirect commitment and appeal.

Existentially it is impossible to live our lives in pursuit of purely rationalistic purposes and goals of definable happiness. If the transcendently related communication defaults, for example, we feel an existential desolation of existence that we can neither adequately state nor purposely remove. But communication occurs in everyday life, in openmindedness and in a readiness that is not merely rationalistic; it occurs in the distinction of essentials and nonessentials, in agreement on that distinction, or in a conflict about it that will be instantly transposed into asking questions and being able to listen. Herein lies the possibility of a philosophical life whose veracity will be jeopardized at the same time, by the urge to be direct. However often our mental poverty may keep us from being direct, it is not the only barrier. What may be permitted to a prophet who breaks through all historic existence and reenters it from another world, so to speak, can be visualized in philosophy as an alien possibility; but it cannot be done in philosophy. Faith in ciphers does not lie in being voiced and preached.

Cipher Script
and Ontology

When I want to know what being is, I want to conceptualize this knowledge. Ontology, the doctrine of being as such, would necessarily give me profound satisfaction if I could come to myself in a knowledge which, *qua* knowledge, demonstrates its truth.

1. Ontology in the Great Philosophies

Ontology has been the basic intent of most philosophies, at least of those under the spell of Aristotle's *prima philosophia* that became the traditional skeleton of philosophical thought; and it has continued to be the form of philosophy even when that basic intent was rejected in principle. Ontology will not let go of us and will not cease, for in us lies an indestructible urge to know, and thus to possess, the essence of all things. That philosophies, despite their ontological structure, strike us as true philosophizing is due to their unification of something which only our situation has set apart: in the same train of thought they provide *cogent knowledge* of existence, *transcend* mundane existence to its ground, *appeal* to a listener who is free to take or refuse them, and *form a cipher* that comes to reveal transcendent being. It is the unheard-of power of the great philosophies that their basic thoughts touch these different sides at the same time. Conferring knowledge, volition, and vision in one, they touch the entire human being. Subsequently, then, it is the isolation of specific sides, the endless arguments that result, the transformation into academic subjects—in short, it is an appalling existential confusion that makes it hard to get a clear, original idea of these philosophies. They will be taken in their shells instead, will be robbed of their content, and will thus necessarily wither.

Kant's understanding of the form of all objective existence, and of the modes of its validity for us, is derived from their conditioning by the capacities of the human spirit, whose pivotal point is the self-being of the I. He makes it possible for us to feel our freedom; he understands both the necessity of beauty and its content in the supersensory substrate of mankind; he comprehends science, its point, and its limits. The edifice of his thoughts is meant to be cogent insight insofar as it elucidates human existence and its reference to being-in-itself. He determines being by its possibilities and draws up an anticipatory schema of what can, as a matter of principle, occur in human existence. In the same thought he transcends existence, bringing its phenomenality to mind by pacing off its limits as an object of knowledge as well as the limits of its perfectibility. All thoughts, however, are to Kant mere premises of the authentic appeal to freedom, of the appeal that is impossible unless that first transcending to the phenomenality of existence has been accomplished. It is from the pathos of this all-pervading appeal that Kant's most peripheral factual discussions derive their weight. Yet in the end, without his saying so, even this thought edifice is a cipher that seems to speak: "Such is being," it seems to tell us; "such as to make this existence possible." My will to know, my sense of freedom, my metaphysical contemplation—all are satisfied at the same time. I learn things I am going to have; I experience the deepest impulse for what I am doing; and I am gently touched by the cipher of transcendence.

Hegel's dialectical circle—of self-being confronting its own objectivity, returning from otherness to itself, and thus, in otherness, remaining with itself—this circle in its abundant variants simultaneously enunciates what existence is, what definitions of being are possible and necessary, and what the transcendence of true being means: namely, the manifestation of God in the presence of philosophical thinking. Hegel's listener is primarily challenged to read the cipher script of this philosophizing, but at the same time he receives an extant knowledge, is contemplatively uplifted from existence to being, and experiences a rather fainter impulse to self-being, even if in Hegel's case this sometimes seems to fade without a sound.

In the first case it is being as a *phenomenon* of existence that occupies the foreground of the one all-inclusive philosophical thought, of the thought that includes all possibilities: Kant circumnavigates the being which I am myself. In the second case the foreground is occupied by being-*in-itself*: this is what Hegel has in mind, what he regards as including existence. But what are constructions of being-in-itself, other than pure ciphers? As objects of cognition they cannot but founder on themselves, since I conceive them in my own existence, whereas being-in-itself passes the bounds of conceivability in existence. Metaphysically, of course, existence is like a mere shadow of being; but to us this shadow is the presence in which generally valid cognition can occur. Even so, almost all of philosophy has sought to take its standpoint in being itself rather than in that shadow. If it was philosophy, however, its thoughts are always reversible: what is said of being can be phrased also as referring to the existential uplift of man. Thus the grandiose ontological philosophy conceived by *Plotinus:* turned into a doctrine, and thus deprived of intelligibility, it seems to present a world image of all being and all existence; but original thinking along the lines of that philosophy will simultaneously discover in it an appeal to possible Existenz and a form of cipher writing. Plotinus takes a metaphysical standpoint in being itself, rather than an existentially elucidative one on grounds of our human situation; but he can manage this only because his construction and deduction of being elucidates Existenz and existence at the same time—an aspect lost in the lectures that transform his thinking into a thing we can know.

Although we cannot repeat this fusion of aspects in the great philosophies, it is by no means a shortcoming. The most substantial speculative ciphers have been written in those philosophies, in ways that would have been impossible without the fusion. To the philosophers, the appeal of existential elucidation formed another link in the thinking that became a cipher—not the thinking of empty logical forms in which thoughts are easily isolated and made stale; not a thinking of something or other; but a thinking aglow with being. In the dichotomy of consciousness, of course, an identity of being and thinking does not make sense, for in that dichotomy thinking aims at something else. But when thinking becomes a cipher, the identity does make sense. Wherever human thought would grasp being proper, the being of that thought was neither being-in-itself nor the subjectivity of random, accidental thought; it was this identity in the cipher—and then in such a way as to remain historic. The thought was the general side of it, but it was this side as a complete thought, with the thinker's being present as well as the thought's. Stated by itself, as a general thought, it became void or trivial, a joke or a curiosity. From Parmenides on, the great, fundamental philosophical thoughts were the ones in which thinking and being were one, the ones conceived in such unity, and a logical dissection of these thoughts was tantamount to desecration. To be accessible as a language at all, they need to be animated by a new self-being. Then we can feel what was really meant and done in them. This thinking itself was reality, and its unreflective, self-understood character was its strength; its limit was that it could never be true more than once. For in any successor who was still thinking the thoughts but was no longer himself in that thinking, the lack of rational self-comprehension in his doings became untruthfulness. He would no longer take a cipher for a cipher, but would regard his thinking as cogent and objectify it unilaterally; he would no longer think with his self-being, only with his intellect. His thoughts, no longer replete with the thinker's own historic fate, would be treated like a knowledge that can be passed on.

2. Ontology Impossible for Us

Ontology is bound to crumble, for our knowledge of existence is confined to world orientation, and objective knowledge as such, to possible definitions of thought in a doctrine of categories. In existential elucidation the essence of knowledge is to appeal to freedom, not to obtain results, and the knowledge of transcendence is a contemplative immersion in unstable and ambiguous ciphers. Nor is it ontology to know about the movement of the inner postures as consciousness at large and possible Existenz—what I get in this knowledge, if I am clear in my mind about the structure of philosophizing, is a grasp on myself rather than a grasp on being. All these are ways of an inconclusive search for being, but they do not make being extant. For me as existence and possible Existenz, therefore, my insight into the disjointness of being puts an end to my desire for ontology and transforms it into the impulse to be myself in order to attain the being I can never gain as knowledge. At first, this self-attainment concerns only the being yet to be decided; it is a matter of free Existenz, not of transcendence. But only this being, which I gain in decision, has access to transcendence. The place of ontological being is taken by the existence of the cipher, which is always historic and never of flatly general validity.

Doing all in one was the depth and grandeur of the original philosophical thought. For us this is no longer possible. Having seen through the fusion of aspects which unconsciously gave these philosophies their unique import, we would be confused by a repetition. Our force is distinction; we have lost the naïve approach. Trying to restore what once upon a time, in naïveté, was marvelously possible and real would produce spurious structures and make ourselves untruthful. To us, the unity of the fusion is deceptive unless it is conscious cipher writing. Ciphers are to us the sublimation of any ontology that has not become a particular definition of mundane modes of being, or a methodical awareness of ways to the ascertainment of being that can never come to a conclusion.

Ontology as a knowledge of what being really is, or as a desire to know this in the form of concepts that would let us construe it, would destroy our real search for being, the search which a possible Existenz pursues in its transcendently related decisions. Ontology deludes us by absolutizing a supposed source of otherness. It ties us to an objectified being and voids our freedom. It paralyzes communication, as if I could achieve my sense of existence by myself alone; it blinds us to really substantial possibilities, prevents us from reading the ciphers, and makes us lose transcendence. In ontology we see being as one and as many, but not as the being of possible Existenz, which can be only this and no other. The freedom of Existenz demands distinction, which puts an end to ontology.

We do not consider the ontology of the great philosophers as the sort that calls for critical negation; it gets to be that sort only when it is transferred—but then at once. This is why the adoption of these philosophers requires us to begin by rending their structures. In these edifices we distinguish elucidation of existence, categorial definition, material world orientation, an appealing elucidation of Existenz, and a reading of ciphers. Not until they have been separated can we make a truly lucid return to the unity of that cipher script. It is a unity restored from its separate elements which we now face, for historic adoption or rejection by our own self-being, and only now can we clearly hear the real voice of a historic self-being as it knew its transcendence. By their elucidation of existence, their world orientation, their doctrine of categories, their existential challenge—all of which they are too, and at the same time—these philosophies bring us in touch with the being of Existenz, as it was for the man who could think in this manner.

3. Reading Ciphers as Distinct from Ontology

Ontology is the way of solidifying being proper into a *knowledge* of being, while reading ciphers is the experience of being *in suspension.*

Ontology continues in the comprehension of being what is possible as a cogent knowledge of finite things. This too, of course, is already of limited solidity. Cognition of empirical existence as it is in fact is inescapable; but in the form of known empirical existence, being is never definitively extant, only grasped up to its current limit, and that faultily. The categories come to provide definitions for all things that can occur in existence and for all men we can meet there; but each of these definitions is finite. The elucidation of existence shows us structures of the existence we are, and yet, although in principle it comprises the whole of consciousness at large, this elucidation is carried by the vitality of each individual being and thus itself dependent: conceived from points of view which are individual in their turn, and out of existential interests already shaping the elucidating thought in the direction of a cipher script. The ontological way, on the other hand, is to complete all these objective definitions and certainties, not to comprehend and to void them within their limits.

In reading ciphers I stay with the basic experience that can be acquired in all forms of definite knowledge: wherever I grasp being, it is relativized by a being I fail to grasp. Ontology disintegrates into a historically evanescent cipher. For where I transcend to the being beyond which there is no path, to the intrinsic being which I am not, but which I can perceive only as my self-being, there I have reached the end of the solidity and determinacy that gives a permanent side to my thoughts of the being which precedes the cipher. A maximum of suspension, too, will be achieved in questions of intrinsic being, because it is present in the most vanishing ways. The extant absolute, the cogent thought, is relative to a mere consciousness at large; but only the loosening of possible Existenz lets intrinsic being be grasped so that all relativity, all sublimation of the modes of being, serves this one suspension that makes me aware of being. My intellect and my vital will would solidify me in existence and detach me from transcendent being. They teach me to see being in duration, and in timeless thought. They push me toward ontology, toward a knowledge of being pure and simple; but as possible Existenz I free myself from these shackles and convert them into materials of being as I read the ciphers, in which being comes into the presence of Existenz.

Ontology originated as the fusion of all modes of thought into one encompassing thought aglow with being; subsequently it became the doctrine that *the one being can be known.* Reading ciphers, on the other hand, reserves the true *unity for acts* of existential reality, because thinking in ciphers does not veil the disjointness for knowledge.

Once ontology is rent, divided into the methods and contents it had been fusing—thus turning in fact into the reading of a currently, historically singular cipher script—the conscious reading of ciphers seems to restore the unity on a new base. We experience it in the inner action of immersing ourselves in the ground of self-being. Read as being, it comprises everything. Objectified, however, it is a unity which on its general side is instantly a mere possibility—not in the sense that transcendent being could possibly be that way (the false procedure of metaphysical world hypotheses), but in the sense that a possible fulfillment of this universal lies in the One of Existenz.

For us, therefore, true unity comes only in historic reality: it lies *in the actions of each self-being* to which the fusion of the modes of thinking becomes capable of achievement in the cipher script. Ontology must be dissolved, to open the way for the individual's return to the concreteness of present Existenz. Not until he goes this way of realizing his being will transcendent being become perceptible for him—perceptible in the ciphers into which his whole existence turns. Clear division in the thoughts that are conceived and uttered is a premise of this existential unity. It is correct that they belong together, are torn apart, and are true only together; but this "together" itself, as a conception, is always untrue unless the fusion of thoughts is the real being of the thinking Existenz and therefore nontransferable. Truth lies in self-being and in its transcendent fulfillment, not in philosophical thoughts in which unity is objectified and conceived as transferable knowledge. There can be no real unity until the thought is torn. In ontology, existence must involuntarily be seen in isolation before a universal known as the union of all; in reading ciphers, on the other hand, the unique universal of transcendence is viewed, in the reader's inner action, out of the uniqueness of Existenz.

Hence, if the content of ciphers is to be *talked* about as we philosophize, *the disjointness will enter into the ciphers themselves as a generalized language.* Not only the order of concepts in the metaphysical language—an order from the realm of world orientation—but the existential appeal of elucidating possibilities remains disjoint In the historicity and ambiguity of each language, transcendent being is not validly extant. We conceive it in steps, but not in a single, regular row of steps. This shows in the many heavens and fore-heavens, in the types of gods with their orders of rank and antitheses, as much as in Goethe's line: "I personally cannot be content with one way of thinking. As a poet and artist I am a polytheist; as a natural scientist I am a pantheist. Should I feel the need of a God for my personality, as a moral human being, that too has been provided for."

False Proximity
to Transcendence

Having taken shape in myths and in speculation, transcendence has come nearer to us, so to speak—but falsely nearer if we believe we have reached it directly, as itself, rather than as a cipher.

We cannot even ask what transcendence is, apart from the human being it is for. This does not mean, however, that transcendence as such might be drawn into existence. Mystics have dared to deny that the deity might be without man; but an Existenz is aware that it has not created itself. The proposition that God as transcendence is even without man seems to an Existenz the inescapable form of thinking negatively what defies a positive conception.

The cipher as transcendent language is the boundary in which transcendence is near to man, but not near as itself. Because the cipher of our world is not legible without leaving a remainder; because, to put it in mythical terms, the cipher of the devil is as visible as that of the deity; because the world is not a direct revelation but a mere language that will not be generally valid, is historically audible to Existenz alone, and even for an Existenz is not to be definitively deciphered—for all these reasons, hiding is the way in which transcendence shows. It is remote because as itself it is inaccessible. It is also alien; since there is nothing to compare it with, it is the incomparable total otherness. Like a strange power, it comes into this world from its distant being, speaks to Existenz, and approaches it without ever displaying more than a cipher.

The tension between Existenz and this hidden transcendence is the life of Existenz. Truth, in this life, is pursued, felt, and seen in questions put to fate and in its answers, and yet, as long as temporal existence lasts, truth remains under a shroud. The tension is the authentic phenomenon of self-being, but it is agony at the same time. To escape the agony, man wants to bring the deity really close to him, to resolve the tension, to know what is, what he can hold on to, what he can give himself up to. He will take that which as a cipher is possible truth and will absolutize it into being.

a. In complete immanence, *man* would make *himself the sole being.* Outside of him there would be nothing but the material he acts upon. He alone would be what matters; by himself he would be what he is. There would be no God, no room for the thought of God. The thought would seem to distract man from himself, to lull him to sleep, and to keep him from realizing his potential.

In this absolutization—an impossible one to carry out—we talk as if we knew what man is. What involuntarily slips in here is the human vitality, the human average, or a specific human ideal. As soon as the question of man is seriously raised, however, he is the being that could be understood only if its transcendence were understood. Man is that which strives beyond itself; he is not sufficient unto himself. To transfigure the world does not mean to make it an absolute, and neither does the proposition that whatever has being for man must be present in man mean that man is all. Man is not the ultimate, although he is what fascinates man, although in his world he is the crux. His concern is indeed he himself, but only because he is concerned with something else. He experiences this when he never finds peace with himself, only with transcendent being.

b. In an immanence expanded beyond our present temporal existence, the world of *human history* would be the process of the deity. The world would turn into the *God who comes to be.* In it, the deity would be advancing to truth and creating itself in struggle. We would be fighting for or against this truth, whose currently possible height would have been achieved in us. The otherness that concerns a man seeking to come to himself would not be transcendence but a deified mankind.

At bottom, this absolutization of mundane being implies equal ignorance of what mankind is and of what it ought to, and wants to, become. It remains absolute in time, yet transcendence is beyond time. Though wholly obscure, transcendence does not depend on what for us are ultimate dependencies; it is the abyss before which truth is possible for us, although beyond our cognition.

c. Mythical representation or speculative construction make a specific being of the deity—a being that will now confront the world, but confront it so that the deity itself remains immanent in this anticipation. Mythically it becomes *a personality;* speculatively it becomes *being.*

If man turns to the deity in prayer, it is to him in his lonely abandonment a thou with which he would like to enter into communication. It takes for him the personal form of a father, helper, lawmaker, or judge. In analogy to his existence, in which being proper is self-being, God involuntarily became a person; but as the deity this person was enhanced into an all-knowing, almighty, all-merciful person. Man is less, and yet akin to it insofar as, having been created in God's image, he reflects God's infinity. Only in his personal form is God really near.

As a cipher, this mythical personal conception may become a presence for a moment, and yet a genuine sense of transcendence will balk at conceiving God as a personality. I quickly shrink from the impulse that would make the deity a thou for me, because I feel I am profaning transcendence. The very idea entangles me in delusions. After all, personality is the mode of self-being that is by nature unable to be alone; relations are its essence; it must have other things, persons and nature, besides itself. The deity would need us, would need mankind, to communicate with. In the idea of God's personality, transcendence would be diminished into an existence. Or the idea of its personification does not leave the deity self-contained: it promptly turns into a number of persons who occupy the realm of their self-being jointly, whether in free, indeterminate polytheistic notions or in defined trinitarian ones. Finally, communication with the deity tends to inhibit communication among men. It establishes blind communities without a growth of individual self-being. Communication between one self and another, the truly present reality in which transcendence can come to speak, is paralyzed when transcendence is brought too close, as a direct thou, and is degraded at the same time.

The personal God is difficult to reduce to what he is as a cipher. God as transcendence stays remote. In the cipher which I as a human being create myself, in the second language, he comes closer to me for a moment. But the transcendent abyss is too deep. This cipher does not resolve the tension. It is fulfilling and dubious at once; it is and it is not. The love I bear the deity as a person can only metaphorically be called love; it truly becomes love only in the world, as love of an individual human being, and it becomes enthusiasm for the beauty of existence. Worldless love is love of nothing, an unfounded bliss. I really love transcendence only as my love transfigures the world.

When the deity is brought closer *in speculative construction* rather than in prayer, it really is not a deity any more. "Being" is not "God." Philosophy is not theology. Speculation—true as a play on ciphers—makes an object, being, of that which as transcendence lies beyond any thought we can lay down. Whether we conceive the world architect who produces the machinery of existence, in analogy to human dealings with external things, or whether the *logos* comes to be in a circular motion of the concept with itself, in analogy to our dialectically conceived self-being, or however else speculation may be solidified, it is always a supposed cognition of God that puts an end to transcendence. Everything becomes divine, or else the divine becomes the world. Worldlessness and godlessness are simply two poles that belong together on one level—whereas ciphers, when they make transcendent being immanent, will neither void it nor turn it into an ossified possession. They let the immanence remain historic, rather, as the phenomenon of transcendence for Existenz.

In fact, transcendence is voided in the three characterized forms of bringing it closer, and in other forms as well. What has possibilities as a cipher congeals as an existing deity; along with transcendence, man is about to lose his self-being. Whether it is he himself, mankind, or the personal God that he posits as absolute being, he always gives himself up to something other and lets himself be deceived by the fleeting, flaring happiness of relief from the inconceivability of self-being. For he is himself only in the tension of the most distant transcendence and the most present presence, of cipher and temporal existence, of freedom and the gift of self. It is as if man were running away from himself when he bows to his idols. No idol, only the deity as true transcendence demands that man be himself in the tension. He must not shrivel into nothingness—neither before the idol he makes of himself when he turns himself into an image, nor before mankind, nor before a personified deity. Against all these and other forms, even against the deity that appears as a cipher, he is to uphold his right, which the transcendent deity bestows on him from afar and confirms: God as transcendence wills me to be myself.

Lest man profane the deity—and in order that he may be himself, as he should—he must keep transcendence pure in its concealment, its distance, its strangeness. The true peace of being is to him the goal of reading ciphers, the ones given to him as well as the ones he wrote himself; it is not taking a rest with an illusory being that has stepped out of the world.

PART TWO
THE WORLD OF CIPHERS

Survey

1. Universality of Ciphers

There is nothing that could not be a cipher. Throughout existence indistinct vibrations and voices seem to express something, although the question may be what, and whence. The world—natural or human, stellar space or history—and our consciousness at large do not merely exist. Whatever exists can, so to speak, be viewed physiognomically.

Attempts have been made to describe a whole that does not fit in any known field of world orientation, a whole that is grasped as the context of a temporary image. These attempts have led to a physiognomy of nature, of plants, of animals, of landscapes; then to one of historic ages, of civilizations, of social and occupational strata; finally to one of human personalities.

There are methods for any description that will serve a scientifically determined end, but there are no methods for the physiognomic comprehension of existence. Rather, the things that go by the name of physiognomy are heterogeneous in themselves. The word is used for the intuitive anticipation of a knowledge that will be verified later, quite unphysiognomically, by rationalistic and empirical means. We use the word for understanding the expression of a psychological existence that is equally accessible in other ways; for a grasp on the character of historical structures of nature and of the spirit of times and groups in human history; for the mood, the feeling for things, that we call "empathy" if we conceive it as an infusion of our own psychological life.

While all of that is expression, it is not a cipher yet. It is as if there were expression after expression, a sequence of strata that ends only with *the cipher's own uninterpretable presence.* The cipher, unlike physiognomy with its indefinite possibilities, is subject to rules. First, it anticipates nothing that will be known later; whatever we know serves only to sharpen the edge of the cipher, since the cipher's life is kindled by a knowledge it will never be. Second, it does not express a human psychological reality: this reality becomes a cipher only as a whole, together with its expression. Third, the cipher is not the character of natural forms, nor the spirit of human structures, though these may turn into ciphers. Fourth, the cipher is not the life of a soul we empathize with. To Existenz, it is an objectivity expressed by nothing else and comparable with itself alone; it is the voice of transcendence, not just of an intensified and broadened human soul. What becomes intelligible in expression is therefore not a cipher. To make the cipher script intelligible means to void it. To see the unintelligible as such, in exact form, by understanding the intelligible—this is what permits transcendence to be touched through the cipher when that unintelligibility becomes transparent.

2. Arrangement of the Cipher World

Physiognomy is an attempt to read current concrete existence, not in order to obtain results couched in general statements, but to let general elements show the way to characterization. This is why physiognomy cannot remain true as a systematic arrangement of contents. A system of its images would cover only the outward forms of its existence. Attempts to logicize the physiognomy of existence, to raise it to the status of a knowledge, have been futile; what may look in them as though it might be subjected to rules and plans, like an object of scientific insight, will in short order dissolve as a research object and disappear as an existing whole. In putting comprehension into words, we perform a concrete act; aside from that act, we can only ponder the forms of possible comprehension.

Where the physiognomic element becomes a cipher, however, it defies conversion into a well-ordered knowledge not only because of indefinite ambiguity and total concreteness, as does physiognomy itself. Like everything in which not only existence but Existenz plays a part, the physiognomic cipher fails to yield any knowledge because of the existential source of our view.

Arranging the cipher world in an intentional order will not help to control or survey it. All that such an order would do is to void the cipher character of that world. The being of ciphers lies in the historic fulfillment of their unsurveyable depth; as general forms of existence they are reduced to mere shells.

If we want to look at them anyway, to "get the feel" of them, so to speak, as we philosophize, we discover a natural sequence of things that become ciphers. It begins with whatever exists in world orientation, with the superabundance of *nature* and of *history*. There follows our explicitly elucidated *consciousness at large* with the categories that articulate being. The last to turn into a cipher is *man*, potentially all things in one and yet never exhausted.

a. World orientation requires no reading of ciphers. Ciphers do not expand it; they threaten, rather, to make it unclear in itself, since its evolution has occurred precisely in critical detachment from the cipher character of existence. The reading of ciphers produces not the slightest knowledge that might apply in world orientation. The facts of world orientation are possible ciphers; but what is a cipher, and how, depends on Existenz, not on any science.

Without a scientific world orientation, metaphysics will be fantasizing. Science alone can give us the standpoints and the known contents that may serve us metaphysically to express real transcending in our historic situation. The metaphysical quest gives a retroactive impulse to world orientation when I see the cipher in reality, when world orientation comes to be of the essence. The search for transcendence, therefore, is at the same time a relentless will to know reality, the will behind

an insatiable exploration of the world. As a direct metaphysical statement, the transcendence I see in reading ciphers grows stale. It fulfills
me in my real world orientation, not in a supposed metaphysical knowledge which someone else imparts to me on the basis of *his* world
orientation.

Although a true reading of ciphers presupposes universal world
orientation, although the true reading takes place in the reality that
has been clarified by means of world orientation, it still does not happen
in scientific results which somebody tells me. Instead, I read the ciphers
in reality itself—in the reality to which I return on grounds of the
methodical knowledge I needed to gain access to reality at all, having
previously strayed all about it, blind and unmoved. I can read ciphers
only where I am concretely, methodically engaged in the knowledge of
world orientation. Mundane knowledge and transcending in ciphers
were linked from the outset, and after their critical separation they can
be truly united only in their roots, not in results, established facts, and
theories.

Scientific world orientation isolates its objects under certain points
of view, *divides them,* and transforms them by construction and hypothesis and by reducing them to measurability, to a visuality that
can be photographed, or to concepts with a finite number of charac-
teristics.

The reading of ciphers—which initially accompanies the world
orientation of an Existenz and will take its place for long times, in
unclear confusions—goes by current *entirety,* by immediate presence, by
unreduced abundance.

The pictorial objectification of this entirety may be a symbol in the
second language, and as an image it turns into a deceptive departure
from things as they can be known. For once the pictorial object has
supposedly become a known one, it will interject itself between the
world and the I, befogging the world for my world orientation and
extinguishing the I in a view of pictures that have turned imaginary.

Once my world orientation has been critically clarified, my reading
of ciphers will be pure and conscious also. I am going to stick to the
facts, and to the bounds of world orientation as the precision of facts
and methods makes them visible—in other words, to the remainder
which reality always leaves. But although reading ciphers restores an
immediate entirety, it does so without claiming any objective import in
world orientation. It is only in the symbolic pictorial view that I see a
whole in the cipher.

Reading ciphers, I am originally with an individual reality. But just as mundane knowledge makes me pursue an encyclopedic unity of all that is knowable, reading ciphers makes me seek an entirety of all that is directly real. I do not want to remain isolated in particular realities; I want to be open to all reality, to achieve a direct sense of transcending in the whole of the world to which I have gained historic access. I do not want to neglect any facts cited by opposing authorities. I do not want to draw a deceptive picture by picking out a purely accidental train of realities and shutting my eyes to others.

Hence two principles of reading ciphers: to want to know all that is real, and to want to apply this knowledge personally and methodically in present, concrete reality. Or, to put it another way, to be wholly involved and not to keep things at a distance—neither by interposing results as generally knowable nor by interposing images as congealed symbols of a past reading of ciphers.

Existence as a cipher is that which is wholly present, absolutely historic, and as such a "miracle." Externalized and rationalized, a miracle is what happens against laws of nature, or without them. But whatever happens in existence is subject to questioning about the legalities according to which it had to happen this way. Nothing that occurs in contravention, or in the absence, of a law of nature will ever be a cogently determinable fact; the illuminable character of consciousness at large, in which all existence occurs to me, makes that impossible. Direct historic reality, on the other hand, is not known and is not just a fact; being endless, it cannot be totally resolved into what can be generally known. I do not doubt that up to the limits of my scientific cognition everything happens naturally—that is to say, in accordance with intelligible rules and laws—and it does not contradict this that reality in its impermeable presence becomes legible as a cipher. As a cipher it is the miracle: that which happens here and now, cannot be resolved into a universal, and yet has decisive relevance because, to the transcending Existenz, it reveals being in existence. All existence is a miracle insofar as it is a cipher to me.

In the cipher, *questioning has an end*, as it has in the unconditionality of existential action. There is a kind of questioning ad infinitum which amounts to empty intellectuality because it lacks an existential impulse. Questioning has its true place for us, and it is boundless in world orientation, but before the cipher it fades. For the questioned object would promptly cease to be a cipher; as mere existence it would be the cipher's shell and refuse unless question and answer as such became materials of cipher reading by an Existenz transcending in those materials. Where questions are the downright ultimate, we can no longer see a cipher.

Questioning becomes the ultimate in the detached, objectifying act of thought; but as this thought comes solely from consciousness at large, it is not the ultimate. Questioning may be like an evasion of the presence, here and now, of Existenz before the cipher.

b. Consciousness at large is a form of being that has already been gained as I transcend, a form that is not explored in world orientation but verified in my own action. The activity and the logical structure of this action, of this thinking which thinks itself, make it a cipher of a sort heterogeneous to all being to which world orientation grants access to me as existence.

c. Man is an existence for world orientation, he is a consciousness at large, and he is a possible Existenz. He is all three of them in one. "What is man?" is a question raised and answered on each level of a knowledge of being, and in the end it is transcendently manifested in the cipher of man's individual being.

Nature

Nature is the inwardly inaccessible existence I meet, the spatially and temporally extended and infinitely interrelated reality. Yet at the same time it is the superior power that includes me, the power I feel concentrated at this point of my existence, and which to my possible Existenz becomes a cipher of transcendence.

1. Nature as Otherness, as My World, and as Myself

To me, nature is first downright *otherness*—that which I am not and which is without me as well. Next, it is *my world in which I am.* And lastly it is *I myself* insofar as I am my own, given, dark ground.

Nature as out and out otherness has sprung from *roots of its own.* It was a world, after all, that existed millions of years ago, when the dinosaurs frolicked in tropical swamps and there were no human beings. To us it is pure past; but it would be absurd to think of its remnants as made along with the creation of human existence in the world, as an eternal past that had never been a present. If we reduce nature to insignificance, compared with being human, we rob it of its own being whose voice we hear all over. We are shown only aspects of this difference between ourselves and nature; we do not know the difference itself. However incomprehensible it may be as such: to us, nature will always be our world.

It becomes *my world* as I act in it. I may seek to dominate it for purposes of my existence, to process it, from the simple manual toil of husbandry and handicraft to technological control. Or my activity may let me be at home in a nature I want to *see*, not to make use of. I roam; I travel; I look for places of special proximity to nature; I cross its every border and would like to know it all. There is no end to the tension between the downright otherness of nature and that which it is as my world. For all my dominance I stay dependent upon it. It seems as though it were aimed at me, as though it were my carrier and my servant. On the other hand, I evidently am a matter of total indifference to it, for it will heedlessly crush me.

I am nature myself, but I am not nature alone. For I can confront myself with it, can master and adapt the nature within as well as the nature without me, can accept it as mine and be at home in it, can succumb to it or hold it off and exclude it altogether. Self-being and natural being confront one another as parts, each of the other.

2. Nature as a Cipher

In the cipher, a nature lover sees the truth of a being that is not to be measured, is not generally valid, but can be embraced along with every reality. The dawn and the puddle in the street, the anatomy of a worm and the Mediterranean landscape—all these contain something which mere existence as a scientific research object does not exhaust.

As a cipher, nature is always a whole. It begins as the landscape in which I am right now, in this specific situation of my existence on earth. Next, it is the world entirety, the one vast cosmos as I think and conceive it. Then there are the realms of nature, the realms of particular beings: of the forms of minerals, plants, and animals; of the elementary phenomena of light, sound, and gravity; finally of the phenomena of life as the modes of existing in an environment. The whole is always more than we can conceive and explain.

In particular historic form, the cipher of nature is the earthbound quality of my existence, the proximity of the nature in which I was born, in which I have come to myself. As such a cipher it is incommunicable, because I alone—and most intensely, therefore—will feel the nature in it as familiar, as the landscape of my soul, and as totally strange in distinction.

From there the circle expands. I am receptive to the spirit of places, which communication shows me in the past and present roots of any other Existenz I meet. I am receptive, moreover, to the alien landscape as such, relying on the core of solitude in a nature still untouched by human hands. The globe turns into my home; the urge to travel, into a search for ciphers in global form.

The historicity of nature, although capable of limitless expansion, is concentrated in the singularity of landscapes that are always new. The more general our view of the type—of the North Sea coast with marsh and heath and moor, of Homer's maritime landscape, of the Campagna or the Nile, of mountains and deserts, of the polar world, the steppe, the tropics—the less real is it as a cipher. The cipher is manifest only when I am involved in the infinity of present things; the abstract type can do no more than awaken me and point the way. There is no surveying the possibilities of ciphers without obscuring the ciphers themselves. Steeping myself in my place, keeping faith with my landscape, being ready for the strange things that come into my presence—these are the postures in which I hear the historic voice of nature.

Nature speaks to me, but when I put a question to it, nature stands mute. It speaks a language that will not unveil it, a language that is like a halting start. It is the language of the unintelligible—not of its stupid factuality, but of its depth as a cipher.

In the cipher lies a sense of present reality without an objective effect. What I experience in the cipher does not exist empirically. It does not depend on causes and is not to be known by results. It is the pure self-presence of transcendence in immanence.

3. Reading Ciphers by Means of a Philosophy of Nature

General statements about the cipher of nature have been ventured from olden times on in philosophies of nature. Such philosophies sought to bring nature closer to man, so this animated proximity would make him feel the unapproachable side of nature as an otherness above his human potential. That nature cannot possibly be meant for man, as being for him alone, and that it cannot possibly be self-sufficient either—this was the conundrum tackled by the speculative thought.

First, nature was viewed as *one universal life*, as if it were a closed system. Then the unity of nature was allowed to *break up* in the knowledge of world orientation, so that it seemed to point to something else. And finally, in a new unity, nature was conceived as a *gradation* structured within itself, and the conception as an *encompassing* sequence of steps, with nature sublimated in something else.

a. In universal life, nature is the *ecstasy of becoming*. There is no question of its whence and whither; in the endless passing of all things it is the being that eternally maintains its rapture. Knowing neither person nor fate, nature is the surrender to the engendering tide whose delight entwines with the pain of absurdity: nature is the *wheel of agony* that seems to rotate on the spot. Nature is time, and yet it is not true time, because nothing is settled in that ceaseless, endless devouring and giving birth. Each individual thing is as nothing in the immense wastage.

Nature is the urge that does not know what it wants; it faces us as the joy of becoming and as the sadness of bondage. Its cipher is ambiguous rather than definitive.

On the one hand, nature is clarified into a calm, extant balance of forces. A silent harmony seems to receive me when I follow it. Coming to be, it has arranged its existence in a plethora of clear-cut, inexhaustible forms, and whatever came into being was doomed to blind, relentless destruction. And yet, nature may appear as infinitely comforting, as the one great, creative life, indestructible, forever new in its appearance, forever the same primal force of the world soul. Universal life seems to attract me, tempts me to dissolve into the flow of its entirety. Its forms in the animal and vegetable kingdoms seem akin to me. But nature does not answer; and so I suffer and balk, left with but a faint sense of being sheltered, with a longing to be sheltered in it.

And the unapproachable nature contains the other possibility: the menace of unleashed elements; the crushing weight of total strangeness; abysmal animal figures with which I no sooner let kinship identify me for a moment than they become frightful or ridiculous masks. If one side of universal life suggested a mother I trust, the other resembled a devil who makes me shudder.

Unrest is the aspect of universal life. The rigidity of rocks and shapes is nothing but petrified restlessness. In the endless shimmer and glitter of waves curling in the light and mica platelets on a sunlit rock; in the dance of raindrops and in the radiance of dew drops; in the circling and twining of hues on the aimlessly moved water level; in the surf on the sea shore; in the clouds, the formed spatiality of their existence not tarrying for an instant in width and narrowness, light and motion— everywhere this surface of natural being is as enchanting as it is destructive.

b. *The unity of nature must break up.* If universal life seemed to be the one nature, *knowledge* shows me the unity in particular forms: as mechanical unity, the universal natural legality that makes all things comprehensible by number, measure, and weight; as the unity of morphological forms, each of them a whole of possible forms; as the unity of life, of each individual vitality of a whole that is infinite in itself. But it is precisely this firm grasp on some specific unity that shatters the one of nature. Universal life is not a lasting concept, merely the cipher of a unity that may seem so self-evident to our direct consciousness that nothing short of an insight into the impossibility of its conception will make us give up this cipher of the natural One. The definite knowledge of natural science clarifies the cipher of natural disjointness.

c. Once the unity of universal life has broken up, we look for it again in speculative thoughts that will link naturally heterogeneous things in a *gradation* of natural forms, in the process of historic becoming. These forms are conceived as a timeless sequence (as if built and produced atop one another) in the realms of gravity and light, of colors and sounds, of water and of the atmosphere, of crystal, plant, and animal forms. In line with the idea of timeless evolution, the gradation of natural existence is deemed an increasing liberation from determinacy, an increasing internalization, concentration, and possible freedom. Becoming, then, is seen as a temporal, teleological evolution which also includes the attempts that miscarried, the grotesque and absurd goals which nature seems to have, and which in turn make a closed system of one nature forever impossible.

The result is the conception of a more encompassing sequence of steps, of a cipher of being in which nature is a link pointing back and forth from itself. Looking backward, the *ground* of nature is pondered as the inaccessible depth of transcendence that makes natural existence possible and subsequently real. Looking ahead, one sees in nature the germ of what will become of it as *the mind*. The mind, which later will spring forth from nature as itself, seems visible already, bound and unconscious, in the cipher of nature. It is stirring and cannot find itself as yet—hence the agony. It prepares the soil of its reality—hence the rejoicing. Nature is the basis of the mind; there is a mental side to nature as there will be a natural side to the mind wherever it is real.

What later, in the mental medium, will come to be existential freedom seems already present—really, if unconsciously—in the cipher of nature as a germinating mind. A creative vision proceeds without consciousness, as a plan without an intellect to do the planning. Nature is more than planning, due to the depth of reason in the unconscious; it is less than planning when it seems at a loss if suddenly required to make adjustments, as a living creature in new situations of existence. In the cipher of nature lie both reason and demonism—reason as a mechanism, demonism as the creation and destruction of forms.

4. Scant and Deceptive General Formulas for Ciphers of Nature

All modes of a definite knowledge of nature can substantially fulfill the cipher formulas—provided only that their knowledge is not meant *qua* knowledge, but that the known *facts* are meant as a language of being. The material of the cipher of nature, however, will always be *visuality*, the mode in which nature occurs to my *senses* in *my* world. The knowledge of nature comes to speak only in retranslation into a visual image. For example, the extension of curved space in Einstein's universe may be mathematically cognoscible as a vast motion of the world entirety, obscure as to origin and goal; but it does not speak as a cipher until we ask about the further cause of the motion and about the location of the curved space, thus turning the theory into the boundary concept of an inconclusive world.

In their proper sense, if not in their visual fulfillment, the speculative formulas of the cipher of nature are independent of specific natural cognitions in the march of science. And yet, if they appear advancing claims to a cognition of empirical reality, they deceive us because we may mistake them for things known in world orientation. No mundane cognition of any kind is accomplished by these formulas; and if they induce us to act upon their supposed knowledge of nature, the desired effect is to be produced by magical operations as the conceived ciphers (universal life, for instance, in the form of the philosopher's stone and finally of particular compounds) are used like effective forces in the world. In the end, the confusion leads to a denial of the value of scientific world orientation, that is to say, of a particular and relative one, whose distinct but isolated and imperfect knowledge seems infinitely inferior to the supposed knowledge of the whole. But if I want to achieve something by acting in the world, I succeed only insofar as I apply a particular, methodical knowledge according to plan, with foresight, and in awareness of its limitations. How to get the most out of the soil is something I learn from biology and chemistry, not by reading ciphers of nature in speculative thought. The prevention and cure of infectious diseases and the surgical treatment of injuries and growths are matters of medical science, not of sympathetic remedies, incantations, and other procedures from a supposed knowledge of universal life.

The formulas are scant, moreover, for every natural cipher lies only in the historic presence of real nature as it is here for me. I read the cipher in a certain realm of nature, coming to know the life of that realm by my own activity in all seasons, at all times of day, in any weather. Only thus do I grow into the natural life, by treating it as this locality. What I observe and arrange, do and experience in this association with nature—without something else, some rule, some mechanism, being interposed—lifts me out of the human world. It is like a return to inaccessible primal days, but a return by way of the knowledge made possible by natural science, the key that unlocks what I can experience. Now I comprehend nature with all my senses and become familiar with everything visible and audible, with everything that can be smelled and touched. I turn myself into a motion that is nature's own and lets me vibrate with its vibrations. To have guidelines for dealing with it—guidelines from which I depart when I come really close to nature—I become a hunter, a collector, a gardener, a forester. With rational world orientation to furnish the rungs of the ladder and protect me from confusions, I come to the true cipher that makes all philosophy of nature pale as a mere thought, even though that philosophy knows how to direct me and to call attention to things. It is thus, by making a realm of nature my own beyond any purpose, that I come to face nature itself; and this is why the millennial philosophy of nature has always blended the indispensable reiteration of a few thought motifs with the infinite joy of really reading the ciphers, without whose riches my thoughts would not be true.

5. *Existential Relevance of the Ciphers of Nature*

In nature I am possible Existenz. Facing it, therefore, I *decline in two directions* from the substance of my potential. If I regard nature as just an object to work upon, a resistance that lets me show my mettle, a material to make something out of, I slip into unsubstantial activity; I come to exist in a formalism whose hostility to nature will cost me the contents of my life as well as my self. We cannot conceive nature purely as material for us without causing our own roots to wither. Even the big city with its sea of concrete, its lights, its noise—even that is still processed nature and preserves my opportunity to look upon nature.

Conversely, if I regard nature as true being and myself as its product, my enthusiasm for it makes me self-oblivious. I forget that my own proper being is to be myself.

It takes the most positive self-being to fight both forms of decline, to cultivate pure love of nature without confusing it. Nature can be neither a derivative of our existence nor a better self we should turn into. It comes from its own self and is for ours. Kant regarded feelings for nature as signs of a good soul. What shocks us in brutalities against nature is not the hurt to nature, as a rule, but the state of mind that made such conduct possible. It sickens us when a stroller swinging his cane decapitates the flowers by the roadside, though we do not mind seeing the farmer mow a whole field.

Yet love of nature is an existential peril. If I give myself up to it as to an unfathomed cipher, I always have to retrieve myself from it —for this love tends to plunge me into thoughtless self-alienation. Viewing the abundance of the world is bliss; surrendering to this bliss for more than a moment is a betrayal.

To the man who loses himself in isolation, nature is a substitute for communication. Shunning human beings, he seems to find a refuge in riskless devotion to his sense of nature. Yet nature will enhance his loneliness. There is something pensive about a sense of nature; its unresponsive unconsciousness makes it seem a delusion, like a companion in sorrow. Language is to us the measure of all things, for as possible Existenz we come to ourselves in communication only, but speechless nature is the uncommunicative realm. Shakespeare's Lear joins the elements when he is cut off from all communication; his maddened mind turns everything into language. The unintelligible becomes intelligible to him as he grows unintelligible.

Living alone with the cipher of nature is the torment of sheer possibility, like the promise of a future. It therefore implies hope and suits the young, whom the sight of the cipher of nature protects from the waste of premature realities and from the demands of a human world they are not yet able to master. To the young, nature is like a companion with whom they can hold on to themselves and live; devoid as yet of clear communication, they have a vague experience of their own depth. But then nature becomes the world I live in, without its cipher being life to me; it becomes the space in which my self-being communicates with other self-being, the field of my activity, the stage of my fate. Hence my connection with nature as the jointly fulfilled world, the historically animated landscape. When it accompanied my happiness, I have transformed it as though moving away. I hear it as the cipher of the dark background as long as my present Existenz and another are in true proximity.

Coming back again to pure nature, it pains me to see in its sheer beauty a possibility beyond realization. As I enjoy it, repetition is like a memory without a future. I suffer the speechlessness of nature. It arouses longing in me, a sense of shortcoming, an emotional movement without present satisfaction, because the cipher of nature is no longer crucial for itself once Existenz has entered into existence.

History

In scientific world orientation, history is the sum of the conditions and events in the past life of nations and of the accomplishments of active men. To an objective observer, what occurs empirically is endless in every respect. We can select at random what we describe and narrate; we can arrange it constructively in the direction of predetermined goals; and we can investigate it causally, as a part of existence only.

If history affects me inwardly, however, there will be Existenz accosting me from the past. Contents will be illuminated; some realities will come near me; the rest will move into a gradually darkening background from which only a faint shimmer suggests that my eye might reach that far.

Transcending goes beyond historical knowledge and existential impingement, but I find it only in these two, as ciphers. Without having theoretical insights yet, whether descriptive or causal, and without perceiving the decisive choices of any Existenz, I feel through both of them a jolt in the historic changes, and I feel it as a transcendent event. As a historian I know: This has happened; so it is definitive reality. As possible Existenz I sense the acts of men: This is done and cannot be undone. Both become ciphers. It is as if transcendence were revealing itself, as if an old god were unveiled and dying, and a new god were being born. There is nothing left to ponder, and there is nothing to justify. The cipher character of history may concentrate for me in specific events. It reveals more than I know, more than I can tell. The great historiographers are those who speak in realities only and allow them to become transparent indirectly, without intent or purpose—as distinct from a rhetorical presentation that merely thrills, and from a mythicizing historiography that consciously produces an intentional and therefore untrue history.

We have come to doubt the mode of reading ciphers in which another, mythical reality was placed beside the empirical one. We do not go along with the objective recital of a supplementary myth and its departure from empirical reality; the intervening powers do not strike us as distinct figures any more. The Greeks could say, "A god did this," and we understand the thought, but we can no longer express it that way in dead earnest. And finally, if a further leap turns the single historical event into the singular articulation of a supersensory entirety —and if that entirety is told as the story of a transcendence remaining in the beyond but revealing itself in the material of this world—too much has been stated. We do not know an original cipher that might, for us, fulfill such a total expression.

To read the ciphers of history, we try to reach *the beginning and the end*. But we see that about the past we can know only what is evidenced by such remnants as documents, monuments, or tools, or what facts allow us to presume as probable in the world—while the future always remains a matter of mutually exclusive possibilities. We never reach *the* beginning, or *the* end. The cipher is legible only in the historicity *between* an imaginary beginning and end. To begin and to end is the mark of all that is historically relevant to us because, embedded in endless duration, it has an existential appeal and speaks as a cipher. A cipher of history is the foundering of the essence. It must lie between a beginning and an end, for only nonentity endures. We see the view that holds with success: the view that what has come to be is best, that it is justifiable, as necessary, because it has come to be. This is the view that lauds power as the sole truth and legitimizes it as a violence full of meaning. But we also see how the cipher being of history will be lost in this view, in favor of mere positivistic knowledge. Truth will founder, but it can be reiterated, recaptured, revived. This is not the chance that something extant might endure, nor the chance that effects on events in the world might have historical import—it is the continuing struggle of the dead, whose being remains unsettled as long as the torch of a seemingly lost cause can be picked up by new men, to the point of definitive failure. World history is not the last judgment, as gleefully believed by the triumphant victor—as believed by the masses, always content to exist, and by self-righteous pharisees who live in fact and think they live because they are the best. There are many ways to interpret what has happened. World history as a sum is a vapid factuality; to conceive it as a single whole is an empty rationality; to relate it to present realities is to be disloyal and oblivious to what belongs together in the mystical body of self-being spirits.

Compared with nature, which is alien to me, history is the existence of my own essence. Empirically, of course, it is quite dependent on an all-obliterating nature; but where nature must serve history, it becomes a relatively conquered object. Nature is impotent because it is aimless; its eventual rule in time, as mere duration, expresses its impotence. History is empirically impotent because in time, overwhelmed by nature, it will have an end; but this impotence expresses its power as the historic phenomenon of transcendence in human Existenz. The power of nature is what is always extant and yet not in being; the power of history is that which vanishes in time and yet has being.

Consciousness at Large

From all world orientation I turn back to the existence in which everything occurs to me. I elucidate the form of this existence to myself as consciousness at large. Consciousness at large is the sole medium in which whatever is can be for me. In it, being takes inevitable forms, which I bring to mind as categories meant to be valid for everyone. On this side, human consciousness is identical no matter how many times it may exist.

What in nature is the arrangement of things by number, measure, and weight has an equivalent in each existence: an articulation of objective, categorially formed being that can be defined in some way. The natural scientists have been reading nature's book as one written in mathematical characters, and so, in some sense, all existence in the world is objectively and identically conceivable for everyone. Consciousness at large, in which I take an impersonal part if I exist at all, creates the possibility of unequivocal understanding, and thus of community in the objectively valid realm. We live in reliance upon this order, trusting in things to follow their natural course. We are aghast when the order seems really disrupted, when everything threatens to plunge into chaos. But in our lucid consciousness at large we know that this cannot be.

Order, rule, universal law, the very things that seem to void all symbolism and to compel a merciless severance of reality and illusion—these become ciphers themselves. *The fact that existence is such as to involve order, and this kind of order, is the cipher of its transcendence.* To us, this order is the most self-evident one, some part of which will be present and used at each moment. We marvel only when we make ourselves aware of its universality.

The accuracy of this order is like a cipher of transcendent truth, and the mystery of its validity, like a reflection of transcendent being. All accuracy has a glow of truth; it is not simply itself, but the seeming luminary of what makes it possible. This glow is deceptive, however. At the moment of contentment with its validly accurate truth, we would experience an endless waste of mere accuracy and would promptly lose the cipher. My former bulwark against arbitrariness and chance would become a tight net in which I am merely trapped.

Consciousness at large with its valid forms is the acid test for everything else, the resistance which all other things must overcome. It is the skeleton of existence, without which there is no understanding and no continuing certainty. It is the water of existence, without which nothing can live. These comparisons rob it of its independence, but in their varying ways they do characterize its indispensability. Every step in which we would leave or ignore consciousness at large goes against our existence itself. The self-esteem of our existence requires that it be tied to its universal; yet any contentment with it, as with being proper, robs our possible Existenz of substance. The accuracy of consciousness at large is truth, and as such it is a cipher, but the cipher itself is the form that makes us feel at once the glow of truth and the discontent of existence.

The necessity of universal legality is a support and a comfort. When everything seems to be crumbling into chance, the law is the place where I can gain a solid footing. If being threatens to sink out of sight, I can seize it in this law of all existence. But the law will be a cipher, then, and ambiguous as any cipher. It will lure me into the void of accuracy and endlessness, will seem to free me from the risks of possible Existenz, will invest me with the dignity of a rational being. I can hold on to it, but not definitively and not absolutely. As in any cipher, I must steep myself in this one without ever touching bottom. In a merely objective retention of its validity I no longer see the cipher.

Every category can become a cipher *in its particularity;* this is the existential import of the several categories. What I am becomes clear to me in the categories I prefer—prefer because to me they are peculiarly transparent.

Specifically, it is the primal categorial antitheses that express an unfathomable meaning. The ultimate dichotomy in consciousness at large is that between logical forms and their fulfilling material—yet even so, the logically impermeable remains material to consciousness at large. Matter is not being, no more than the categories are. It is alogical, but not transcendent. But the fact that existence shows this split in existence is a possible cipher. My speculative aim is to push through to transcendence for a moment, through matter and then through the logical forms; but it is only where the two are one—where matter becomes form and the diversity of forms becomes matter, or where the sundering thought is abandoned in formal transcending—that the cipher will light up.

Man

What we are would seem to be what we can know best of all; yet we never know it.

Anthropologically we conceive man in his physical makeup, as a link in the realm of life, and in his races as anatomical, physiological, and physiognomic types. We conceive him as consciousness, both as consciousness at large—known in man alone—and as psychological existence. As this makes him an object of logic and psychology, his quality of arising always from his tradition and in mutual intercourse with others makes him an object of sociology. Explored as an object, man is never just a biological type. There is a leap between him and the animals. He is a creature of the mind, the creature that speaks, masters nature, and finally includes itself among the things of its making.

The ways in which man turns himself into an object—the anthropological one, the logical elucidation of consciousness, the psychological and sociological ways—are inseparable from one another. Each one makes us feel things to which only the next will give us real access. Encompassing them all, however, man is *the knower who is always more than he knows of himself.* His very knowledge brings him new possibilities, so that by understanding himself he will come to be another. It is on one side of my being only that I am what I know of myself; as a known being I am not yet my real self.

To himself, man is nature as well as consciousness, history as well as Existenz. *Being human is the node* of all existence, the spot where all things tie in for us, the standpoint from which everything else becomes conceivable for us. To call it a microcosm says too little; man's transcendent relation goes beyond any cosmos. He may be conceived as the *central link* of being in which the remotest things meet. The world and transcendence entwine in man, in the Existenz that occupies the borderline between them. What man is cannot be ontologically stated. Never sufficient unto himself, not grasped in any knowledge, man is to himself a cipher.

He comes nearest to transcendence when he perceives it thus, through himself as a cipher. The mythical way to put this is that he has been created in God's image.

Man has no access to any closed system of being. Both nature and history are therefore inconclusive, with consciousness mere appearance and Existenz remaining a possibility. Man does make images to himself, pictures of the whole; but to the question what counts, the One and the whole or the individual, he will of necessity give a contradictory answer. Along the lines of the relation to a whole, he will say, the individual is depreciated; but the breakthrough of the independent individual's self-being in turn depreciates every entirety—into which man never goes anyway, without leaving a remainder. Every unity will be called into doubt: the natural world's unity in the cosmos, that of history in Providence, and that of individual Existenz. Reading the cipher in himself, man conceives *transcendent* unity without knowing or understanding it.

All existence, his own included, is unstable and unready. He reads the cipher of transcendent unity, entwining all in himself as the node, and as he himself is that cipher, the unity he reads defines his being. *United*, his otherwise separate sides strike him as a cipher.

1. The Cipher of Man's Unity with His Nature

My natural side, adopted and pervaded by my self-being, is more than nature. To live as nature in nature, aimlessly in the present, in the *élan vital* of mere life, may become banal in short order, but the taking of that risk and the self-denial it requires are conditions of man's becoming a cipher to himself. What I am and what I know must become flesh and blood for me. The ever-present life of my senses, the seeing and hearing in the up and down of tension and fatigue, not only gladdens me as living nature; it has the depth of possibility at the same time. The ciphers of my existence are written in the sensuous mode. Sensuosity, of course, is only the material of the cipher language, but without entering into it at each moment, I cannot have the supersensory in mind.

Eroticism is the part of man's natural existence which most clearly expresses the cipher of his being. He may turn it into an indifferent natural process subject to regulation—in that case it is a vital tension and satisfaction, an empty gorging that will not be a cipher even if it is bacchantically enhanced. As mere perception and the mere intellect are blind, so is erotic satisfaction as such nontransparent, however vastly enriched by stimuli.

Eroticism does not acquire the character of a human cipher until it serves existentially to express communication in its transcendence. As pure nature it splits my humanity and debases it in the other; but as a cipher in existential communication it becomes a part of man's humanity. The manner of his eroticism decides his being.

The phenomenon of love makes erotic surrender a singular, unconditional entrustment of one's own nature. In a rationalistic view it is biologically interchangeable and can be repeated under erotic stimuli—and then it is pure nature, and artificially formed nature at that—but surrender as a cipher is possible only to one sole human being. No intellect and no psychological acumen enables us to understand this exclusivity, which in absolute consciousness and from the cipher point of view is the most self-evident of things. The exclusivity is a cipher only if it is voluntary—though never as a matter of the will alone (since an exclusive will could only be violent) but as an incomprehensibly bestowed necessity of being. Hence the impossibility of a repetition in the same sense. It ruins this cipher if the one and only human possibility of one side is wasted because the other knows only the richness of life and its possibilities, and thus knows only change—wasted, perhaps, without either being aware of what has been done. As I have only one body and cannot change it, so does the physical union as a cipher mean the only way for humans to belong to one another.

It is in existential love—in cipher form, as a uniquely singular bond, each time as an incomparable possibility—that nature comes to fulfill Existenz in its unilluminable present existence. When a tendency to become nature threatens my humanity, I can turn essentially human in the cipher. This cipher, the product of freedom as much as of dark nature, breeds possibilities of tenderness in silence and in oppressive situations. Altogether inwardly, open to the inwardness of others and sensible for them, it is hard and impervious to protect itself from brutality. Against the sheer laxness of humanitarian conventions it dares to carry detachment to the point of inhumanity. As human beings who give in to nature, we can see this cipher of being human even when our own is dimmed. The determinant of man's every posture is whether he has been capable of this cipher and ready for it.

Pure eroticism makes man give up his own self; but if each of two people is the only one for the other, their union seals the absoluteness of the One. Eroticism is a cipher as the sensualization of humanity in unconditional communication. It is the vanishing surety for all time, nontransferable, not to be given twice and many times.

2. The Cipher of Man's Unity with His World

I am not a human Existenz unless I am received by a world, form myself in that world, saturate myself with it, and act upon it. The humanity of one who starts afresh at his own peril is not brought to an end by his detachment, but it is reduced. It becomes a sensible cipher only in the present, when society and the state become positive realities for the man who identifies with them. This makes him aware of being human: the resolute Now, not the universal contemplation of all possibilities and realities of history and of his time. Man becomes human in the unity of the cipher—by being something, not by gingerly touching things that remain strange to him anyway, and not being himself in the end.

Man's natural side seems to shackle him to the most alien of things, and so does his social and historic situation in existence. He cannot deny nature without destroying himself; his own depths will radiate nature if he would make his adoption of it subject to conditions; and neither can he, without blurring, reject society, marriage, family, his trade, his state. Only by entering into all those can he find himself. He may succumb to them, as to nature, and forget that there is something besides work and pleasure; but when the bustle grows stale, when everything has been reduced to intellectual and empirical objectivity, it will become a vessel of being human and thus a cipher if carried by one whom it serves to come to himself. Then man is received into this present reality and simultaneously bound to it, and by its possibilities which he must fathom. He is subject to the laws of an existence with which, to grow fully human, he must be as one. Since this identification comes from possible detachment from the world, however, it may take in-between forms—such as going along with the bustling world, giving it its due, but maintaining one's reserve until the historic point where identification will realize the substance of the bustle and turn it into a cipher in its world.

3. The Cipher of Freedom

In the man who merely exists, there is no one cipher of being human.

The rise of that cipher requires the passionate unconditionality that turns a man's existence into an Existenz *at one* with its nature and its world. Without a life of the senses and without a world there is no present Existenz, only a possible one, and neither, without Existenz, is a sensory mundane existence truly human. To keep faith, on grounds of absolute consciousness; to take the long view, though living wholly in the present; to be able to wait; to go in for self-education, fitting yourself for ends yet unknown; to take time to reflect; to decide resolutely; to dare—these and all other words for the inner action of Existenz describe the free man who can be a cipher to himself, as distinct from empirically existing man whose cipher is his natural being or his consciousness at large, not his being human.

Freedom is not an object, but it is the presence of self-being, the only being *for* which there is a transcendence—and for the free, in turn, freedom is a cipher of transcendence in two possible ways.

We have seen in the elucidation of freedom that it is autogenous but not selfmade. Antinomies of the will may leave it at a loss, and its utter difference from transcendence may make man feel corrupt and wholly dependent on grace. Or an assurance that freedom is transcendently related may give him confidence in his own ground.

I may live with a sense of my corruptness, watching my rotten existence. I think I loathe myself because I know what man is in general: prey to the ambiguity of all his motives. Good itself turns into evil, for I note its goodness and pride myself on my merit. Either my good will remains equivocal or I know what is right and fail to do it anyway. No matter what I do, it will be reversed. Desperately I admit my ever-recurring guilt until divine grace shows me the way out by a revealed warrant, an undeserved gift of something I could never achieve. It seems presumptuous to consider myself free when everything is God's will.

Or I may live with the sense of an innate nobility that makes demands on me and encourages compliance because I trust it (*De commendatione nobilitatis ingenitae*, Julian; cit. Augustine X, 735, Migne). In this case I respect myself. The good, to me, lies in my being, which my doings heed and serve. I return to myself where I am true. I have left myself where I backslide. What dominates me is not pride in a given being, but confidence in a being that seeks realization even if it means peril. I cannot bear committing acts of disloyalty against myself; their reality gnaws at my selfhood and will not let me rest. I accept what I have done and try to make amends for what I have ruined. I cannot become self-satisfied. But it seems a self-diminution unworthy of man to hate myself and to seek salvation in grace rather than—in keeping with the will which the deity appears to indicate by hiding—to let my own freedom help me, because in its true being I may love myself.

The antithesis of consciousness of grace and consciousness of freedom does not coincide with that of a sense of corruption and a sense of nobility. And yet the two antitheses are related. In corruption I search for grace; in the sense of nobility I am sure of my freedom. But just as there must be a trace of freedom in my corruption if I am not to be hopelessly mired in the indifference of things that are not my fault, so must the sense of nobility have some of the gift of selfhood in it if a proud *hubris* is not to make man believe in his own divinity.

But it is neither by revelation nor by an objective guarantee that I am given to myself. It happens at moments in which my will comes to a decision—a decision prepared for by my adoption of historic tradition, by example and guidance, and grown lucid in communication. Transcendence comes to man as he makes ready for it, and this advent, along with the mode of possible readiness, is the transcendent cipher.

Art as a Language Born of Reading Ciphers

The communication of what men have read in natural, historical, and human ciphers is art when it occurs in visuality as such rather than in speculative thinking. Since art lends a voice to ciphers—since what it says can be said in no other way, though dealing with the same intrinsic being that all philosophizing is about—art becomes here the *organon of philosophy,* as Schelling put it. In the metaphysical philosophy of art we think in art, not about art. Speculative thinking does not turn art into an object, as does the scientific theory of art; to that way of thinking, our contemplation of art becomes an eye, rather, to gaze upon transcendence. Philosophical thoughts in the contemplation of art can be philosophically conveyed in declining generalizations only. There, philosophy lives at second hand. It does not lead; it teaches appreciation of things it cannot do, though they belong to it in substance. Where we think that our philosophizing will take us to the crux, we must content ourselves with disquisitions that are downright failures. When I philosophize, I am better able to hear what Shakespeare, uninterpreted and uninterpretable, says in the foundering self-being of his original characters; but I cannot translate it into philosophy.

1. Art as an Intermediate Realm

Where the cipher is just a beginning, doomed to swift destruction that will let me be one with the transcendence from which the cipher parted me, there is mysticism. Where the hidden deity is heard in the factual action of self-being, there is the decisive temporal existence of Existenz. But where I read eternal being in the cipher, where pure contemplation endures in view of perfection—in other words, where the tension of my separation from the object remains and temporal existence has been left just the same—there is the realm of art, a world *between* timelessly submerged mysticism and the factual present of timeless Existenz. The mystical I dissolves into the undifferentiated One; in temporal existence my self-being succumbs to the hidden deity; but a self-being that contemplates art reads the cipher script of being and in doing so remains pure possibility. Mystics slide into an objectless pantheism; artists realize in their ciphers the diversity of the divine in its immensely rich forms, none of which is solely and wholly divine. But the one God of Existenz shatters art, reducing the life of its ciphers to a game of possibilities.

The satisfaction I feel in the imaginative viewing of art lifts me out of mere existence as well as out of the reality of Existenz. It is an upsurge of absolute consciousness that frees me from the misery of existence: Hesiod has the Muses begotten "to bring deliverance from sorrow, and relief in woe." But imagination does not commit me. Instead of causing me really to be myself, it creates a space in which I can be, or a presence whose being changes my inner posture without my taking any real existential step in it. Savoring art, man is "swiftly oblivious of grief, nor will he think further of sorrow; thus he has been transformed apace by the goddesses' gifts." An Existenz is not oblivious, however, and what transforms it is not distraction, not a fulfillment derived from something else, but its own acceptance and adoption of reality.

Yet Existenz cannot manage this authentic transformation unless it gains a space of its own by interposing that art-bestowed self-obliviousness in the contemplation of being. In the noncommitment of art lies potential commitment. Truth ceases only when all seriousness becomes impossible, when I esthetically enjoy strange things at random, things that are never to enter the realm of my own possibilities, that are destined only to serve my curiosity, my desire for variety, and the rise of emotions that will never be my own. It is then that the reality of existence and Existenz is veiled by existentially depleted pictures from artistic languages, that nothing of the essence is seen any more. But the possibility of such degeneration does not argue against the original right to felicity in viewing art, for without that noncommittal viewing I am not free to be possible Existenz. Entirely immersed in the reality of existence, or solely concerned with the reality of my Existenz, I would be as though in chains. Immobilized and consumed by my incapacity, I would burst into acts of blind violence. As Existenz, facing original ciphers, I would never be redeemed for freedom unless these ciphers come to speak. Without a moment of voiding reality in the language of art I could not freely seize upon reality as Existenz.

Reality is more than art, since in reality an Existenz is tangibly present as itself and in earnest about its decisions. But reality is also less than art, because it comes to speak only in the echo of the cipher language acquired by way of art.

2. Metaphysics and Art

Metaphysical thinking impels a man toward art. It opens his mind to the beginnings, when art was meant seriously, when it was not just decorative, playful, sensually pleasurable, but a reading of ciphers. Throughout his analyses of the form of works of art, throughout the accounts of their worlds in intellectual history, throughout the biographies of their creators man is seeking to make contact with an Existenz —not with his own, perhaps, but with one that was asking questions, seeing things, and forming them in the ground of the being he too is searching for. A caesura divides all the things we call works of art, according to the external characteristic of their being man-made: speaking in those on one side are ciphers of a transcendence, while the others lack depth and a ground. Only in metaphysical thinking will man perceive this caesura in reflected consciousness and believe in his own serious approach to art.

3. Imitation; Idea; Genius

To be able to express what he has read as a cipher, the artist must *imitate* realities. Mere imitation is not art, however. It plays a part in cognitive world orientation, as anatomical drawing, for instance, as the depiction of machinery, as the design of models and schemata. Here it is the thought alone that guides the language, with an empirical reality or a consistently meaningful design as criteria. This imitation merely expresses something rational in visual form, transparently and succinctly.

The artist perceives more than empirical reality and cogitative construction. In all things lie the infinite *ideas* of entireties and forms that are universal and yet are not to be adequately depicted. Schemata in types and style forms express abstractly and unfittingly—but in ways appropriate to rational world orientation—what is continuously disseminated in the world as the substance of the ideas. Art brings to mind the powers represented in ideas.

Although these powers are universal, the artist cannot universally express them. In works of *genius* they find a singular concretion that is absolutely historic, noninterchangeable, and yet understood as the universal that defies repetition. This alone is the voice of a transcendence that has been grasped by a historic Existenz and thus become a cipher.

Repetitions by disciples lose the magic of original truth, of the truth in which a genius may seem to have brought transcendence itself down from heaven. What remains in the end is imitation, of realities or earlier works or things thought up by the intellect.

The *imitation theory* of art covers only the material of its language; *esthetic idealism* explains the general powers; the *theory of genius* goes to the root. But the concept of genius is ambiguous. Does it mean the creative talent—which is subject to an objective appraisal of its achievements—or the historic Existenz, the source of the transcendent manifestation? Existenz is the being that appeals to me through the work, the being whose language strikes me as a form of communication, while talent has a remote, objective meaning. But it is where man can touch the ground of being and can, in ciphers, say what is— it is there that Existenz and talent come to be one, as genius.

4. Transcendent Vision and Immanent Transcendence

In art, the cipher either comes to visuality as a transcendent vision or becomes visible in reality as such, as immanent transcendence.

Mythical persons outside the natural world, or as special beings in the world, receive their forms from the artist. Herodotus said that the Greeks had their gods made for them by Homer and Hesiod. Such historic beings are not thought up, not invented; they amount to the original creation of a language analogous to the language of words, but used for the understanding of transcendence. As powers, taking shape only in fetishes and monstrous idols, they remain symbolic and arcane. Turning into human figures, they seem like enhancements of human existence but are conceptions of the divine by way of man: man is the invariably flawed image of the gods revealed in this transcendent vision. The Virgin-Mother-Queen, the suffering Christ, saints, martyrs, and the immense realm of Christian figures, scenes, and events all are seen in such mythical visions; the form which transcendence assumes here is the *disjointness of empirical existence,* not its possible perfection. But the visual object of the myths is always a divinity in human form that sheds everything merely human, a specific world beside the merely real world, the miracle next to nature.

The *immanent transcendence* of an art that seems to represent nothing but empirical reality as such is another matter. True, all art speaks only in visualities of empirical origin, but mythical art turns elements of reality into another world: where it is genuine it will let us see things that could not result from those elements, a world which those elements would not suffice to construe. It is really another world, and to dissect it into its empirical elements would be to destroy them. But the art of immanent transcendence turns the empirical world itself into a cipher. It seems to imitate things that occur in the world, but it makes them transparent.

The *world of a cult* is a premise of the art of transcendent visions. It presupposes a community of practicing believers, and thus a dependence of the artist's own vision; its depth is due precisely to the fact that the individual rests not on himself alone, that he expresses things he knows jointly with all others. The art of immanent transcendence, on the other hand, is tied to the *independence of the individual artist*. He has his original view of existence, may decline into mere imitation or cognitive analysis of reality, and uplifts himself by his own freedom to a vision of things that no cult and no community has taught him. The artist of pure transcendence gives form to traditional ideas; the artist of immanent transcendence teaches how to read existence anew, as a cipher.

The hitherto greatest artists managed to combine the two possibilities. They did not drop the mythical material; they carried it over into reality, which their own freedom let them rediscover in transcendence. This was the way of Aeschylus, of Michelangelo, Shakespeare, Rembrandt. To them, the original connection of myth and reality became an enhanced reality, one that could always be seen and shaped only once at a time. Through them, the myths—taken from a tradition that has fallen silent—are now speaking again in loud and different voices. They gave reality a share in powers we can no longer conceive in the language of reality alone. On the other side stands van Gogh who dropped all myths, confined himself totally to reality, and thus lent transcendence a voice which of necessity is infinitely poorer, but is true for our time.

5. Diversity of the Arts

Music, architecture, and sculpture let us read the cipher in the realities which they produce, respectively, in temporality, spatiality, and corporeality. Painting and poetry express imaginings that are unreal in the world, with the first confined to every visible thing which line and color can bring to an illusive presence on a flat surface, while the second, free to imagine whatever can be seen and thought at all, must express it in words.

In music it is the form of self-being as *temporal existence* that becomes a cipher. Music makes transcendence speak in the inwardness of a being that assumes temporal form as it disappears. It is the most abstract art in the sense that its material is not visible, not spatial, not imaginable, and thus least concrete; but it is the most concrete art in the sense that this material of it has the form of always producing and consuming itself in time—the very form of temporal self-being which in the world, to us, is being proper. Music touches the core of Existenz, so to speak, when it turns the universal form of existential existence into its own reality. Nothing, no object, gets between music and self-being. Each musical reality may become the present reality of the performing or listening participant who will allow his temporal form of existence, structured and filled by the sound alone, to grow transparent. Music is the one art whose being depends upon human performance. (To the dance, being danced is so essential that it permits not even a notation that might make its transferable; it can be taught only from person to person, and its cipher, if it does contain one, lies in its musical side— just as all music has something that lends itself to accompanying movements of the body. The drama, on the other hand, need not necessarily be put on stage; the most profound dramas such as *King Lear* or *Hamlet* hardly bear staging.)

Architecture structures *space* and makes spatiality the cipher of being. It challenges my modes of moving in space and requires my successive acts in time to come fully to mind—and yet, to my mind it is precisely that which endures, not that which vanishes like music. The spatial form of my world with its delimitation, its structure, its proportions, becomes the cipher of rest, of lasting permanence.

Sculpture lends a voice to *corporeality* as such. From fetishes and obelisks to the marble human figure, the sculptural cipher is not an image of something else; it is the existence of being, rather, that is condensed in the three-dimensional mass. Because that existence makes its most concrete physical appearance in human form, the human figure has become the dominant object of sculpture—not as man, however, but as the deity in the superhuman form of a bodily presence in this sculptural cipher.

Music, to fulfill time, needs the material of sound; architecture, to fulfill space, needs delimiting matter in connection with the point and purpose of this spatiality which serves as the world of our real human existence; sculpture, to experience its corporeality, needs the material of contents represented in that form. The cipher pales, and art becomes unessential, whenever this fulfilling element is hypostasized: in the musical imitation of natural sounds; in the sculptural representation of random things, the depiction of objects in general; in the architectural isolation of purposive forms, now grown mechanically, rationally transparent.

While music, architecture, and sculpture depend upon the real presence of their elements to make their ciphers speak, painting and poetry move in visions of things now unreal, of possibilities freely drafted in the direction of infinite worlds, with such objectivities as color and the language of words used as dependent means to other ends.

This is why the impact of the first three arts lies in their sensory presence—in my factual acting-out of temporality when I listen to music; in my factual ways of living and moving in space when I take in an edifice; in the gravity and tangibility of corporeality when I grasp a sculpture. These arts seem unwilling to grant us any real access; their limited abundance has a depth that opens only to persistent self-discipline. I must be involved as myself if there is to be a revelation of the cipher. The activity of the self aims straightways at this cipher being, without any other object being interposed. If I succeed at all in gaining access to those three arts, therefore, I find self-deception easier to avoid than in poetry and painting.

Painting and poetry make the infinite space of all things, all being and nonbeing, accessible with playful ease. The activity of the self now seeks primarily to gain an imagined illusion; only secondarily, through this illusion, is it aimed at the cipher. The endless variety of things on display makes it more difficult for the cipher to have an impact. The easy access is deceptive, due to the effortless diversity.

On the other hand, painting and poetry manifest the wealth of the real world. They let us read not only the ciphers of time, space, and corporeality, but the ciphers of fulfilled reality, in which they imaginatively include the three first-mentioned realms along with all other real or potential being. The interposed objectivity in which they move serves to remove painting and poetry from the elemental force of the proximity of being; but the interposition lets those arts deal with existence as an intermediate being, the way it is to us everywhere. In the cipher they detach us from being, but they bring us closer to the way in which we really meet the ciphers in existence.

Cutting across this division, music and poetry together can be opposed to the other arts. They are the two that move us most directly. They may deceive us, make us lose the cipher as emotions—sensuality in music, a variety of suspenseful experiences in literature—are quickly stirred up; but they also move us truly, because in the most abstract material of sound and language they call most forthrightly for an active involvement accentuated in time, for action that will make the cipher felt in the arousal of present self-being. The spatial arts are more detached, more cool and, in that sense, more noble. They reveal their cipher to a contemplation whose approach to them is more subdued.

PART THREE
THE SPECULATIVE READING OF CIPHERS

The Being of Transcendence: Arguments for the Existence of God

No empirical determination and no cogent inference can assure us that there is a transcendence at all. Transcendent being is encountered in transcending, but it is neither observed nor conceived.

I doubt transcendent being when I try to think of it purely in terms of consciousness at large and am simultaneously motivated by possible Existenz, for which alone my doubt has relevance. Now I want to make sure. I want to prove to myself that there is a transcendence. These proofs or "arguments for the existence of God" have coagulated in typical forms over scores of centuries. They fail, for transcendence is not as such; only for Existenz does it have the being of a historic cipher.

And yet the arguments are not mere fallacies if they elucidate an existential ascertainment of being. To think them is not yet the existential uplift of relativizing all existence that is not more than existence; but thinking of the arguments will clarify that factual uplift. Their form, of course, is to start with a being and to arrive at transcendence, but their point is to make an intrinsic sense of being clear.

The arguments fool us if they become known results that take the place of existential ascertainment. Even if they do not fool us, their rationalistic objectivity makes them like extreme dilutions of a clarification of being. Conceived as real in the echo of existential fulfillment, the arguments themselves are *ciphers of the thinker*, ciphers that unite his thought and his being.

But it is from the knowledge I have when I am truly aware of my being that I take the *content* of the arguments as if I had it still, even when that awareness is no longer present. Their content is the indefinite depth of transcendent being, stated in *negations;* it is the sublime, the absolute ideal, the most perfect being, the maximum in every sense, something I cannot conceive or imagine but can bring to mind by *en-*

hancing whatever fulfills me; and to the specifically religious individual it is the "thou" he turns to, the thou he means to hear as the subject of those heights and depths when he is *praying*.

The negations express my discontent with all existence; the enhancement, a fulfillment by reality; and prayer, the relationship into which trancendence enters with me. The awareness is either the ceaseless urge to transcend, with transcendence indefinite but real (expressed in negations), or the positive glow of being whenever I see truth, beauty, and good will (expressed in enhancement), or finally, in prayer, the turn of Existenz to the being which is its ground and shelter, its measure and succor (expressed as the personal deity).

As a rational statement, the argument now takes this form: *what is present, as being, in my existential awareness must be real, or I could not come to be aware of it.*

In other words: the being I conceive—which is what this awareness amounts to—is the being which an existential unity makes identical with the conception of it, thus demonstrating the reality of the conception.

Or: if the conception of this existential being did not imply the reality of its content—transcendence—it would not even be a being I conceive. Yet it is such a being, and so there is a transcendence.

Or: Existenz has being only with the thought of transcendence. Their union is, first, the existential one of being and thought in the thinker, and then the cipher of the union of thought and transcendence.

In every other case throughout the world, a thought is not yet a reality. To consciousness at large the two remain separate, rather, and reality must be established. Here and here alone the separation of being and thinking is deemed absurd because in case of such a separation the sense of that cogitative awareness would be voided, its factuality denied. To possible Existenz in existence, transcending is only another possibility that leaves realization by self-becoming a matter of free choice; but now the transcending of Existenz is deemed a reality identical with the assurance of transcendent being. I can deny the factuality of the cogitative awareness (and I do so as a psychologist, when I turn the awareness into a phenomenon, investigate its origin and its conditions, and let it go at that—in other words, when I consider only the empirical reality of a lived experience, not the existential being). But this factuality as well as its denial is a matter of freedom. As possible Existenz I cannot deny its possibility; as real Existenz I cannot deny its reality; as Existenz I cannot fail to transcend. The most I can do is freely to negate transcending—and yet, in negation, to perform it.

This general form of the argument can be modified, as in the following variants.

The *greatest conceivable being* is a possible thought. If it is possible, the greatest conceivable being must be real also, for if it were not, I could conceive a being greater than the greatest conceivable one—namely, the one that *is* real also—which would be a contradiction.

This thought would be impossible to carry through, however. No more than I can conceive "the greatest number" can I conceive any other "greatest" thing; the very thought would take me beyond each limit. I cannot substantially complete the thought of any "greatest." Yet the greatest conceivable being is not just an empty or impossible thought; it is a fulfilled thought which then is necessary, a thought I must think when I am really in being.

Or: I conceive the thought of *infinity*. I myself am a finite being and in existence I meet only finite things. That I harbor that thought, and that I come to be aware of being finite, must be due to a reason that cannot lie in my finiteness alone. The reason must fit the enormity of the thought. In other words: there must be the infinity I think, else I could not understand that I think it.

In these and other modifications of the thought which Kant termed the *ontological argument for God*, the speaker at the crucial point is Existenz, and thus—despite their objectifying rationality, which is itself not compelling—the probative character of the modifications is impaired. As mere rationalisms they would be circles and tautologies used to figure out logically impossible objects. But their rationality can be fulfilled, replete with the clarity I carry in myself, and though this will never give it the meaning of proof, it can mean a cipher for transcendent being. Because that rationality is null and void as proof in the sense of argumentation, its only meaning can be to express the utmost universality in stating a sense of being. In substance, therefore, the rationality of the arguments is never one and the same. As a detached logical form —the form in which proof is one and the same—it is a matter of indifference. But in its intrinsic quality it is historically fulfilled and therefore not to be possessed in any knowledge. It is a language, rather, which in each instance must be lent a new voice of its own.

The arguments for the existence of God are neither empirical nor logical. They cannot be intended as calculations to unlock transcendent being in the sense of something that exists somewhere. Instead, what lies in these arguments is being for a self-being—a being that is experienced but takes freedom to be experienced, and that is also stated but in the statement is conceived as a cipher.

The forms of the ontological argument refer to transcendence as such. They envision no individual thing but start out from my sense of being in existence. I, the thinker, come to be a cipher to myself. To be fulfilled, however, this cipher needs what I simultaneously am and see and believe. This is why all particular arguments for God are applications of the ontological one, starting out from a particular being that is existentially approached and thus characterizes a specific uplift.

The *cosmological* argument starts out from the existence of the world, which does not consist of itself. The *teleological* one starts out from the purposive design of life and the beauty of mundane things. The *moral* argument starts out from good will, which postulates transcendent being as its own ground and goal. Each time, the rational form and the visual being constitute only the medium in which the experience of discontent brings forth the argument proper. Looking through the veil of the rationalistic language, we see the font of each argument in the existential sense of being it expresses.

If the probative base of the arguments is allowed to wither in our thoughts, our statements grow empty. The only strength of the arguments lies in their existentially fulfilled content, in the present being in which transcendence is heard as a cipher.

Because the arguments are intended, not as real proofs, but as ciphers that must be fulfilled historically, and because they turn so easily into trivia, they do not keep us from doubting that there is transcendence. They are not means to refute our doubt—when they do claim to refute it, they invite it, rather—but to clarify and strengthen our awareness.

How can the being of transcendence be doubted at all? It may be doubted because our sense of being has strayed into the blindness of mere existence: there has been a failure of Existenz. It may be doubted because of the possibility of an empty, formal thinking in which nothing is truly thought: our doubt consists of words only. And transcendent being may be doubted because of a failure to notice that something which is not transcendence, which was substituted for transcendence, has in fact been posited as absolute after all: our doubt merely shields an unclarified unconditionality.

I cannot refute my doubt; I can only act against it. Transcendence is not proven; transcendence engenders. The cipher is to me the voice of transcendent being, but it will not become a reality without my doing. Discontent and love are the fonts of my active realization of the cipher that is not yet, or of my contemplative reception of the cipher's appeal to me.

It takes free acts to bring transcendence to the mind of a philosophical self-being in the world. The transcendence of one who philosophizes is no more demonstrable than is the God of religion found in a cult.

The Being of a Cipher:
Speculation on Becoming

When formulas of transcending are used to express transcendent being, with cogitative experiences transformed into ontological knowledge, the result may be as follows.

There is a transcendence. Being as such is absolute, for it depends on nothing else, and it is not related to anything else, for it has nothing outside it. It is infinite. To being, what to us is split is one. Being is unity pure and simple—unity of thought and being, of subject and object, of accuracy and truth, of being and the ought, of becoming and being, of matter and form. Yet if this one, this whole being is self-sufficient, an Existenz that finds itself in existence will ask: Why is there an existence? Why the split, the division of subject and object, of thought and reality, of what I ought to be and what I am? What sort of road led from being to existence, from the infinite to the finite, from God to the world?

There are playful answers to these questions.

We can say, for example, that being would not be intrinsic if it did not *manifest* itself. A self-sufficient being is unaware of itself; it is only a possibility unreally revolving about its own axis. Not unless it enters into existence and then, from all the divisions, returns to itself will it become both manifest and real. It is not a whole unless even the utmost dichotomy, its own split from existence, is integrated and united in it. What it is, being must be as becoming in time. It is not infinite unless it includes the finite. It is supreme power and perfection when finiteness and division are granted an independent being of their own and yet encompassed by the being in which all is as one. The highest tension harbors the deepest manifestation.

This reply, this harmonization of everything, will be rejected in view of all that is dark, evil, absurd. A new playful thought will counter that being was indeed bound to reveal itself, but what exists now is not manifest being. This existence need not be. A catastrophe has occurred in transcendence, an *apostasy* by beings which, though part of being, wanted their own being anyway, beyond the established measure. Thus the world came about.

Existence, in both of these thoughts, is *history*. As the self-revelation of being it is timeless history, an eternal present; the manifest expanse in time without beginning or end is the phenomenon of being, which is identical with itself at all times, eternally giving itself and returning. As apostasy, on the other hand, existence is temporal history, with a beginning and an end, with the beginnings conceived as pernicious and catastrophic and the end as a restoration, and thus as voiding existence.

As naked objectifications, these answers have the *defect of starting out from the imaginary point of a transcendence known as being*, as if there could be a cognition of being. The phrasings of a self-sufficient being that might have remained undisturbed in perfection and would not have needed to come into existence—these phrasings are projections of thoughts into an absolute duration; as thoughts, they have real meaning only insofar as they express a categorial transcending or an existentially elucidative appeal. The very posing of the question is dubious because its point of departure is the being of the imaginary point of transcendence, as if that were extant.

To Existenz, existence becomes a cipher. An Existenz cannot even clearly fulfill the question why there is an existence; the question only makes it dizzier as it seeks to combine meaning with the words. But that existence is a cipher is a matter of course to an Existenz for which there is a transcendence. All things must be able to be ciphers; if there were no cipher, there would be no transcendence either. The unities of the dichotomies lie in reading the cipher, although this reading never gives us access to a being detached from existence. This is also why we do not arrive at a starting point for the question why being comes into existence. From our existence we can rise to the cipher, but we cannot descend to the cipher from transcendent being. *The fact that there are ciphers at all is to us identical with the fact that there is transcendence at all;* existing, we do not grasp transcendence otherwise than in existence. For us, the question why there is existence is replaced by the question why there are ciphers. And the answer is that *for an existential consciousness the cipher is the only form in which transcendence appears to such a consciousness.* It is the sign that from the sight of Existenz transcendence is indeed hidden, but has not vanished.

The depth of inconceivability receives its due in the cipher, as against the supposed knowledge of a supersensory origin of transcendence itself, and of its becoming a world. *The cipher is the existence I must recognize, the existence in which I find myself and can in truth become only what I am.* I would like to be something else; I would like to presume that I am the equal of all that is noble—or, rather, better than all; my being irks me; I should like to be God himself if there is one. But I can harbor these thoughts and desires only when I am not reading ciphers. Ciphers make me profoundly aware of my existential possibility at this point of my existence, and they let my self-being come to rest in the cipher view of being as incomprehensible, and in my subsequent, free, total effort to become what I am and can be. I come to feel the flatly destructive self-deception that lies in cerebration without transcendence and in volition by instinct, with all things supposed to be different from the way they are, and with reality no longer in full focus. In this self-deception I lose what a commitment on my part would really let me change.

Present Reading of Ciphers: Speculative Remembrance and Foresight

And yet, truth is not wholly lacking in the question why there is existence, and in the playful answers to it. The question comes to express a sense of having become: *the historicity of Existenz is universalized into the existence of being as such.* The process of manifestation, known to me solely from myself in communication, turns into the reflection of a transcendence in which it will not be lost. The thought of apostasy, existential only as a reality of freedom, strikes roots in transcendence because my Existenz will not make it sufficiently clear to me—because I seem to fathom it as in a memory of choosing myself before the beginning of time, at the original departure of all things from transcendent being. The historicity of existential becoming has turned into a cipher.

But the lucid cipher of historicity is no sooner objectified into a known origin of the world than all of it grows deceptive. The world's existence is an object of scientific world orientation only, even when we are dealing with the beginning and the end. Research is boundless, and its premise—which we cannot think of voiding—is that the world is temporal existence, endless without a beginning or an end.

I have, in the present, what being is; but I do not have it purely present.

What it is comes to mind in remembrance, as what it was. And it comes to my mind in foresight as what it may come to be, what is still unsettled.

Remembrance and foresight alone give me access to being. If I grasp the cipher in both, they become one. What I remember is present as a possibility that can be regained in foresight. What I see in foresight is empty unless it is remembered also. The present no longer remains simply the present; if I read the cipher in a foresight permeated by remembrance, it becomes present eternity.

1. Remembrance

Psychologically, to remember is to know things I have learned, to recollect people and things, events and situations I have experienced. It is dead remembrance as the mere having of things I can represent and reproduce; it is a remembering process as the unconscious or conscious aftereffect of experienced life, as complete adoption and penetration, as the forgetting of things by transforming them into general knowledge or by locking them out as if they had never been experienced.

Historical remembrance is the adoption of tradition. My psychological memory of a limited time span is able to break through my own existence, to grasp a being outside my own, a being that was when I myself was not yet. I share in the memory of mankind by receiving an existence that comes to me in documents. I expand beyond the existence I am, into boundless eons. My existence remains the situation from which I start out, my standard of measuring myself, and my point of reference, but my existence itself is changed by my way of historical remembrance. As an unconscious tradition this remembrance molds me from my first awakening. As objective knowledge, and as my idea of the past in the wealth of its figures, it becomes a link in my cultivation of my mind. From the point of view of mere research and observation the past is extant, a petrified act that is the way it came to be; but historical remembrance is a living thing to which the past is still present as a reality of possibilities in flux. I share in them and play a part in deciding what has truly been. In itself, of course, that which has been is settled; but it is not yet definitively that which makes it our concern. Hence the unfathomability of what has been. It is extant in itself, but to us it is an inexhaustible possibility.

In the psychological and historical realms, remembrance becomes existential when he who remembers ties himself to the remembered thing. In my memories I freely accept what I am, as given. I am what I was and what I want to be. Fidelity, the historic sense of my fate as inseparable from the persons I came to be with; awe of the foundations of my own existence; the strength of reverence for what appealed to me as the true being of Existenz—these are phenomena of the existential self-identification I need to be really I, not just an empty I in consciousness at large. A denial of remembrance would uproot me.

None of these remembrances is the metaphysical one. But in each one it may happen.

It is an experience—though putting it into words makes it only an interpretation—that an insight which becomes clear to me is self-evident, as if I had always known it and were now merely having it lucidly. The insight is like an awakening to myself, a return of something I had unwittingly carried.

For long periods of time my understanding of past history simply means to take external cognizance of it; but when the understanding becomes lucid, it is like a remembering for which the documents merely provide the occasion. Something in me responds to the outward impressions that make me conscious of it.

There is remembrance in everything that turns for me into an existential presence. It amounts to a realization of what I had not wanted to be before and yet really am, unknown to me. In deciding about my being and fulfilling it, I remember eternal being.

Here the sense of remembering lay in *present reality*. It does not become remembrance till I read it as a cipher—factually in original awareness, interpretively in subsequent communication. It is not otherness that I remember. I do not penetrate a beyond, a strange world beyond the cipher. Cipher being means precisely to read only in the cipher itself, in its unity of existence and transcendence. Remembrance is a form of access in which I feel existence turn into a cipher.

This remembering accompanies my existence as a constant awareness of the depths of the past. In the cipher the past becomes being. The being that was is no more, and yet it is not nothing. Remembrance comes to be my access to it, through the factuality of present things. In the world itself this world of memory becomes a presence of the inscrutable past. What to world orientation is only something now, a new existence in the endless flux of coming and going, is to my Existenz a phenomenon of the being I recall in it. Outwardly speaking, existence is a sign of being; inwardly, as a cipher, it is steeped in remembrance. Goethe could express this cipher being in incomprehensible terms of love: "Ah, it was in times before this life that you were my sister or my wife"; and Schelling, the impassioned reader of all existence as a cipher, could speak of "being privy to the Creation," which man attended and thus can remember now. This remembrance is a longing one; it is the impulse of readiness that can move us even in early childhood, when we scarcely have a past and have not lost anything yet.

It is from this point that certain psychologically conditioned experiences—fairly frequent as such, and irrelevant in themselves—may occasionally come into the context of a recollective cipher reading if an existential content fills them: the *déjà vu*, for example, and the waking from sleep with a sense of emergence from crucial depths of the past. Profoundly struck by the shuddersome mystery that seemed to unveil intrinsic being, I want to hold it fast; but with progressive awakening it flattens out, and by the time I am fully conscious, I may still feel oddly ready, but that which was has been reduced to nothing, after all.

2. *Foresight*

In foresight I look at that which is to come. If I *expect* an event that will happen of necessity, I make a *forecast.* If I want to *realize a goal,* I picture the whole that is to become real, and within this picture I draw up a *plan,* relating means to ends. If my foresight *determines my actions in undetermined situations,* it becomes *speculation:* on the ground of merely probable prognoses, proceeding by invariably suspended and flexible ways, I do what may have the desired result in each instance.

The future is what is possible, and foresight is thus a conception of possibilities. Even when I predict things that are bound to happen, the infinity of possible conditions leaves a margin for doubt: what is not yet can always come to be different from the most assured expectation. Factual world orientation expands the realm of the possible by acquainting us with more distinct expectations and more abundant images; but at the same time it restricts that realm by drawing the line between definable objects and the haze of unlimited possibilities.

An enclave in the possibilities of the future is *that which depends upon me,* and the crux of the future is that things remain to be *decided.* What I really am in the future depends so much upon me that I feel responsible for it. My sense of impotence regarding the course of the world is as original as my sense of freedom where I am concerned; but while remembrance is the inescapable bond in myself, foresight gives me freedom within the realm of the possible.

I know what exists by what will happen; I know what I am by what I decide. If all future existence were completed, being would be finally revealed. As it stands, however, future being is the suspended cipher which I either fulfill in an anticipation or read in its indeterminacy, as a trend.

In metaphysical play I anticipate the end of days, perfection as the coming of a timeless spirit realm, the recovery of all losses, a manifestness past all processes. But in temporal existence any picture of a future existence that shows a definitively extant realm of perfection and is meant to be real is a utopian absurdity. For in the world of time the last word belongs to world orientation, and what world orientation shows, more and more bluntly, is the impossibility of a calmly enduring existence, along with constantly new possibilities. Only as a metaphysical language can the game of transcending temporal existence have an evanescent import.

In this game I read the direction of being *qua* future being: being is the concealment that will be revealed; what is will see the light of day; existence already harbors the germ of what will become, and then will show, what is. Things to come are in being as things now.

I drop all the chains of a knowing world orientation by conceiving them boundlessly expanded as I transcend: to me, infinite possibility comes to be the reflection of infinite being.

Being is what lies in the future. Foresight is my form of access to it.

3. Contrariety and Unity of Remembrance and Foresight

Remembrance and foresight are in contrast with each other. In remembrance the past is extant; man assumes a contemplative posture, going back only to that which is; with nothing left to be decided, time as such becomes a matter of indifference. In foresight the future is that which concerns me, which my decision will help to bring about, but in itself it is the being to come. In both cases an isolation of either past or future robs the present of its being. The *depreciated present* is interpreted as a low point and a transition: as the deepest fall to look back from, or as the farthest distance from which to look ahead. The present itself is nothing. I live by stepping out of it: I look for myself in my past ground, or I live in expectation of the future I need to confirm my being. *The sense of present nonentity in turn renders past and future ambiguous.* The past is the depth of perfection to which I feel urged to return, or it is the horror I have incomprehensibly outgrown and never want to return to; the bond of my past may be the substance of my being or the curb on my potential. The future is the golden age when all will some day be resolved, or it is the abyss—whether as the end or as an empty endlessness or as the onslaught of every terror I face in despair.

There is a link between the isolation of past or future, the depreciation of the present, and the ambiguity of all that is not present. Together they are the decline from an incipient reading of ciphers to a cipherless objectivity. Remembrance and foresight are modes of cipher reading only when they *unite in present eternity*, in the Now as the focal point of existential being.

Only the most resolute grip on time itself will let an Existenz overcome time. As the place of decision, time is neither a low point nor a fall; it is the present which I am cast back upon in order truly to be. In the unconditionality of decision, the Now casts radiance from the being which that unconditionality makes me love in the form of the presence, the present transparence, of man and of the world. In decline the present is never intrinsic, being always either no more or not yet, and the empirical reality of the present remains an unattainable limit of world orientation; but the reality of transcendence in the being of ciphers is each present time. It is the *nunc stans,* the eternal present borne by a past remembered and illuminated by a future foreseen, and only in union with both of them will it permit us to feel being in the cipher.

The transcendence in the cipher is the past being that comes toward me from the future—or, differently put, the being I remember as I look ahead. Hence the closing of the circle: *what merely passes in time rounds into being.* But it does so only as a cipher, not for some kind of knowledge; and it carries the risk that as a thought the cipher may detach me existentially from time in favor of a metaphysical contemplation which will grow vacuous, and that the only ground on which this cipher has been visible may be destroyed.

Remembrance occurs, first, in the *personal historicity* of my life, which brings me what I do myself, like a homecoming. The existentially decided course of life is an ascertainment of what I have been. The uplift to being as I embrace things to come is my union with the future as the being to which I have always been joined. What comes to me from the future into the present has a persuasiveness not derived from correct thoughts and facts, nor from the efficacy of a course of action, but from present reality as eternal reality. What I encounter is quite new, in the sense that I never thought of it and never had a picture or an idea of it; and it is quite old, as if it had always been and were merely found again.

Next, remembrance occurs in *history,* in the past of the human race. There I remember in viewing this ground of my existence as the realm of every Existenz that has awakened me. I no longer see the random material of past worlds; instead, what I meet in history is either recognized as that which I eternally belong to or it will be dropped as irrelevant. Throughout my existence, my life with history is one sole course of awakening by communing with spirits, and only thereby is it the possibility of striking roots in the present, whose future can be of substance to me only now.

4. Speculation in the Philosophy of History

As a detailed thought structure, metaphysical speculation is a rare growth from the depth of human remembrance. Those engaged in it speak of a transcendent being they have originally read in the ciphers of their own existential existence. In history—a history for which the past explored by the historical science of world orientation is no more than material—they read a cipher of existence as a whole, from the beginning to the end of days.

To science, each total conception of history is defined by a certain point of view. If man, for instance, is conceived as fundamentally the same always and everywhere, historical understanding is considered possible because my own possibilities and those of others are identical everywhere, however vast the differences in their unfoldment and realization.

Or we speak of a world history in the sense that all existence hitherto dispersed is drawn into a single context. Or we admit endless changes in the multifarious existence of man, but assume within these changes a certain typicality of varied processes that have come and gone without relating to each other and without an adequate memory of the whole, because there is no whole.

The cipher of the whole is different. Historic itself, it is a speculation in which Existenz comprehends itself in the totality of its accessible existence. The sense of being can be expressed in a *supersensory philosophy of history* that encompasses past and future in order to understand everything as a language of present eternity. Thus, evanescent structures were speculatively conceived in the Christian history of the world from the Creation and the Fall to the Last Judgment; others followed, dependent on the Christian one at first, but finally changed altogether in Hegel's philosophy of history—whose cipher throughout is the past and the empirical event only—and in Schelling's mythicized history that comprises past and future and only slightly touches the empirical realm. The only meaningful way to test such speculations is to test them existentially. Their proper content is not subject to scientific investigation.

If the rounding here seems too definitive, the world too definite, the form too objective, and if the peril of decline into a knowing possession of the whole is therefore such that an Existenz that gives in to it will perish almost at the first perception, we can seek a more indistinct cipher. But this too will stay all but mute.

There, my remembrance refers to a *spirit realm* that lets me enter as the man my actions make me. The remembrance is at the same time a kind of foresight: as the question whether or not, and how, I join this spirit realm. I feel I may be in a community that I hear in my inmost conscience, in a community long in being, yet never closed and definitive.

Wherever I felt on the point of contact, historical figures and contemporaries would become untouchable to me. I listen in silence whether the other has this untouchability—and whether we come silently together, having gained access to such ranks without the help of any objectivity, of anything that can be laid down in words.

It is not being that becomes visible as a whole here, not the super-sensory history of all things. But I remember the spirit realm by be-coming myself in the future, and it is this remembrance that comes to be present as a cipher—though there is no point to articulating a thought-out history, location, or population of that realm. Only in the cipher of real existence is access to it to be gained.

And yet, all great metaphysics has been more than that. It has been *an articulated reading of the cipher script,* an explicit statement of what being says in existence, and what, therefore, it is. We shall have to review this questionable enterprise, which nonetheless must never be totally spurned if a historic word out of the solitude of cipher-reading Existenz is sought at all.

The Cipher of Existence
as a Whole:
Speculation on Being

What being might be without existence is flatly inaccessible. That there is a transcendence at all has been speculatively conceived in trains of thought misleadingly called "arguments for the existence of God," and that there are ciphers in existence at all could be understood as incomprehensible. The present reading of ciphers, finally, has become clear in speculative remembrance and foresight.

But what about the cipher of existence as a whole? What this really tells us would, if we could have it as a speculative knowledge, bring the deepest insight possible in existence. Yet existence as a cipher remains ambiguous. It does not become a definitive entirety. And what it says, therefore, will again take only the form of a thought movement in which possible Existenz resorts to ciphers for the positive fulfillment of its sense of transcendence.

As possible Existenz I explore reality in world orientation and try to unveil by a comprehensive hypothesis what underlies the whole. In *positivism* I seek cognition and a knowledge instead of the cipher.

In *idealism* I explore throughout reality while being existentially conscious at the same time of a thoroughly interrelated unity of the idea—of the whole which I rediscover everywhere in countless variants.

Or I see that hypothetical cognition will necessarily founder and that there are limits to unity and ideal entirety. I do go back to positivism with its unmerciful eye for all empirical reality, but I do not take this reality for outright being; I grant that a sense of unity and ideal entirety is relatively valid, but I break it up when it becomes absolutizing and anticipatory. For as Existenz I must stay in the one place where I can be real: in the temporal existence that shows me a diverse being, an undefinable transcendence, an ambiguous cipher. Only in historic concreteness can I believe what I do in fact as the *cipher reading of existential philosophy*.

1. Positivism

The strength of positivism lies in its will not to ignore any empirical reality. A positivist will reject all means to make a reality unreal by calling it accidental, irrelevant, unessential, diseased, abnormal. But he has a weakness: he wants to explore the unexplorable. Behind his world hypotheses—which are scientific fallacies—stands the impulse to interpret the cipher of existence. Since his method makes him misconceive that impulse, he will lose its transcendent source: rather than with ciphers, he will end up with empty conceptual mechanisms or with an empty not-knowing.

Positivism is the soil of the sciences that give us our bearings in the world. The impulse behind them is to see what is; their metaphysical significance is a succinct demonstration of the facts that may become ciphers.

2. Idealism

The strength of idealism is that it envisions the unity of the immaterial whole. An idealist wants to let nothing exist in isolation; he wants to understand the entirety of things, to connect each one with every other. But his weakness is that he ignores whatever would disturb his unity. While seemingly ranging all over the wealth of existence, he ends up with a tranquillizing view of a supposed universal harmony, a view devoid of transcendence.

All unities and entireties, the original ciphers of the unity of being, cease to be ciphers for the idealist as he comprehends them. To him, the whole is the unity of antitheses. The synthetical unity of what seems mutually exclusive constitutes his true being, and it is precisely in negation that what seems mutually destructive brings itself into substantial existence for him. What in isolation looks like discord is but an enhancing element in the harmony of the whole. This harmony is an organic, self-structured unity in an evolution whereby that which is impossible simultaneously comes to be possible in sequence. Everything has its destiny and its place—like every character in a play, every organ in a living body, each single step in the execution of a plan.

This unity is initially motivated by the basic experience that to me *my world always becomes entire*. In space it is not a rubble pile; it is a structure that strikes me as beautiful everywhere, provided it is properly viewed. Wherever I am, I see a whole come into being: in the arrangement of my space, in corporeal structure, in the atmosphere of the landscape which includes that which in isolation would be unstructured. This entirety is not only of my making. Nature promotes it, covering the most disjoint and jarring things with a blanket of unifying peace. The world entirety—conceived in the cosmos, brought to mind in images—turns analogically into the world landscape, the one fulfilled spatiality of existence.

The second basic experience is the *unity of the mind,* the fact that understanding brings all there is into the context of self-consciousness. The cosmos, instead of being read in the unity of spatial nature, is real in the ideal unity of an absolute spirit in which spatial nature is but a link. This spirit, manifested in existence as history, is always present in myself as intelligibility.

But the decisive motive behind unity is the *will to reconcilement.* There is harmony because a possible Existenz pacifies its sense of being in restoration from the negativity of untruth, of moral and physical evil, of pain, of suffering. In the world there is this negativity, of course, but only as part of a process in which being comes to itself. Confined and imperfect, I occupy a place in the whole where I have to perform my specific tasks, to bear the corresponding negative side of my particularity, and to dissolve it in the whole. The negative, of whichever sort, is not real in itself at all; it is an articulation of the positive. The negative in my place—my own suffering—is senseless in this place if viewed by itself alone, but when I view it in the whole it will make sense. I must achieve the serenity of contemplation, in which I see myself in my place in the whole, aware of a confinement as well as of a calling, and know that everything is all right. In this serenity, freedom is nothing but the concordance of my inner posture with the whole. Beauty is the perfection of being in the work of art, a perfection that can never be attained in our confining existence.

Idealism is the philosophy of happiness. The idealist lives with a sense of the real entirety that lies in the ciphers of existence as the One and All, rescinding all negativity. He does know tensions, but only the tensions for which a solution exists. Marriage, family, the state, the occupational and social entireties, and finally the world entirety—these make up the substance with which it seems possible to live in close accord. Every defect is compensated for by something else. Struggle is only a means of evolving union. One thing enhances the other. Through dissonance we move toward harmony.

3. Cipher Reading in Existential Philosophy

No definitive, pictorially or speculatively rounded knowledge of transcendent being can be attained in existential philosophy. This philosophy is philosophizing in existence, and the disjointness of being leaves it with no alternative other than to achieve the one being as Existenz, by way of historicity. In existential philosophy I know that a supposed perfection would mean that I had stepped out of existence without seeing a realization of the whole, and of the One for all men. *The permanent world of philosophizing is existence in time*, with the sense of having a future and a whole to which I belong by choosing.

Philosophizing takes me back to positivism, to an unlimited readiness to acknowledge facts; initially, all it asks of a fact is that it be that way. Factuality, ever new and ever-changing, remains an impulse to philosophizing.

When I philosophize, I enter into the absolute historicity of Existenz, and thus into boundary situations and into communication. As a positivist or an idealist I know the one truth, and therefore only a relative historicity and a secondary communication in that one extant truth; there is no original communication where truth and the deity are revealed, where historicity is only a special case or a concretion of the universal. Existentially, however, communication comes to be the awakening, the contact, the conjunction of truths which are nothing but themselves and are lost to us when we conceive them as entireties. Since the deity stays hidden, our only firm support lies in Existenz taking the hand of other Existenz.

To Existenz in phenomenal temporal existence, this *temporality itself is a cipher*, but not an unequivocal one. An Existenz can neither, for itself, anticipate the reality of its realization and of its foundering nor anticipate the whole in that which as a cipher is already called "the end of days." To Existenz, eternity is present, athwart its present temporality—but again in temporal ciphers only, as decision, resolve, probation, or fidelity.

The world of the ciphers, which once upon a time were meant directly and immediately, can be retained by Existenz as the realm of its own possibilities. Even that which idealists conceived as a system and considered a matter of knowledge may now, as a whole, become a possible cipher. It is as such ciphers that the grand aspects of being devised by Plotinus and Hegel are still relevant—not in the sense that they might commit me, of course, but as a possible language for existential moments and as a back-drop of the strangeness, the otherness, that has its own truth even if it is not mine.

When we think of the whole—narratively, in the world of ciphers, or constructively, in speculation—the existential origin of our thinking makes us treat a metaphysical system as if it were mythology. Instead of drawing on world orientation, on the systematics of the sciences, for merely relative world images from existence, we conceive one being as the ground of all things. There are two ways of doing this. It may happen in naturalistic, in logical, in dialectic-ideal forms that are akin in the basic posture of envisioning a tranquillizing unity of the universal whole. Or it may happen on the borderline of conceptuality and visual myth: when a positive transcendent story is told in a different basic posture, with the whole viewed as unfathomably historic and every intrinsic part of the whole as individual and noninterchangeable, not deducible from a universal, but rooted in transcendence.

Possible Existenz today can no longer solidify the ciphers, and yet they need not be nothing. And no matter what they are, they will be infinitely ambiguous once they become objective, and in order to be true they must withstand the final cipher, that of foundering. They must hold up under a ruthlessly positivistic view of the facts of foundering, and under an existentially serious approach to it in boundary situations.

PART FOUR
Vanishing of Existence and Existenz as the Decisive Cipher of Transcendence: Being in Foundering

The Many Meanings of Factual Foundering

All forms of the corporeal world are transitory, from fabrics and rocks to the suns; what remains in their unceasing transformation is the matter they were made of. Death comes to all living existence. Man learns in his life and from his history that everything has to end. Realizations become untenable as social conditions change; thought possibilities are exhausted; modes of intellectual life fade out. We see greatness annihilated. We see profundity evaporate, with its effects seeming to continue after it has turned into something else. In history as a whole there has been progress only in technology and in the rationalization of existence; in the areas of true humanity and of the human mind, a history that brought forth the extraordinary has simultaneously been the triumphal parade route of destructive forces. Were mankind to develop without limits, no stable state, no permanent mundane existence could be achieved without destroying man as such. Inferiority and vulgarity seem to facilitate survival amid mere change. Lacking a unity of meaning and of continuity, the evolutionary course would have no chance to become entire; what would be realized and then destroyed is only what no remembrance need ever recall. The existence of living people to whom this past was only a futile, forgotten Before, not a premise of their consciousness, would be like the existence of a few hot embers that might as well be left from the fire of Rome as from the burning of a rubbish heap. Should a fantastic technology accomplish things still inconceivable today, it would be capable of equally fantastic havoc. If the technological wrecking of the foundations of all human existence were a possibility, there is small doubt that some day it would be a reality. By our activities we can impede things, put them off, win periods of grace, but all the experience of human history suggests that some day, somewhere, somebody will do the worst that can be done.

Foundering is the ultimate, according to an inexorably realistic world orientation. More yet: it is what ultimately comes to mind in thinking of all things. In logic, validity founders on relativity; at the bounds of knowledge we confront antinomies that finish our ability to think without contradictions; what emerges beyond knowledge, encompassing knowledge, is a truth that is not rationalistic. For world orientation the world founders as existence, being not comprehensible by and in itself; it does not become a closed, intelligible being, nor can the cognitive process round itself into a whole. What founders in existential elucidation is the being-in-itself of Existenz: where I am really myself I am not myself only. In transcendence, thought will founder on nocturnal passion.

In such visualizations of becoming and passing away, of destructibility and assured destruction, of frustration and failure, the source of confusion is the undifferentiated diversity of what we mean by foundering.

For pure existence there is only a passing away of which it has no knowledge. Foundering requires knowledge, and then a reaction to it. The animal is subject only to objective transitoriness; it exists completely in the present, sure of its instincts, perfectly adapted to the things it does under living conditions that suit it; but when these are denied there will be bursts of ferocity or brooding silence, or dull, unwitting and unwilling fear. Man alone can founder, and this capacity is to him not unequivocal: it challenges him to react to it. *In itself,* I might say, nothing founders and nothing remains; I let something founder *in me,* by my cognition and recognition of foundering. If my knowledge of the end of all things is submerged in the undifferentiated unity of an abyss that is sheer darkness, an abyss to which I want to shut my eyes, I can regard the animal as the pure, present fulfillment of an ideal existence and lovingly, longingly raise it above myself. But I cannot become an existing animal. All I can do is to give myself up as a human being.

If I remain in the human situation, I make distinctions. What founders is not just an existence passing away. It is not just cognition shattering itself in the attempt to grasp being, pure and simple. It is not just action lacking a final purpose that might last. The boundary situations reveal that all our positives are tied to corresponding negatives. There is no good without possible or real evil, no truth without falsehood, no life without death. Happiness is tied to pain, and realization to risks and losses. The depth in man which lends a voice to his transcendence is bound up in reality with destructiveness, sickness, or extravagance, but this vastly variegated bond does not exist unequivocally. In all existence I can see its antinomical structure.

The ways of foundering are thus objective realities or thinkable inescapabilities, and in some sense, therefore, they mean a foundering in, and of, existence. The foundering of Existenz lies on a different plane. When I come freely from existence to an assurance of being, it is precisely in the acts of my most lucid and forthright self-being that I must experience its foundering. For the impossibility of being absolutely on my own does not arise only from a factually destructive bondage to existence, but from freedom itself. My freedom makes me guilty in any case; I cannot become entire. Truth proper, which I comprehend because I am and live it, cannot possibly be knowable as generally valid; general validities are timeless and could endure in ever-changing existence, but intrinsic truth is the very one to go down.

Self-being proper cannot maintain itself alone. It may default, and it cannot compel its coming. The more decided its success, the clearer the limit that will make it fail. Failure in its search for self-sufficiency prepares it for its otherness, for transcendence. But when transcendence defaults, when my trust in the transcendent relationship in which I ultimately hope to find myself is disappointed—I never know what was my guilt, then, and what I must bear as having happened to me. *I can founder on myself,* and philosophical trust will not help me, nor will divine words and religious promises, for all the readiness and veracity in which I seem to exist.

The question in the diversity of foundering, however, is whether it means outright destruction—whether that which founders is perishing in fact—or whether it reveals a being. In other words, whether foundering can mean not merely foundering but eternalization.

Foundering and Eternalization

My natural, vital, matter-of-course existence aims at duration. It not only seeks to keep from foundering but presupposes the possibility of extant being—of an empirical being that evolves into a boundless future, preserves what has been gained, and advances to better things; of a being that is logically accessible without leaving a remainder; of a being I can think without contradictions. On such a premise, foundering will not be necessary. It is a risk, but one that can be overcome. When the individual dies, his work remains, taken into history by others. Nowhere does contradiction need to turn into an inescapable antinomy. It is due to error, and clarity and improved experience will void it.

But I must be intentionally blind to cling to this premise. Foundering is the ultimate.

It was because all empirical phenomena proved transitory that my existence, in its quest of being proper, turned to the objectivity of valid and timeless things; but insofar as such things become accessible to me, it is precisely in their timelessness that they are not merely unreal but empty. I turned to subjectivity, to give fulfillment to valid things in their reality; but I see this reality trickle away in the flow of mere life. I want a being that makes eternal, and I look for it in duration: in my progeny, in works that will remain effective beyond my life. But even here I cannot blind myself to the fact that all of it means only an extension of existence in time, not absolute duration. I must be thoughtless to confuse prolonged existence with imperishability.

At last, faced with the transiency of all things—though they may pass only after thousands of years—my possible Existenz in existence will see true being only in the concrete, present reality of my own self-being. And this is where even destruction and perdition turn into being, if only I freely embrace them. Foundering, which in my existence I merely suffer as though by accident, can now be embraced as intrinsic foundering. Instead of spurning it, my will to make things eternal seems to find its goal in foundering itself.

As a vital creature I have the will to last, and losses make me seek new support in something extant; but as possible Existenz I want the being I can embrace even as I go down, without its being extant. Regarding *destruction suffered* when the best-loved disappears, unfinished, I can accept what happens, and in clear-sighted suffering I can feel that a moment of present fulfillment may be past, but is not lost. Then, of course, if my transfiguring imagination entwines being with perdition—in such thoughts as that he whom the gods love dies young, or that giving form to a thing makes it eternal—Existenz will balk. If all that is left to it is passive suffering, a contemplative tranquillization cannot satisfy the Existenz whose sense of being proper stays unfinished in the pure contemplation of not being lost. It must have taken itself into its foundering, rather, beginning with its own activity, with the risks that entails, and then in its own failure. It is not in contemplation, in which I merely accept, that the cipher is clearly revealed; it is revealed to my Existenz which freely produces the cipher in going down as existence. In its own ruins Existenz will find its ground in transcendent being.

As a phenomenon, foundering remains contradictory. The solution is not known. It lies in being, which remains hidden. The man who has really climbed the existential steps in his own proper fate comes up against this being. It cannot be presupposed. There is no authority that could be its administrator and mediator. Its eye is upon him who dares approach it.

A *direct will to founder* would be a perversion, a renewed total obscuring of being into nothingness. The true, revealing foundering does not lie in random perdition, not in every destruction, not in each instance of self-abandonment, resignation, or failure. The cipher of eternalization in foundering is lucid only when I do *not* want to founder even though I take the risk. I cannot plan to read the cipher of foundering; I can plan only for duration. The cipher unveils, not when I will it, but when I do all I can to avoid its reality. It unveils in the *amor fati*; but a fatalism that surrenders prematurely and thus does not founder any more would be untrue.

If the random plunge into foundering is thus sheer nothingness, the foundering that overwhelms me when I truthfully do all I can to avoid it need not be mere foundering. In this foundering I can experience being if I have done all I could to resist in existence, if I take full responsibility for myself as Existenz, if I make the utmost demands on myself—but not if the sense of my creatural nonentity before transcendence makes me resign myself to the being of a creature.

Just as flagging in the struggle for existence and ignominious abandonment of self-being are stabs at the void, so is a direct *willing of the end of all things* an embrace of the end as the obliteration of existence, not as the being of eternity. There is a deceptive temptation in the nihilistic and sensual ideas of the end as a delightful wrecking of this wretched world. The cipher of being in foundering marks the goal of a road shunned by those who take this attitude, who proclaim: "We believe in the end; we want the end, for we ourselves are the end—or at least the beginning of the end. In our eyes lies an expression never seen before in human eyes." That the note struck in these words may seem akin to the uplift of existential foundering in the world serves only to make them a more frightening display of the false pathos of worldless passion.

Being may be experienced in peril and extinction, but I pervert this experience when phenomenal existence comes to be not merely evanescent but irrelevant to me—when I seek my true being not in a constructive life in the world but in the arms of *adventure*. I absolutize daring, destruction, perdition even when there is nothing at issue—precisely then, in fact—with the idea that this kind of consciousness will take me to being. I regard anything in which the world is taken seriously, all duration as well as all timelessness, as deceptive. The adventurer feels only scorn for all orders of life; he despises the status quo. The extravagant loosing of all bonds, the reckless gamble, the surprising, the unexpected—to him who jubilantly embraces or smilingly suffers his downfall, all this is truth.

When I exist as possible Existenz, however, I shudder not just at the void of merely objective validities, not just at the delusion of a supposed permanence, but at the unsubstantiality of mere perdition in adventure. Objectivity and duration are nothing in themselves, but they remain the phenomenal body of Existenz in temporal existence. Pure perdition is nothing: the one thing that really perishes without realization in the world is a chaotic subjectivity. And yet it remains true that essentials perish as phenomena and that perdition must be received in me to reveal the depths that let me see the ground of being proper. Eternalization would thus be the building of a world in existence with a continuous will to abide by norms and to achieve duration—but not only with a sense of the perdition that is eternity's entrance into the phenomenality of time, not only with a readiness for it, but with the full knowledge of risking it.

Only this true foundering, this unreserved knowledge and open acceptance of it, can become a fulfilled cipher of being. Whether I shroud reality from myself or dispense with it in heading for my downfall—in either case I miss the genuine foundering as I founder in fact.

To Realize and Not to Realize

The sense of foundering need not turn us into passive nonentities. It may be possible in consequence of it, to engage in true activity: *what perishes must have been*. Only a mundane reality can really perish; otherwise it would be just a possibility that disappears. This is why I put the full stress of my being on realization in existence, on permanence in my doings, and why I believe in this as something to be done. I want permanence in order to experience the fulfilled foundering that lights up being for me. I go into the world and extend myself in its abundance with all my strength, to get an original view of the world's disjointness and perishability and not to know of them in abstract thoughts only. Unless I enter the world without reserve, suffering whatever mundane havoc may be wrought upon me, I cannot really experience foundering as a cipher. Otherwise there would be only the groundless, indifferent perdition of all things.

To the sense of being of a possible Existenz the world is the area in which it learns what really is. I turn to the society in which I live, cooperating in the fields where I can be effective. I seek communicative permanence in family and friendship. I address objective nature in its legality and technical governability. As existence I breathe in a world; as a human among humans I produce that which fulfills existence. All fulfillment is transitory, yet it is in and through fulfilled existence that I read the cipher script of being.

I might seem to have reason to think: *Everything founders; I need not even begin, for everything is senseless anyway.* This thought presupposes duration as a standard of value and absolutizes mundane existence. But although for existence—and thus for each one of us—the will to be lasting and extant is inescapable, although the thought that all things founder will initially express despair in the boundary situation, an Existenz cannot come to itself if it has not been in boundary situations.

The sense of a resolute refusal to realize is another matter. There my Existenz can see no compelling need for this existence in the world: while finding myself in existence, *I can still fight existence as such.* Mundane existence can be truly, consciously embraced only by an Existenz that has been touched by the question of this negative resolve. One must have potentially left the world and come back to it, to have it positively as a world—in its splendor and in its dubiety and in its character as the sole place for the appearance of Existenz, the place where it can understand itself and other Existenz.

I am not alone in existence. It is this fact which makes that negative resolve to call mundane existence into doubt so doubtful, since all I do in it is to plunge worldlessly and uncommunicatively into the transcendent abyss. But Existenz in existence is the will to communicate; since communication is a premise of its being, it can neither stand absolutely on itself nor cling directly to transcendence. There is no individual salvation. No truth will let me reach the goal for myself alone. I share in being what others are; I am responsible for that which is outside me, because I can address it and enter into active relations with it; I am a possible Existenz for other Existenz. I therefore reach the goal of my existence only if I grasp what is around me. I have not come to myself until the world with which I can establish possible communication has come to itself with me. Freedom depends upon the freedom of others. The measure of my self-being is my neighbor's self-being, and finally that of all men.

Only the eventual foundering of *this* realization will reveal what being is.

Interpreting the Necessity of Foundering

Wherever we look and whatever we touch, the end is foundering. This makes us ask whether it must be so. The answers we can give are not possible insights but attempted clarifications of being in the cipher.

1. Freedom a Bar to Firm Validity and Permanence

True being does not lie in the validity of that which we can think without contradictions. If it did, its extant immobility, its monotonous identity with itself, would be like the being of death, which I cannot believe in. For the unknowable but intrinsic truth of being to break through to me, all extant logic has to founder on antinomies.

Nor is true being an endless duration in time. If it were, there would again be nothing but dead existence; for mere duration, the monotony of the same, would become another kind of timelessness. Instead, in temporal existence the fact of being must take the form of a motion aimed at foundering. When phenomenal being attains a peak in existence, it will instantly be a mere point recoiling into disappearance to save the truth of the peak, which would be lost in continued existence. Whatever has been perfected will pass; there is no stopping its passage. Being proper is either not yet or no more. We cannot even find it as anything but the dividing line between the way to perfection and the way from perfection. The impossibility of lingering causes the whole of a fulfilled existential reality to spin around this vanishing point. The moment as such is all, yet it is but a moment. The truth in reality does not lie in the isolated peak but in the spread of the before and after.

But this motion is not comprehensible yet as the elimination of a pall of endless boredom which its absence would cast over all things, from the dead existence of validity and temporal duration. The crux is, rather, that *free* being can never come into *extant* existence. Free being lies in achieving itself, and it ceases when it has come to be and would last. Completion is its extinction. The fact that endless duration and timeless validity founder is the chance of freedom, which exists in the motion of passing away as existence when it really is. Transcendent being too is present in existence as its transparency, but in such a way that the transparent existence disappears as existence. What really is will enter the world in a leap and disappear from the world as it is realized. This is why lesser things seem more durable than free nobility, which will not remain extant—as when the form of matter outlasts life, life outlasts the mind, and the mass outlasts the historic individual.

2. The Antinomy of Freedom

Freedom is only by nature, and it is against nature. Therefore, it must fail either as freedom or as existence.

There is no freedom unless there is nature. Without meeting resistance, and without being grounded in itself, freedom would not be. What becomes overpowering in mental illness, for instance, destroying man as though extraneous to him, belongs to man's existence as his dark nature, which produces him but must be striven against. He may come into the situation of not recognizing himself in what he has done. It is as if something else had deranged his mind, but the deed was his and he must answer for it. His genius calls on him to be receptive and accessible to all things and thus to come freely to his resolutions; but his nature, which hears the genius, is not assuredly present at each moment. This is why good will in communication requires not only patience in the process of elucidation and disentanglement but recognition of possible Existenz despite the entanglements, and finally in the entanglements. There is this tremendous cipher of being in existence: that nature and freedom are not just two embattled powers, but that it takes nature to make freedom possible. In the ideal of free humanity the dark ground is not merely tamed; having been tamed, it remains the motivating force. Its excesses, taken for failures and challenges by the affected Existenz, are the indelible shortcomings whose ground remains the ground of Existenz itself.

Transcendence, therefore, lies not only in freedom; through freedom, there is transcendence in nature as well. As the otherness of Existenz, it is a cipher indicating the encompassing ground from which I too have arisen, but not I alone. To me, the mundane reality that covers more than the existence of possible Existenz seems like the mere material of my freedom; but then it seems to proclaim a natural being of its own, to which I too am subject. The unfathomability of the whole, of the One that defies cognition, forbids me to take Existenz for all there is—as I would in the narrowness of an existential philosophy secluded on the basis of self-being. Afraid of the nature in existence and of self-obliviously succumbing to it, such philosophizing would void the surrender that becomes possible when an Existenz is listening to its own otherness, to that which is neither Existenz itself nor a reality due to Existenz.

When a narrowing of Existenz tends to turn nature into mere material for its freedom, nature's initial reaction is a revolt of the natural ground of Existenz. But since the freedom of Existenz is bound to put it on that course, it *cannot help* splitting on the rocks of existence because it transgresses against nature. This is the antinomy of freedom: to become one with nature will destroy the freedom of an Existenz; to transgress against nature will make it founder in existence.

3. A Finite Vessel of Intrinsic Being Must Fall Short

In unconditionality an Existenz seeks to transcend the finite measure; in the end, therefore, existential uplifting will ruin finite existence. This is why foundering is a consequence of proper being in existence. Existence is a coexistence of many things which must mutually allow each other possibilities and scope; the world's arrangement in measure, restraint, acquiescence, compromise is that which makes it relatively stable. For proper being, however, I must upset this stability. My unconditionality does not know about measure. The guilt of unconditionality, which is a condition of Existenz at the same time, will be atoned in destruction at the hands of an existence bent on permanence. This is why throughout the world there are two forms of the ethos: one claiming to be generally valid and expressed in the ethics of measure, of prudence, of relativity, without a sense of foundering; the other holding nothing to be impossible, expressed in not-knowing, in the questioning ethics of free unconditionality, and seized by the cipher of foundering. Both forms mutually call for each other and delimit one another. The ethics of measure becomes relatively valid for duration and stability as the premise on which freedom may exist; the ethics of unconditionality becomes relative as the exception, whose different being stays acknowledged when it is wiped out.

An Existenz must take up its finite existence, outside of which there is nature and other Existenz. But as possible Existenz it necessarily wants to become entire, to realize, to complete its work and itself. Its unconditionality is to want the impossible. The stricter its compliance, its ban on adjustments, the stronger its will to break out of finiteness. Its highest measure is no longer measured. That is why it must founder. The fragmentary character of its existence and its works becomes the cipher of its transcendence for other Existenz that looks upon it.

4. A Speculative Reading of Ciphers

If we conceive being as the infinite One, to become finite is to become individual. Since the individual is not entire, it must return—that is to say, it must perish. Becoming finite would as such be guilt, with self-will the ineradicable characteristic of this guilt in individual being. A *hubris* of self-being led to apostasy. The principle of individuation in itself would be evil; death and all kinds of perdition would be ciphers of the necessity to return and atone for the guilt of being finite.

Freedom is lost in the abstract unequivocality of this mythical thought, which is like the objective knowledge of an occurrence. Since finiteness is universal, covering not man alone but each particular existence, it cannot be properly experienced as the guilt of self-will. Self-will belongs only to my own existence, in which it is the blindness of my self-preservation. But here self-will must not necessarily have the last word for an Existenz; it may be forced to bow to the existential unconditionality. The unavoidable guilt will then be experienced only in this unconditionality, which allows not only a control of self-will but a transcending of the finite measure.

In mundane existence, being is thus not only veiled but perverted. Because the world lasts only by constantly reproducing the force of the will to exist, it is as if this concern with mundane realization were the sole form in which being exists. Yet this is the source of the basic fallacy about being—of the fallacy that it is this existence itself—and so it is not until its existence founders that being will reveal itself. The fallacy is the inevitable intermediate link, the moving agent behind the forces whose foundering will void the fallacy and thus make being felt. For us, without this fallacy it would have remained in the darkness of possible nonbeing.

Being, barred from perception in finite existence, has in a sense arranged it so that in seeking it we feel obliged to produce it as existence, whereas it is in eternity. For what shows being to us, by way of realization in existence, is the exploding of the fallacy that it is existence—in other words, the real occurrence of fulfilled foundering.

5. What Defies Interpretation

Every interpretive thought which we hold to be true and realize will let us see the cipher of being in foundering. Every such thought expresses the uplifting of absolute consciousness. But only things of which we can think as fulfilling will go into the interpretations.

What does not go into them, to start with, is the *senseless end*. As negativity is overcome, it may become a source of true reality; it can be awakening and productive. But the negativity that simply destroys; the sterile suffering that fails to awaken and does nothing but confine and paralyze; the mental illness that merely overpowers man as otherness, all out of context—these cannot be interpreted. There is not only productive destruction; there is flatly ruinous destruction.

Another thing that will not lend itself to exegesis is the *denial of possibilities*—when something founders that has not even existed yet but has already manifested its potential for existence.

There is indeed a sort of conquest in which the possibility denied to a self-being can be transmuted into another fulfillment. Foundering is then the source of a new being caused by nothing else. Nonrealization becomes an existential reality where any realizing would be fated, in the actual situation, to be a decline: because there is no compromising on essentials, there is the heartache of unrealized possibilities. Where an incipient reality was cut down early, for instance, there is the painful fidelity that shuts the door to vast new possibilities. That the cause is not lack of talent but an abundance of unfathomable memories—this is what casts a mysterious shimmer on the substance of such nonrealization. Existenz is truer here than in compromise, in the choice of a broad sham reality to which there is no absolute link. In the world it is granted, such an Existenz without reality will have the exclusive love of a few.

It lives in a state of lonely, unceasing torment, for the contrast between its potential and its reality will not let it rest. It cannot blind itself to the fact that phenomenal Existenz finds its fulfillment nowhere but in the expanse of a mundane existence. To make up for its deprivation, the reality left to it will be animated by a consummate humanity brought forth by inner action, by a detachment from the reality of the situation that is not a passive denial but intrinsic activity. If such an Existenz appears to others like a blessed spirit in the world, if it remains mysterious like a creature enchained, this Existenz itself will dread being idolized and thus robbed of its last human contacts. It knows the dangers of violence and unnaturalness. But because its refusal to compromise was a matter of its own Existenz rather than of a rationalistic moral principle, its entire being in the face of those dangers has become gentle and self-evidently natural, albeit incomprehensibly disrupted now and then, and borne by insoluble guilt feelings for which it cannot give any rational reasons. This Existenz cannot understand itself, has no pretentions, and—unlike an impotence trying to give itself weight and a profile—eschews recognition. It lives an unresolved life of unknown heroism in a reality of negativities and possibilities; it may convey a closer proximity to the depths of being than others who come to regard it like an oracle. The historicity of its appearance, of its fate of nonrealization, has become the depth of its existence.

This sort of foundering by nonrealization leads to a new substantiality. And yet, the foundering that flatly ruins a potential will leave us nothing but an aching, uninterpretable void.

Beyond exegesis, finally, is the *historically terminating destruction that ends the chance of human continuity by burying all documents and traces*. Our passionate will to save the phenomenality of being proper drives us to rescue its documents, to keep it extant, preserved in the spirit of history. If what has been remains in memory, if its very downfall makes for its presently continuing effect in preservation, definitive destruction ends the chance of remembering. Whatever realities there were of human greatness, existential unconditionality, and creativity will be forever forgotten. What we remember historically is a random selection that must substitute for all that has been lost. There is no interpreting the ruin of oblivion.

The Cipher of
Being in Foundering

Time and again, everything that we have gained in philosophizing will be thrown into doubt by the extinction we cannot interpret. It seems that one who really sees what is must be beholding the stark blackness of the void. Not only does all of existence forsake him—what foundering itself comes down to is the being of nothingness. It no longer speaks the transcendent language of a cipher. If it remains this Mene Tekel, everything is sheer opacity in empty night. The threatening extreme of uninterpretable foundering is bound to crush whatever had been envisioned, conceived, constructed behind the blinders of deceptive happiness. There is no longer a reality we can live by.

The transcending that was still interpreted seemed to give us a grasp on a being we could hold on to. This is now like a mirage, for if we are truthful we resist all dreams that would convey a fanciful knowledge of being. We must reject all constructions that aim at the whole, but shroud reality instead. Without transcending, however, we can live only in a radical despair that leaves us nothing but the void.

This is the final question: what sort of a cipher of foundering is still possible today? How can it be, beyond all exegeses, if what foundering shows us is not the void, after all—if it is transcendent being? The question is whether a being can shine out of total darkness.

1. The Uninterpretable Cipher

Finiteness is not a thing I can pass by, except in foundering itself. When I expunge time in the metaphysical contemplation of foundering, without experiencing it in reality, I only fall back so much harder into finite existence. But one who expunges time in genuine foundering does not return; inaccessible to those he leaves behind, he demands that finite existence leave transcendent being untouched. We cannot know why there is a world; we may come to feel it in foundering, perhaps, but it is no longer something we can *say*. When we, as existence, deal with being, the extent of foundering brings language to an end, along with thought. The only answer to the silence in existence is silence. And if we do break it, we speak without saying a thing.

a. An answer to senseless extinction may take the form of the simple sense of being. Just as the passing of all mundane forms leaves matter, that which is flatly other but indifferent, so does the foundering of all existence and Existenz leave the inaccessible being proper. "It is," says the silence—a statement which in substance is null and void.

b. Regarding the potential killed in the bud, silence is an urge to hear the being that was before there was time—the being that *includes* what failed to become real.

c. On the irretrievability from oblivion: even as we want to rescue and remember what was lost, we know that what is affected by loss and rescue is not the *being* of the forgotten or remembered Existenz, but its *existence*. What has been lost, from the standpoint of the silence of transcendence, is *only what was never in transcendence.*

Finally, the uninterpretable cipher is the only one in which the world's end becomes being. Any end we know is in the world and in time; it is never an end of the world and of time. But the silence before the uninterpretable cipher of universal foundering relates to transcendent being, before which *the world has passed away.* What is revealed in foundering—the nonbeing of all being accessible to us—is the being of transcendence.

None of these formulas says anything. Each of them says the same. All of them say merely: *Being.* It is as if they were saying nothing, for they are breaks in the silence they cannot break.

2. The Last Cipher as a Sounding Board for All Ciphers

Rendered doubtful by a foundering beyond exegesis, any cipher that brought real fulfillment and thus revealed being must live backwards from the font of the silently experienced being, or else it must wither. For foundering is the encompassing ground of all that ciphers are. The sight of a cipher as a reality in being springs only from the foundering I experience. This gives their final confirmation to all the ciphers I do not reject. What I submerge in annihilation can come back to me as a cipher. When I read ciphers, I let them rise from a view of the ruin which in the cipher of my foundering will give its resonance to each particular cipher.

A passive not-knowing remains no more than the painful possibility of nothingness or a critical reservation against false ontological knowledge. But in the experience of uninterpretability, not-knowing becomes active in the presence of being. It becomes the source from which all proper consciousness of being springs in the infinite riches of mundane experience and existential realization.

Uninterpretability is the ultimate cipher, but it is no longer a definable cipher. It remains open, hence its silence. It may as well become the absolute void as the definitive fulfillment.

3. Peace in Reality

In view of foundering, it seems impossible to live. When fears are aggravated by a knowledge of reality, when hopelessness makes me melt away in my fears, the inescapable factuality seems to turn fear into the last thing there is. The real fear is the one I take for the last, the fear from which there is no escape any more. The leap to a fearless being strikes me as an empty possibility: I want to jump, but I already know I am not going to make it. I'll only plummet into the bottomless chasm of definitively final fear.

The leap from fear to serenity is the most tremendous one a man can make. That he succeeds in it must be due to a reason beyond the Existenz of his self-being. Undefinably, his faith ties him to transcendent being.

It is only in the fear from which I manage the leap to serenity that I can see mundane realities without reserve. Realities are shrouded both by sheer dread and by sheer serenity: my fear of them blurs my perception of foundering; holding on to supposedly known realities makes me faithless; the fear of which I make a factual ultimate in this fashion is hidden from me by a tranquillizing knowledge I possess. In this extant whole, this counterfeit reality, I dream of a false harmony, formulate an ideal ought, hold truth to be unique, and know that mine is the right one. Such serenity springs from untruth. It could arise because

I closed my eyes to fear—making my fear the hidden but unconquered cause of my serenity.

The basic fact of our Existenz in existence is that neither without fear nor without the transition from fear to peace of mind can reality, the source of the obliterating fear, be seen as it is. That man can at the same time see reality, be a reality himself, and yet live without fading out in fear—this makes his self-being dependent on his being utterly realistic, but in an interminable process in which being afraid is not the ultimate and neither is being unafraid, and no reality is definitive reality. To see reality, I have to feel the utmost fear in myself. This fear alone enables me to make the most difficult, the least comprehensible leap: to a peace that leaves reality uncovered.

There is no solution for a truthful sense of being. There is no answer in the great silence, no justification for what is, and for the way it is; there is no tranquillization, no unveiling in the cipher. The road to peace is long-sufferance. Passive suffering is empty, merely a form of resistless self-relinquishment, of letting things take their course; but active sufferance allows me to experience the foundering of all existence and yet to engage in realizations as long as an ounce of strength remains. In this tension I gain composure. Sufferance sustains the world of one who is receptive to reality and has become sensitive to transcendent being. In sufferance lies the not-knowing of the kind of faith that makes men active in the world without any need to believe in the possibility of a good and definitive world order. The cipher of foundering may pale for such a man when it appears to him to be abysmally senseless, when no form of cogitative uplifting seems to give him access to it any more; but sufferance means that he will cling to being *in spite of* his foundering, where the cipher of foundering fails him.

Not until he has made sure of this transcendence, not until the darkest turning point finds him able to do even without the transcendent language, has a man the support in existence that will give him peace—a peace which no longer deceives. His assurance depends upon the presence of Existenz and cannot be constituted in time as an objective warrant. It is bound to vanish time and again. But when it is there, nothing daunts it. That there is being suffices. Whatever we think we know about the deity is superstition; truth lies where a foundering Existenz can translate the ambiguous language of transcendence into the simplest certainty of being.

Only in this final peace, at vanishing moments, can one have the vision of perfection without deluding himself. True proximity to the world has always sprung from readings of the cipher of perdition. The transparency of all things had to include their foundering before Existenz would be quite ready to open itself to the world. Its eyes would clear, then; in unbounded world orientation it would see and search whatever there is and has been; it was as though the veil were lifted from things. Now, the love of existence made men capable of tireless realization; now the world's transcendently grounded abundance became unspeakably beautiful—but the horrors of the world remain, and they keep making it a question which in temporal existence will never be answered forever and for all men if an individual's clear-eyed sufferance lets him find his peace.

What trips off the tongue is never quite brought to mind. Any anticipation of the thought makes it untrue. It is not by reveling in perfection but by suffering, by seeing the grim features of mundane existence, by unconditionally being itself in communication that my possible Existenz can achieve what I cannot plan, what becomes an absurdity when I wish it: in foundering to experience being.

Index of Persons